THE CITY OF LONDON AND SOCIAL DEMOCRACY

OXFORD HISTORICAL MONOGRAPHS

The *Oxford Historical Monographs* series publishes some of the best Oxford University doctoral theses on historical topics, especially those likely to engage the interest of a broad academic readership.

The City of London and Social Democracy

The Political Economy of Finance in Britain, 1959–1979

ALED DAVIES

OXFORD
UNIVERSITY PRESS

OXFORD
UNIVERSITY PRESS

Great Clarendon Street, Oxford, OX2 6DP,
United Kingdom

Oxford University Press is a department of the University of Oxford.
It furthers the University's objective of excellence in research, scholarship,
and education by publishing worldwide. Oxford is a registered trade mark of
Oxford University Press in the UK and in certain other countries

Published in the United States of America by Oxford University Press
198 Madison Avenue, New York, NY 10016, United States of America

British Library Cataloguing in Publication Data
Data available

Library of Congress Control Number: 2016960542

ISBN 978–0–19–880411–6

Printed and bound by
CPI Group (UK) Ltd, Croydon, CR0 4YY

Acknowledgements

I am grateful to the University of Oxford and the Arts and Humanities Research Council for giving me the opportunity to undertake the doctoral research on which this book is based. I am also thankful for the financial support provided by the Winton Institute for Financial and Monetary History.

I wish to express my utmost gratitude to Ben Jackson for his enthusiastic support for this project, and for his help and assistance throughout. In always providing invaluable guidance, but never seeking to direct my research, he has been the ideal supervisor and editor. I would like also to thank Jim Tomlinson and John Davis for examining my doctoral thesis, and for recommending it for publication. I am grateful to John Watts and the Oxford Historical Monographs committee for agreeing to publish the book, and to the anonymous referee who provided such useful feedback on the original thesis. I would like to thank Hugh Pemberton for his support and guidance while I turned my dissertation into this book, and I am also grateful to both Roger Middleton and Martin Daunton for their helpful feedback and advice.

This book owes its completion to the support and encouragement given to me by my colleagues, friends, and family. The staff and students of the Oxford University Economic and Social History group have been a source of intellectual inspiration and academic assistance throughout. I am particularly grateful to Harold Carter, Nicholas Dimsdale, Rui Esteves, Anthony Hotson, Jane Humphries, Nick Mayhew, Avner Offer, Deborah Oxley, Florian Ploeckl, and Kevin O'Rourke for their support. In preparing this work I have also benefited from the comments and suggestions made by attendees of various seminar and conference papers I have delivered in Oxford, London, Paris, and York. I would also like to thank the archive and library staff at the various institutions listed in the Bibliography, and Michael J. Oliver and Gordon Pepper in particular for their assistance in researching Chapter 5. Furthermore, I am grateful to Cathryn Steele at Oxford University Press for her support throughout the publication process, and to Hilary Walford, whose copy-editing skills have been invaluable.

Mansfield College provided a friendly, egalitarian, and supportive working environment while I was in Oxford. I am grateful to all the college staff, and especially to Kathryn Gleadle, who was a great source of encouragement throughout. Undertaking doctoral research can, at times, be a lonely and difficult experience. If not for the friendship of many people in Oxford I would have struggled to complete the original thesis on which this book is based. Special mentions must go to Keian Noori, Chelsea Sutcliffe, Colin Seepersad, Julien Labonne, and Andrew Seaton.

I am grateful to Jane, Gerwyn, and Catrin Davies for their patience and support while I researched and wrote this book. I am especially grateful to my Dad for lending his bike to me while I was living and working in Oxford. I would also like to thank Jill and Ian Cherry for all their support and encouragement.

Finally, I would like to thank Kate Cherry. Without her constant support I would never have started this project, and I certainly would not have finished it.

Contents

List of Figures, Table, and Boxes

FIGURES

TABLE

BOXES

Abbreviations

AES	Alternative Economic Strategy
APEX	Association of Professional, Executive, Clerical and Computer Staff
ASTMS	Association of Scientific, Technical, and Managerial Staffs
BBC	British Banking Corporation
BEB	British Enterprise Bank
BIA	British Insurance Association
BIBA	British Insurance Brokers' Association
BNEC	British National Export Council
BOE	Bank of England
CBI	Confederation of British Industry
CCC	Competition and Credit Control
CLCB	Committee of London Clearing Bankers
COIE	Committee on Invisible Exports
DCE	Domestic Credit Expansion
DEA	Department for Economic Affairs
EAG	Economists Advisory Group
ECI	Equity Capital for Industry
EEC	European Economic Community
FCI	Finance Corporation for Industry
FFI	Finance for Industry
GEC	General Electric
ICFC	Industrial and Commercial Finance Corporation
IEA	Institute of Economic Affairs
IMF	International Monetary Fund
IRC	Industrial Reorganization Corporation
ISC	Institutional Shareholders' Committee
LIFFE	London International Financial Futures Exchange
LSE	London School of Economics
MLR	Minimum Lending Rate
MTFS	Medium-Term Financial Strategy
NAPF	National Association of Pension Funds
NBPI	National Board for Prices and Incomes
NEB	National Enterprise Board
NEDC	National Economic Development Council
NIB	National Investment Board
NUBE	National Union of Bank Employees
OECD	Organization for Economic Cooperation and Development
OPEC	Organization of Petroleum Exporting Countries

PPS	Parliamentary Private Secretary
PSBR	Public Sector Borrowing Requirement
SET	Selective Employment Tax
TGWU	Transport and General Workers' Union
TUC	Trades Union Congress
USDAW	Union of Shop, Distributive, and Allied Workers

Introduction

The City of London and Social Democracy

This book is a study of the political economy of Britain's chief financial centre, the City of London, in the two decades prior to the election of Margaret Thatcher's first Conservative government in 1979. The primary purpose of the book is to evaluate the relationship between the financial sector based in the City, and the economic strategy of social democracy in post-war Britain. In particular, it focuses on how the financial system related to the social democratic pursuit of national industrial development and modernization, and on how the norms of social democratic economic policy were challenged by a variety of fundamental changes to the City that took place during the period.

It is intended that the research findings presented in this book will contribute to answering the broader question facing historians of post-war Britain of how, and why, the nation transitioned from a social democratic to a 'neoliberal' political–economic settlement in the final third of the twentieth century. The incipient debate on this issue has so far focused primarily on the role of 'neoliberal' ideas (favouring free markets and limited state intervention in the economy) in challenging the social democratic settlement and constructing an alternative consensus. This literature has concerned itself either with the ideological origins of 'Thatcherism' within the Conservative Party, or the import of trans-national neoliberal ideas into domestic politics via think tanks.[1] It is

[1] See, e.g., Richard Cockett, *Thinking the Unthinkable: Think-Tanks and the Economic Counter-Revolution, 1931–1983* (London: HarperCollins, 1994); Radhika Desai, 'Second-Hand Dealers in Ideas: Think-Tanks and Thatcherite Hegemony', *New Left Review*, 203 (1994), 27–64; E. H. H. Green, *Thatcher* (London: Hodder Arnold, 2006); E. H. H. Green, 'Thatcherism: An Historical Perspective', *Transactions of the Royal Historical Society*, 6/9 (1999), 17–42; Ben Jackson, 'The Think-Tank Archipelago: Thatcherism and Neo-Liberalism', in Ben Jackson and Robert Saunders (eds), *Making Thatcher's Britain* (Cambridge: Cambridge University Press, 2012), 43–61; Florence Sutcliffe-Braithwaite, 'Neo-Liberalism and Morality in the Making of Thatcherite Social Policy', *Historical Journal*, 55/2 (2012), 497–520; Keith Tribe, 'Liberalism and Neoliberalism in Britain', in

hoped that the findings presented in this book will provide an alternative perspective that broadens and complicates this existing narrative. It is particularly pertinent to focus on the City of London, as, by re-establishing itself as one of the world's largest international financial centres, it has been one of the chief beneficiaries of the 'neoliberal' consensus.

The key argument set out in the book is that substantial changes to the financial system during the 1960s and 1970s undermined a number of key components of social democratic political economy that had been embedded in the economic policy norms of the British state since the 1940s. The institutionalization of investment; the fragmentation of an oligopolistic domestic banking system; the emergence of an unregulated international capital market centred on London; the breakdown of the Bretton Woods international monetary system; and the popularization of a City-centric, anti-industrial conception of Britain's economic identity, all disrupted and undermined the social democratic economic strategy that had attempted to develop Britain as an internationally competitive industrial economy since the war. However, the research findings presented in this book also demonstrate that social democrats were not simply ignorant of the changes, or fatalistic in response to the challenges arising from them. Instead, it is clear that they instead sought to reformulate and reconstruct their economic strategy in the 1970s in an attempt to advance the social democratic project beyond the post-war settlement. This book discusses some of the ideas and approaches developed during this attempted re-evaluation, and considers the reasons for their ultimate failure. The decision to focus on social democratic ideas and intentions is a deliberate challenge to the commonplace tendency to view the 1970s through the prism of a triumphant neoliberalism that came to dominate in the 1980s.[2] It forms part of an attempt to rescue the aims and aspirations of British social democracy in the period from the 'condescension of posterity' to which subsequent Thatcherite (and 'New Labour') narratives have condemned it.[3]

Philip Mirowski and Dieter Plehwe (eds), *The Road from Mont Pelerin: The Making of the Neoliberal Thought Collective* (Cambridge, MA: Harvard University Press, 2009), 68–97; Adrian Williamson, *Conservative Economic Policymaking and the Birth of Thatcherism, 1964–1979* (London: Palgrave Macmillan, 2015).

[2] James Vernon has argued that 'the central historical problem in twentieth-century Britain was . . . the brief life of social democracy' James Vernon, 'The Local, the Imperial and the Global: Repositioning Twentieth-Century Britain and the Brief Life of its Social Democracy', *Twentieth Century British History*, 21/3 (2010), 418.

[3] E. P. Thompson, *The Making of the English Working Class* (New York: Random House, 1964), 12.

Before proceeding, we must first define the terms 'social democracy' and 'City of London'.

SOCIAL DEMOCRACY AND THE POST-WAR SOCIAL DEMOCRATIC STATE

'Social democracy' emerged as a transnational political project in the second half of the nineteenth century—ideologically rooted in a mixture of socialist and liberal thought, and endorsed by a coalition of organized labour, intellectuals, and social reformers. In contrast with international revolutionary Communism, social democratic parties broadly sought to overcome the inequities and inefficiencies of capitalism via a reformist, democratic strategy conditioned by the specific political, economic, and social conditions of their own countries. This was especially so following the break-up of the Second International in 1916, and the Bolshevik Revolution in 1917.[4] Transnational European social democracy was a diverse project consisting of multiple political parties and pressure groups pursuing a general set of ends within the social democratic tradition. Many of the policy themes and approaches of social democratic parties converged and overlapped during the twentieth century, yet their political organization and policymaking were all shaped by their national contexts.[5] In Britain the dominant social democratic political party during the twentieth century was the Labour Party.

Though the extension of the franchise following the end of the First World War enabled social democratic parties to gain political power during the interwar period, their success was limited by the severity of the period's financial and economic crises.[6] However, the onset of the Second World War offered social democrats a political opportunity to advance their cause, as the demands of total warfare, and the subsequent need for economic and social reconstruction, necessitated the expansion of state action. In reconstructing the post-war world, especially the war-torn European continent, economic policies designed for the benefit of workers

---

[4] Stephen Padgett and William E. Paterson, *A History of Social Democracy in Post-War Europe* (London: Longman, 1991); Ben Jackson, 'Social Democracy', in Michael Freeden, Marc Stears, and Lyman Tower Sargeant (eds), *The Oxford Handbook of Political Ideologies* (Oxford: Oxford University Press, 2013), 348–63; Geoff Eley, *Forging Democracy: The History of the Left in Europe, 1850–2000* (Oxford: Oxford University Press, 2002), 223–9.

[5] For a general overview, see Donald Sassoon, *One Hundred Years of Socialism: The West European Left in the Twentieth Century* (London: I. B. Tauris, 2010).

[6] Of course, there were social democratic political achievements, but they were hard won and precarious.

gained the ascendancy as new Keynesian demand management macroeconomic techniques offered the means to resist unemployment; labour market regulation was advanced; redistributive taxation created a more egalitarian society; and state expenditure on public goods and services all became prominent norms for advanced industrial nations.[7] By displacing the previously dominant political forces of conservatism and orthodox economic liberalism, these achievements reflected the democratic success of social democracy in the decades after 1945. Benefiting as they did from a period of unprecedented sustained global economic growth, these decades are understood as the golden age of social democracy.[8]

The landslide victory of the Labour Party at the 1945 general election heralded a radical shift in British politics that spearheaded this international trend: a commitment to macroeconomic interventionism in pursuit of full employment; extensive and 'progressive' taxation; and a large public sector encompassing public services and public ownership. Labour's success in the 1940s, combined with the impact of the war on British society, served to shift the political 'middle', and in doing so redefined the types of government activity deemed, in the words of Kavanagh and Morris, 'administratively practical, economically affordable and politically acceptable'.[9] In the critical juncture of the transition from war to peace under Labour, social democratic priorities were implanted into the normal operating functions of national governance, thus serving to reconstitute the British state as what can be termed a 'social democratic state'. This is not to suggest that policies did not vary or change over the course of the post-war era; however, the key goals and basic approaches were fixed in the 1940s. The result of this reconstruction was to impose constraints on the opposition Conservative Party, which, though ideologically resistant to the new governing norms, was forced to accommodate itself over the following three decades—with a great degree of electoral success.[10]

---

[7] Jackson, 'Social Democracy', 352–7; Tony Judt, *Post-War: A History of Europe since 1945* (London: Vintage, 2010), 360–90; John Callaghan, *The Retreat of Social Democracy* (Manchester: Manchester University Press, 2000), 1–25.

[8] Judt, *Post-War*, 324–90.

[9] Dennis Kavanagh and Peter Morris, *Consensus Politics from Attlee to Thatcher* (Oxford: Blackwell, 1989), 12; Mark Blyth, 'Moving the Political Middle: Redefining the Boundaries of State Action', *Political Quarterly*, 68/3 (1997), 231–40.

[10] The extent to which there was a consensus in post-war British politics has been debated at great length. For example, see Kavanagh and Morris, *Consensus Politics*; Harriet Jones and Michael Kandiah, *The Myth of Consensus: New Views on British History, 1945–64* (Basingstoke: Macmillan, 1996); Kevin Jefferys, *The Churchill Coalition and Wartime Politics, 1940–1945* (Manchester: Manchester University Press, 1991); Stephen Brooke, *Labour's War: The Labour Party during the Second World War* (Oxford: Clarendon Press, 1992); Paul Addison, *The Road to 1945: British Politics and the Second World War*, 2nd edn

This book employs two separate, but related, terms—'social democracy' and the 'social democratic state'. 'Social democracy' refers to the ideology and strategy of the Labour Party. Meanwhile, 'social democratic state' will refer to the fundamental governing purpose and practices of the post-war British state as had been constructed by Clement Attlee's Labour government. The former should be understood as a dynamic and changing political project subject to conflict and disagreement which adapted (or attempted to adapt) to political, economic, and social changes in the post-war era. The latter should be understood as a more rigid set of fundamental assumptions and practices, which, though criticized and challenged at the fringes, were embedded in the political economy of post-war Britain. As this book focuses specifically on economic policy, the following section will attempt to define the economic strategy of the post-war social democratic state, from its construction in the 1940s to its crisis in the 1970s, as well as surveying the shifting priorities and approaches of the Labour Party's economic policies. This overview should clarify the delineated definition of 'social democracy' and the 'social democratic state' on which this book rests.

Establishing the Economic Strategy of the Social Democratic State: 1945–1951

The economic strategy of the post-war social democratic state was constructed by the 1945 Labour government. This strategy was shaped not only by the ideological and political priorities of Labour, but by the practical realities and structural economic constraints imposed upon the reforming administration. The financial and economic turbulence of the 1930s encouraged the Labour Party to put its faith in economic 'planning' as the means by which future national economic stability and prosperity could be ensured. Not only did economic planning by the state seem to offer a superior solution to the supposed anarchy of laissez-faire; it provided an alternative economic model in which collective endeavour and public/worker control could supersede individual competition and private ownership of the means of production.[11] These abstract proposals

(London: Pimlico, 1994); Dennis Kavanagh, *Thatcherism and British Politics: The End of Consensus?* (Oxford: Oxford University Press, 1987); Dennis Kavanagh, 'The Post-War Consensus', *Twentieth Century British History*, 3 (1992), 175–90.

[11] Stephen Brooke, 'Revisionists and Fundamentalists: The Labour Party and Economic Policy during the Second World War', *Historical Journal*, 32 (1989), 159; Richard Toye, *The Labour Party and the Planned Economy, 1931–1951* (Woodbridge: Boydell Press, 2003); Daniel Ritschel, *The Politics of Planning: The Debate on Economic Planning in Britain in the 1930s* (Oxford: Clarendon Press, 1997); Elizabeth Durbin, *New Jerusalems:*

for economic planning were made real with the onset of the Second World War, as the demands of total warfare generated a host of physical controls on prices, consumption, manpower, investment, and production. With the cessation of hostilities in 1945, the new Labour government sought to harness this planning structure, having promised in its election manifesto to 'plan from the ground up'.[12] Yet, despite Labour's near universal commitment to notional planning, in reality the party was uncertain and divided over what planning would actually entail. In particular, it had not concluded whether the state should intervene directly in the economy, or whether to permit the operation of the price mechanism and rely instead on Keynesian macroeconomic techniques.[13]

Keynes's innovative proposals for macroeconomic management consti-tuted an attempt to maintain a free, liberal economy by encouraging the state to take responsibility for controlling employment, inflation, and output through budgetary alterations. Elements of this method, particularly the use of national accounting, had been first adopted in the 1941 budget, and Keynes had had a great deal of influence on the government's wartime economic policymakers.[14] Keynes's approach proposed that economic pros-perity could be achieved without undue direct interference by the state. This was an attractive alternative to those on the left who were not wholly convinced of the government's capacity actually to plan the economy, and were concerned also for the implications of extensive state involvement in daily life. The Attlee government was forced to resolve the tension between its enthusiasts for direct economic planning and those who favoured a more hands-off approach.[15] Ultimately the latter was favoured. The wartime planning apparatus, in addition to new bodies and organizations set up after 1945, was continued until 1947, when a fuel shortage and sterling crisis demonstrated to the government the failings of the planned economy in its current form.[16] In response, Harold Wilson at the Board of Trade

The Labour Party and the Economics of Democratic Socialism (London: Routledge and Kegan Paul, 1985); Michael Cunningham, ' "From the Ground Up?": The Labour Governments and Economic Planning', in Jim Fryth (ed.), *Labour's High Noon: The Government and the Economy, 1945–51* (London: Lawrence & Wishhart, 1993), 3–19.

[12] *Let Us Face the Future: A Declaration of Labour Policy for the Consideration of the Nation* (London, 1945); quoted in Cunningham, 'From the Ground Up?', 3.

[13] Cunningham, 'From the Ground Up?', 5–7.

[14] Alan Booth, 'The "Keynesian Revolution" in Economic Policy-Making', *Economic History Review*, 36 (1983), 103–23; Toye, *Labour Party and the Planned Economy*, 91–113.

[15] Noel Thompson, *Political Economy and the Labour Party: The Economics of Democratic Socialism, 1884–1995* (London: University College London, 1996), 138; Richard Toye, 'Gosplanners versus Thermostatters: Whitehall Planning Debates and their Political Conse-quences, 1945–49', *Contemporary British History*, 14/4 (2000), 81.

[16] Cunningham, 'From the Ground Up?', 8–11.

embarked on a 'bonfire of controls', which sought to liberalize the economy and restore the market mechanism in many areas.[17] Meanwhile, demand management supplanted the existing efforts to control inflation through physical controls on food and prices in the November 1947 Budget.[18] Ultimately 'socialist planning' fell out of favour, as its insufficiently defined methods met substantial administrative difficulties. In particular, there were substantive supply-side constraints on physical planning: the commercial orientation of the newly formed public corporations could not be centrally controlled; the desire to pursue a democratic tripartite approach that garnered voluntary industry and trade-union support; and an unwillingness to create new institutional structures that could oversee central planning.[19] Furthermore, attempts to control consumption were electorally unpopular.[20] In comparison, Keynesian techniques were attractive for their clarity, ease, and proven efficacy during wartime.

Central to Labour's promise of a planned economy in the 1930s and 1940s was the proposal to bring the process of investment in the British economy within the control and direction of the state.[21] The incoming Labour administration in 1945 was convinced of the need to control capital investment. The most significant component of the attempt to achieve this took the form of a proposed National Investment Board (NIB).[22] Such a body had been part of the 'progressive consensus' in

[17] Neil Rollings, '"The Reichstag Method of Governing"?: The Attlee Governments and Permanent Economic Controls', in H. Mercer, Neil Rollings, and Jim Tomlinson (eds), *Labour Governments and Private Industry: The Experience of 1945–51* (Edinburgh: Edinburgh University Press, 1992), 15–36.

[18] Thompson, *Political Economy and the Labour Party*, 142; Alec Cairncross, *Years of Recovery: British Economic Policy, 1945–51* (London: Methuen, 1985), 14–15. The extent to which a 'Keynesian revolution' took place in economic policymaking has been debated at length: Booth, 'Keynesian Revolution'; Alan Booth, 'Defining a "Keynesian Revolution"', *Economic History Review*, 37 (1984), 253–67; Alan Booth, 'The "Keynesian Revolution" and Economic Policy-Making: A Reply', *Economic History Review*, 38 (1985), 101–6; Neil Rollings, 'The "Keynesian Revolution" and Economic Policy-Making: A Comment', 38 (1985), 95–100; Neil Rollings, 'British Budgetary Policy, 1945–1954', *Economic History Review*, 41 (1988), 283–98; Jim Tomlinson, 'Why was there Never a Keynesian Revolution in Economic Policy?', *Economy and Society*, 10 (1981), 72–87; Jim Tomlinson, 'A "Keynesian Revolution" in Economic Policy-Making', *Economic History Review*, 37 (1984), 258–62.

[19] Jim Tomlinson, *Democratic Socialism and Economic Policy: The Attlee Years, 1945–1951* (Cambridge: Cambridge University Press, 1997), 85–7; Stephen Brooke, 'Problems of "Socialist Planning": Evan Durbin and the Labour Government of 1945', *Historical Journal*, 34 (1991), 688; Cunningham, 'From the Ground Up?', 5; Thompson, *Political Economy and the Labour Party*, 140–1.

[20] Tomlinson, *Democratic Socialism*, 80.

[21] Jim Tomlinson, 'Attlee's Inheritance and the Financial System: Whatever Happened to the National Investment Board?', *Financial History Review*, 1/2 (1994), 142–5.

[22] Ibid. 139–55.

the 1930s, with supporters in the Liberal Party and among a small group of Conservatives.[23] The purpose of such an approach was to ensure that investment flowed to the most productive and efficient ends, and would assist in modernizing, amalgamating, and rationalizing British industry. For socialist planners it was intended that the NIB would sit at the heart of the planned economy in order to direct investment funds according to expertise and knowledge beyond the scope of individual firms. Yet, despite its well-established support in the previous decade, the NIB never came to fruition. In December 1945, on the orders of the Chancellor Hugh Dalton, a 'Control of Investment Bill' was introduced 'as part of wider proposals for economic planning'. After 1945 Dalton proposed the establishment of a National Investment Council, which had the limited purpose of providing advice on investment policy.[24] Neither of these schemes lived up to the ideals of those who believed that the state should take a major role in investment decisions. Despite the fact that the post-1945 Labour government brought the Bank of England into public ownership, and oversaw the creation of the Finance Corporation for Industry (FCI) and Industrial and Commercial Finance Corporation (ICFC), Jim Tomlinson has noted that the reforms of the Attlee government were 'remarkable for their mildness'.[25] The NIB was abandoned, and control of investment was instead to be achieved in aggregate through demand management policies.[26] Once again, a key reason for this simplification of approach was the inherent difficulty of agreeing upon how *actually* to plan investment in any real sense. Yet more importantly, as Tomlinson has demonstrated, it was a function of the structure of British capitalism in the 1940s. There was a historic distance between Britain's industrial firms and the capital market in which most investment was undertaken not on the basis of external finance or investment, but through reinvested profits by individual firms. Where the process of transferring savings into investment had been captured by a centralized financial system in other nations, capitalist firms in Britain continued to obtain most of their investment funds from self-generated profits. The investment process was characterized by a model of disaggregated decision-making in which surpluses were recycled within individual firms. As such, control over the national capital

---

[23] Ibid. 142–3.   [24] Tomlinson, 'Attlee's Inheritance', 145.

[25] Ibid. 154; the FCI and ICFC were established by the Bank of England to meet some of the apparent gaps in the capital markets identified by the Macmillan Committee in the 1930s. The former had been instigated by the Bank with a nominal purpose of attempting to fill the 'Macmillan Gap', and the latter to act as lender to special 'large case' firms. These new bodies were essentially rooted in the Bank of England's desire to offset demands for more radical intervention during the final moments of the war.

[26] Ibid. 154–5.

market was not a wholly efficacious approach to directing the overall investment process.[27] Immediately following the war most companies were cash rich and therefore did not require external finance to fund investment, and, although strict controls on such investment remained in place following the war, these were gradually dismantled. As a result, greater emphasis fell on fiscal influences over investment.[28]

Central control of investment, beyond changes to monetary policy through the nationalized Bank of England, was abandoned as a goal of social democratic policy in the 1940s. The methods by which the post-war Labour economic strategy sought to achieve desired increases in investment accepted this basic architecture as given and sought to use financial incentives to ensure that profits generated by capitalist firms were not distributed to shareholders as income but were employed almost solely for reinvestment. This was an attempt to reconcile long-standing socialist hostility to profit with the fact that profits were key to the dynamism of the national economy. The economic strategy of the post-war social democratic state was therefore built upon the accepted necessity of private profit, but determined that any profits generated were subject to the normative assertion that they should be harnessed to meet the requirements of national economic development and not individual consumption or the accumulation of wealth. Under Attlee's government, this originally took the form of a generalized investment allowance scheme that imposed higher taxes on distributed profits. The effect of giving incentives for non-distributed profits was to reaffirm the already established norm of British firms relying on ploughed-back profits for sources of investment.[29] After 1966 this was eventually replaced with an investment grant scheme, which encouraged investment in manufacturing and extractive industries, as well as in geographical areas requiring development.[30] As we will see in Chapter 1, this method for managing the investment process in the economy came under increasing strain in the late 1960s and 1970s.

The Labour government's attempts to resolve the tensions within its planning agenda cannot be viewed in isolation. Instead, it is essential to recognize that they took place within the context of an urgent need to recover Britain's position in the world economy following the devastation caused by the war. The significant costs of waging the Second World War

---

[27] Ibid. 153.   [28] Ibid. 147–9; Tomlinson, *Democratic Socialism*, 81.

[29] Jim Tomlinson, *Government and the Enterprise since 1900: The Changing Problem of Efficiency* (Oxford: Clarendon Press, 1994), 170–1.

[30] Jim Tomlinson, 'The Labour Party and the Capitalist Firm, *c*.1950–1970', *Historical Journal*, 47/3 (2004), 685–708.

had left Britain in severe financial and economic difficulties. The great problem facing the nation at the end of the war was the entrenched gap between dollar receipts and dollar earnings following the US government's decision to end the 'Lend-Lease' programme. This withdrawal of external finance was combined with a reduction in earnings and exports to 30 per cent of their pre-war level.[31] Britain was, in Keynes's words, facing a 'financial Dunkirk'. Massive war debts had accumulated, foreign assets had been sold, and exports were sacrificed for the sake of devoting resources to domestic war production. The nation could not adequately pay for its imports, which resulted in a severe balance of payments deficit. In addition to its desire to maintain economic stability and undertake major domestic welfare reforms, Attlee's government was faced with the challenge of rectifying the nation's dire external position. Labour's solution was to promote an export drive designed to bridge the payments gap. Rather than cutting back on the nation's significant overseas military expenditure (a difficult proposition in the context of the dangerous early stages of the Cold War), the government focused its attention on altering the balance of trade to ensure that, through increased productivity in export industries, enough British goods might be sold abroad to meet the costs of the nation's imports.[32] The aim was to rebuild and revive 'Britain's industrial might', thus tying national revival specifically to manufacturing expansion.[33] This approach was heavily conditioned by the options available to the government (earnings on the capital account had been severely eroded by wartime and post-war constraints on international finance; and the commitment to Britain's foreign military role was steadfast), although Labour's inherent bias towards industry on electoral, cultural, and moral grounds was also significant.[34] Tomlinson and Tiratsoo have demonstrated that in this context the Attlee government was committed to pursuing the modernization of British industry by placing a high priority on raising the level of productivity.[35] The government pursued a variety of initiatives that attempted not only to meet the short-term demands of increased output, but also to ensure the long-term

---

[31] Thompson, *Political Economy and the Labour Party*, 145; Cairncross, *Years of Recovery*, 6.

[32] Corelli Barnett, *The Lost Victory: British Dreams, British Realities 1945–1950* (London: Pan Macmillan, 1996), 46–69; Michael Asteris, 'British Overseas Military Commitments 1945–47: Making Painful Choices', *Contemporary British History*, 27/3 (2013), 348–71.

[33] Jim Tomlinson, 'Balanced Accounts? Constructing the Balance of Payments Problem in Post-War Britain', *English Historical Review*, 124/509 (2009), 866–8.

[34] Cairncross, *Years of Recovery*, 8.

[35] Jim Tomlinson and Nick Tiratsoo, *Industrial Efficiency and State Intervention: Labour, 1939–1951* (London: Routledge, 1993).

efficiency and competitiveness of industry.[36] Importantly, the Labour government did not challenge the orthodoxy that sterling should be restored and maintained as an international trading and reserve currency. As with military expenditure, the purpose of this may have been simply to retain national economic prestige through old imperial ties despite the realities of Britain's post-war impoverishment. However, it was also in part due to a belief that currency stability would encourage international trade and prevent financial instability (the role of sterling is discussed further in Chapters 4 and 5).[37]

The post-war Labour government constructed a new macroeconomic settlement in the 1940s that was the product of its ideological priorities and the structural economic constraints in which the government was forced to operate. Fundamentally, this economic strategy consisted of using the apparatus of the state to encourage the expansion of Britain's industrial economy in order to reclaim and reassert Britain's position as a pre-eminent nation in the international economic order. The aims and techniques of policy that formed the core of Labour's approach were to be deeply embedded in the governing norms of post-war British government for the following three decades.

Consensus and Revision, 1951–1970

The Conservative victory at the 1951 general election cemented the approach to economic policy that the Labour government had implemented since 1947. The Conservatives were more able to reconcile themselves with the removal of controls on economic activity than a Labour Party that still retained a notional commitment to socialist planning, but were also willing to adapt to the new environment in which demand management was deemed necessary to fulfil electoral demands for 'full employment'.[38] Furthermore, the practical problem of Britain's balance of payments problem remained, and the Conservative governments continued to prioritize industrial development, especially in the latter half of the 1950s.

---

[36] Ibid. 1–20; Tomlinson, *Democratic Socialism*, 68–93.

[37] Jim Tomlinson, 'The Attlee Government and the Balance of Payments, 1945–1951' *Twentieth Century British History*, 2 (1991), 47–66.

[38] Ina Zweiniger-Bargielowska, 'Rationing, Austerity and the Conservative Party Recovery after 1945', *Historical Journal*, 37 (1994), 173–97; Anthony Seldon, 'Conservative Century', in Anthony Seldon and Stuart Ball (eds), *Conservative Century: The Conservative Party since 1900* (Oxford: Oxford University Press, 1994), 46–7; Neil Rollings, 'Poor Mr Butskell: A Short Life, Wrecked by Schizophrenia?', *Twentieth Century British History*, 5 (1994), 183–205.

During the thirteen years spent in opposition following the 1951 defeat, the Labour Party engaged in an extensive intellectual and political debate over its purpose and future strategy. Labour 'revisionists' believed that economic affluence in the 1950s demonstrated that radical changes to the capitalist system were no longer necessary in the light of expanding national income and full employment. In Keynes the techniques had been found that would permit the most effective means to ensure stable economic growth and full employment, and working-class prosperity offered the scope for the expansion of freedom in leisure and consumption. More significant to the economic strategy of Labour was the revisionist rejection of public ownership as a necessary condition for socialist advance. The revisionists argued that nationalization was only a means to an end—sometimes necessary and sometimes not—rather than an end in its own right. Anthony Crosland's belief that public ownership was no longer essential to the socialist cause was based on a perceived structural change in the nature of the capitalist economy, with the state, trade unions, and salaried management having removed the untrammelled power of capitalist owners that had characterized the classical model of capitalism. Particularly important was the apparent division between ownership and control, which had been engendered by a new managerial class whose ability to oversee the complexity and technicalities of modern industry was far greater than the largely passive shareholders whose involvement was limited.[39] Many revisionists were dissatisfied with the state monopoly model of public ownership implemented by the Attlee government, and sought instead to promote alternative types of collective ownership, including competitive public enterprises or state share ownership in private industry.[40] Such policies were strongly opposed by defenders of nationalization.[41] However, as Favretto has noted, the party's 'left' was itself divided between fundamentalist resisters and a technocratic centre-left, which emphasized the role of public ownership in improving efficiency (with less moral criticism of consumerism and private ownership).[42] Opposition to revisionism also found a unique criticism from the emergent 'New Left'.[43]

---

[39] Tudor Jones, 'Labour Revisionism and Public Ownership', 1951–63', *Contemporary Record*, 5/3 (1991), 437.

[40] Ibid. 439; Ben Jackson, 'Revisionism Reconsidered: "Property-Owning Democracy" and Egalitarian Strategy in Post-War Britain', *Twentieth Century British History*, 16/4 (2005), 433–7.

[41] Jones, 'Labour Revisionism and Public Ownership', 443.

[42] Ilaria Favretto, '"Wilsonism" Reconsidered: Labour Party Revisionism 1952–64', *Contemporary British History*, 14/4 (2000), 54–80.

[43] Mark Wickham-Jones, *Economic Strategy and the Labour Party: Politics and Policy-Making, 1970–83* (Basingstoke: Basingstoke, 1996), 40–3; Mark Wickham Jones, 'The

These doctrinal debates took place within a context of increased pessimism about Britain's economy. Jim Tomlinson has demonstrated how, in the late 1950s, a bout of so-called 'declinism' (as he has termed it) developed in public and political discourse regarding the British economy. The emergence of new economic statistics (regarding national income, trade, productivity, and so on) made it possible to compare the performance of the British economy with other advanced capitalist nations. Over the course of the 1950s it became widely understood by British officials, politicians, and media commentators that the nation was experiencing slower growth than foreign countries, as well as lower rates of industrial production and productivity. By the early 1960s an economic, social, and cultural critique had developed that alleged that Britain was stagnating in the dynamic post-war world.[44] It was evident that Britain needed to improve in order to avoid losing its international economic significance, and so the already established belief in the need to expand and modernize industry became even more pronounced. This was exacerbated by the difficulty of removing the payments deficit, which constantly threatened the value of sterling on international markets, producing an endemic cycle of 'stop–go' in economic activity.[45] In the light of such concerns with relative economic decline, the Conservative government became more interventionist and embraced 'planning' (through the voluntary cooperation of industry) in an effort to bring higher rates of growth to the national economy.[46] This was inspired by the apparent success of 'indicative planning' across the English Channel, where the French state had overseen rapid economic expansion, as well as by a fearful admiration for Soviet economic performance.[47] Planning of this sort was popular with industrialists, notably the Federation of British Industries, and led to the creation of a National Economic Development Council (NEDC)—a tripartite body that agreed target rates of economic growth and sought

New Left's Economic Model: The Challenge to Labour Party Orthodoxy', *Renewal*, 21/1 (2013), 24–31.

[44] Jim Tomlinson, 'Inventing "Decline": The Falling behind of the British Economy in the Post-War Years', *Economic History Review*, 49/4 (1996), 735–9; Matthew Grant, 'Historians, the Penguin Specials and the "State of the Nation" Literature', *Contemporary British History*, 17 (2003), 29–54; Glen O'Hara, *From Dreams to Disillusionment: Economic and Social Planning in 1960s Britain* (Basingstoke: Palgrave Macmillan, 2007), 9.

[45] Tomlinson, 'Inventing "Decline"', 731–57; O'Hara, *Dreams to Disillusionment*, 10–12.

[46] Tomlinson, *Government and the Enterprise*, 246; Jim Tomlinson, 'Conservative Modernisation, 1960–64: Too Little, Too Late?', *Contemporary British History*, 11/3 (1997), 18–38.

[47] O'Hara, *Dreams to Disillusionment*, 16–22.

to help in overcoming possible obstacles to expansion.[48] The approach of the Conservatives in government confirms the existence of a broad industrial–expansionist 'consensus' in economic policy.

Meanwhile, a deliberate attempt to halt 'decline', tied to Harold Wilson's political strategy of focusing on technological advancement and managerial expertise, created what Wickham-Jones has termed a 'technocratic-Revisionist strategy' for Labour.[49] From these policy debates emerged a proposal for a National Plan that could increase the rate of investment in the British economy and act as a catalyst for technological change and adaptation.[50] The means to achieve the former was sought in fiscal incentives rather than state direction; the latter was overseen by new coordinating institutions and backed by the threat of selective nationalizations where the private sector could not achieve the necessary changes.

Following the 1964 general election, the new Labour government sought to implement its approach through the newly created Department for Economic Affairs (DEA) under George Brown. The department sought to increase the rate of investment by creating a stable environment that would generate business optimism; engage in tripartite consultations to generate plans for investment; assist in consultation and the provision of information; and undertake studies of industries and sectors. The first National Plan, a product of these consultations and investigations, was published in September 1965. It led to the creation of the National Board for Prices and Incomes (NBPI) in September 1965, which was designed to dismantle monopolies and (possibly) oversee the establishment of some form of incomes policy. The Industrial Reorganization Corporation (IRC), created in January 1966, pursued the merger, rationalization, and reorganization of industries to gain the benefits of scale. The National Research and Development Corporation was expanded, and the Industrial Expansion Act of 1968 afforded a new Ministry of Technology the power to provide financial aid for industrial developments that would 'support technological improvements'.[51]

Like their predecessors since 1945, the goal of the Wilson governments was to break out of the constraints imposed upon the nation by a weak balance of payments, and in doing so to overcome national 'decline'. It was intended that the plan would achieve a 25 per cent increase in national output between 1964 and 1970, with an annual average growth rate of

---

[48] Tomlinson, *Government and the Enterprise*, 248–9; O'Hara, *Dreams to Disillusionment*, 44–52.

[49] Wickham-Jones, *Economic Strategy and the Labour Party*, 44.

[50] Thompson, *Political Economy and the Labour Party*, 183.

[51] O'Hara, *Dreams to Disillusionment*, 52—71; Thompson, *Political Economy and the Labour Party*, 186–7.

3.8 per cent. The plan would achieve this through 'purposive economic planning'—using the capacities of the state to work with industries operating within the market economy to coordinate and plan economic development.[52] This was to be backed by an explicitly expansionist macroeconomic policy that would escape the 'stop–go' cycles that had characterized the 1950s. No longer would public expenditure be sacrificed for short-term expediencies.[53] The plan fell short of its growth aims. Between 1964 and 1970 the economy grew by 14 per cent—significantly below the 25 per cent target. Investment grew by 20 per cent, rather than the proposed 38 per cent, with private-sector investment increasing at below half the desired rate.[54] Glen O'Hara has attempted to rescue the plan from its critics. It might not have reached its lofty goals, but, according to O'Hara, 'on every available indicator—real output per worker, GDP per hour worked, the rate of growth of overall productivity, and the annual rate of growth—this was the most successful period Britain's economy was ever to enjoy'.[55]

The economic strategy of the social democratic state in the 1950s and 1960s attempted to adapt to the new affluence afforded by a post-war world of consumer capitalism and full employment, but with an ongoing desire to develop an advanced industrial economy that could achieve national prosperity through export-led growth. Within the social demo-cratic movement, the apparent failure of the Labour governments between 1964 and 1970 generated a great deal of disappointment. This provoked a hostile response from the Labour party's left wing. By 1970 the revisionist strategy was in doubt, and attempts were made to chart a new social democratic course.[56]

Social Democracy in Crisis, 1970–1979

The 1970s was a decade characterized by the onset of global economic turmoil following large increases in the price of oil, a collapse of the international monetary system, vast rates of inflation, and a concurrent growth of unemployment. In Britain, the severity of the inflationary crisis placed the existing methods of inflation control under strain, thus creating conflict between the state and the nation's trade unions. The decade also

[52] Cmd 2764, *The National Plan* (London: HMSO, 1965), 395.
[53] Glen O'Hara, ' "Dynamic, Exciting, Thrilling Change": The Wilson Government's Economic Policies, 1964–70', *Contemporary British History*, 20/3 (2006), 384.
[54] Thompson, *Political Economy and the Labour Party*, 188.
[55] O'Hara, 'Dynamic, Exciting, Thrilling Change', 397.
[56] Wickham-Jones, *Economic Strategy and the Labour Party*, 51–2.

witnessed an unprecedented rate of de-industrialization, as 1.5 million manufacturing jobs were lost, and Britain's share of world trade in manufactures declined to a mere 9 per cent.[57] Manufacturing exports had exceeded imports by 59 per cent in 1970, but this was eroded to only 10 per cent in 1979.[58] In this context, following the election defeat in 1970, the Labour Party's economic strategy splintered. A resurgent left wing began to develop a new analysis of Britain's economic problems, and offered more adventurous solutions, in a challenge to the Wilsonism of the previous decade. In addition to the failure of the post-1964 governments to generate a 'new Britain', Wickham-Jones has argued that the rise of the left in the early 1970s can be attributed to new left-wing political alignments within the trade-union leadership, broad structural economic changes, successful political activism by left-wingers, and the weakness of the revisionist response.[59] The journalist Michael Hatfield has described at length the way in which its leading figures colonized the various committees and subcommittees that made up the Labour Party's internal policymaking process during its years of opposition after 1970.[60] Their primary agenda was to develop and promote a case for greater involvement of the state in the management of the economy in order to resist industrial decline, which threatened to reduce employment and living standards. This took the form of the Alternative Economic Strategy (AES).[61] However, despite gaining strong support from within the party, the proposals for radical economic policy changes faced a hostile reception from the party's parliamentary leadership, who, for the most part, remained committed to the revisionist policy norms that had dominated for the previous two decades.[62] The case for more radical and extensive economic interventionism during the 1970s and 1980s was not simply a phenomenon of the British left. The attempted Meidner Plan in Sweden, and the early efforts of President Mitterrand in France, both represented, in the words of Andrew Glyn, 'a challenge to capital' in this

---

[57] Jim Tomlinson, 'Economic Policy', in Anthony Seldon and Kevin Hickson (eds), *New Labour, Old Labour: The Wilson and Callaghan Governments, 1974–79* (London: Routledge, 2004), 56.

[58] G. Tweedale, 'Industry and Deindustrialization in the 1970s', in Richard Coopey and N. W. C. Woodward (eds), *Britain in the 1970s: The Troubled Decade* (London: UCL Press, 1996), 253–5.

[59] Wickham-Jones, *Economic Strategy and the Labour Party*, 117–20.

[60] Michael Hatfield, *The House the Left Built: Inside Labour Policy-Making, 1970–75* (London: Gollancz, 1978).

[61] Wickham-Jones, *Economic Strategy and the Labour Party*, 53–85; John Callaghan, 'Rise and Fall of the Alternative Economic Strategy: From Internationalisation of Capital to "Globalisation"', *Contemporary British History*, 14/3 (2000), 104–30.

[62] Callaghan, 'Rise and Fall', 85.

period, provoked by underlying changes to the material conditions of advanced capitalist economies.[63]

The AES model, backed by its intellectual guru Stuart Holland, found its fullest expression in *Labour's Programme 1973*, which promised to secure 'an irreversible shift in the balance of power and wealth towards working people and their families'. The document proposed a three-pronged strategy for industrial revitalization and socialist equity—the establishment of a National Enterprise Board (NEB) to invest public money in, and take ownership of, large swathes of industry; a system of planning agreements in which the state would provide public money to businesses in exchange for information on their market and business strategies; and an expanded Industry Act, which would bestow upon the government even greater powers to increase the size of the public sector.[64] The party's industrial strategy was at the heart of what Artis, Cobham, and Wickham-Jones have described as its 'civil war' in the 1970s.[65] Although the idea of a state holding company (NEB) found support across the party, the actual role to be played by such an organization was hotly debated. Many on the party's right wing saw it as an effective means to expand the recently abolished IRC to allow for public investment in companies looking for support, and to stimulate investment in areas of the country and industrial sectors requiring development. This built upon ideas developed by Labour revisionists in the 1950s.[66] The left viewed the NEB as a more radical body that could extend public ownership throughout British industry and pursue national economic planning in a much more direct way than had previously been attempted. By taking equity holdings in successful and promising sectors, it would allow the state to become central to the modernization of the economy and provide a means to achieve public ownership of multinational firms.

With the formation of a minority government following the February 1974 general election, the debate over economic strategy continued. Party unity had been achieved in the campaign by Wilson's willingness to make vague concessions to the left, yet confusion reigned once the Labour took power. At the Department of Industry, Tony Benn attempted to set up the National Enterprise Board, yet reluctant ministers made a concerted

[63] Andrew Glyn, *Capitalism Unleashed: Finance, Globalization, and Welfare* (Oxford: Oxford University Press, 2006), 15–21.

[64] Wickham-Jones, *Economic Strategy and the Labour Party*, 53–85, Wyn Grant, *The Political Economy of Industrial Policy* (London: Butterworth, 1982), 101–6.

[65] Michael Artis, David Cobham, and Mark Wickham-Jones, 'Social Democracy in Hard Times: The Economic Record of the Labour Government 1974–1979', *Twentieth Century British History*, 3/1 (1992), 32–58, at 54.

[66] Jackson, 'Revisionism Reconsidered', 433–7.

attempt to prevent a significant expansion of public ownership through its activities.[67] While the Labour Party sought to construct a more advanced, interventionist social democratic economic strategy in the 1970s, the established practices of Keynesian macroeconomic management came under strain. With the onset of 'stagflation', the 1976 sterling crisis and the arrival of the International Monetary Fund (IMF), and the inability to develop a stable incomes policy with the trade unions, the Labour governments of the 1970s retreated from the norms of post-war macroeconomic management. The efficacy of Keynesianism was rejected, and the application of the social democratic cause appeared to flounder (see Chapter 5).

The economic strategy of British social democracy, and of the social democratic state, was designed to achieve the fundamental goal of a modern industrial economy in which export-led growth could resist national decline by overcoming the endemic deficit in the nation's balance of payments; as well as providing stable, productive, and well-paid employment for all.[68] The means to achieve these ends was a source of great debate and competition within the Labour Party over the extent to which the state should intervene in the private economy, with actual policies conditioned by the external economic and political context in which Labour governments found themselves. The crisis of the 1970s both challenged, and offered new opportunities to, the economic strategy of British social democracy. Ultimately the challenges proved too great, and the social democratic cause in Britain was constrained and corroded by a resurgence of liberal economic policy norms in the final decades of the twentieth century. Pursued by Margaret Thatcher's Conservative governments, this political–economic project attempted to reduce the size and scope of the state, restrain the freedoms of organized labour, and revive the apparent dynamism of the free market economy. In economic strategy it represented an almost total rejection of the principles and practices of the post-war social democratic state in Britain.

THE CITY OF LONDON

References to the 'City of London', or 'the City', are deployed widely in both historical and contemporary discourse relating to the political economy of Britain. But what do we mean by 'the City'? Though one may have

---

[67] Wickham-Jones, *Economic Strategy and the Labour Party*, 93–6; Martin Holmes, *The Labour Government, 1974–79: Political Aims and Economic Reality* (Basingstoke: Macmillan, 1985), 35–64; Artis et. al., 'Social Democracy in Hard Times', 45.

[68] In addition, a key aim of the social democratic project was to reduce class, wealth, and income inequality. See Ben Jackson, *Equality and the British Left: A Study in Progressive Political Thought, 1900–64* (Manchester: Manchester University Press, 2011).

an instinctive understanding of what the City refers to, usage of the term is in fact subject to semantic flexibility and context-dependent shifts in meaning. This confusion is made more acute by the fact that the City has both a literal and a metonymical definition. The latter derives from the former, yet they are not identical, and neither is fixed. Despite this slipperiness and inconsistency, the City remains a vitally important subject for historical analysis, as it has been central to modern Britain's economic, social, and political development.

'The City of London' refers literally to the geographical area and self-contained political entity located within roughly one square mile in the eastern half of what is now central London. Originally founded by the Romans, the City became a self-governing municipality during the medieval period, with the rights and privileges of its citizens first recognized by the Crown during the eleventh century. Yet, despite retaining its unique model of governance to this day in the form of the 'City of London Corporation', the character of the City has been defined first and foremost by the economic activities that have taken place within its boundaries. As a result, the City has developed a commercial identity, in contrast with the governmental and administrative character of neighbouring Westminster. This identity has been shaped by a multiplicity of commercial and financial activities, which have evolved over time. These activities, though highly specialized and unique, grew as part of a complex and interdependent structure. At the heart of this structure, and embodying the fundamental essence of the City, were 'markets'—the capital market, the money market, the foreign-exchange market, and commodity markets. It was through these markets that individuals, firms, institutions, and states were brought together, from throughout Britain and across the globe, in a sophisticated and multifaceted financial system. Although certain other non-financial activities have also taken place within the boundaries of the City, it is the financial aspect that is of most interest to students of modern British economic and social development.[69]

The Origins and Evolution of the Modern City of London

The City of London established itself as a centre of international trade, in which merchants from across the world met to exchange goods and

---

[69] The City has hosted a wide array of economic activities (including cloth-making, printing, etc.) According to Ranald Michie, it was only in the post-war period that it became a predominately financial centre—Ranald Michie, *The City of London: Continuity and Change, 1850–1900* (Basingstoke: Macmillan, 1992), 12–15.

commodities, during the sixteenth century.[70] Traders created markets that subsequently expanded and multiplied considerably as global trade increased throughout the eighteenth and nineteenth centuries. International trade demanded auxiliary services, most notably in insurance, banking, and shipping. Insurance protected against the risks inherent in the global movement of goods, while banking provided merchants with credit and an effective mechanism of exchange.[71] Banking services for trade were provided by so-called merchant banks, though these were also joined by other private deposit-taking banks. From the late eighteenth century these private banks based in the City were particularly important to the domestic British economy, as they acted as agents for the hundreds of new provincial banks that had been established throughout Britain. These local banking institutions were able to make deposits in the City, which, through the incipient London discount market, were lent to other regional banks where demand for credit was higher (primarily transferring funds from rural areas to industrializing areas).[72] As the eventual sole issuer of notes and as lender of last resort, the Bank of England, founded in 1694, was at the heart of this evolving banking and monetary system.[73] The Bank's original purpose as a private institution created to raise funds to meet the state's military expenditure also served to create a capital market in which government and commercial securities could be bought and sold.[74] This was formalized in the London Stock Exchange, which was established in the early eighteenth century.[75]

The rapid acceleration in global trade in the latter half of the nineteenth century facilitated the golden age of the City of London as an international financial centre.[76] The square mile, enveloped within the dense metropolis of greater London, was at the centre of the global trading network. Its markets allowed goods and commodities to be exchanged. The highly liquid money market, backed by the Bank of England's commitment to the international gold standard, and the sophisticated means by which merchant banks issued and discounted Bills of Exchange, ensured that trading was efficient and secure.[77] These banks also specialized in making loan issues on behalf of foreign governments and companies on the

---

[70] Youssef Cassis, *Capitals of Capital: The Rise and Fall of International Financial Centres, 1780–2009*, 2nd edn (Cambridge: Cambridge University Press, 2010), 17.

[71] Geoffrey Ingham, *Capitalism Divided? The City and Industry in British Social Development* (Basingstoke: Palgrave Macmillan, 1984), 43–4.

[72] Cassis, *Capitals of Capital*, 18.

[73] Ibid. 16; David Kynaston, *City of London: The History* (London: Chatto & Windus, 2011), 12.

[74] Cassis, *Capitals of Capital*, 16; Ingham, *Capitalism Divided?*, 47.

[75] Ingham, *Capitalism Divided?*, 48.

[76] Ibid. 43; Cassis, *Capitals of Capital*, 83–101.   [77] Cassis, *Capitals of Capital*, 82.

London market.[78] This ensured that the London capital market was highly internationalized, with foreign shares constituting over 50 per cent of those listed on the Stock Exchange after 1873.[79] Shipbroking and insurance provided essential auxiliary services, which enabled international trade to flourish. On the eve of the First World War, the City of London was the pre-eminent international financial centre at the heart of a globalized, liberal world order, yet the war and its myriad effects disrupted this dominance. The collapse of the liberal trading order, the suspension of the gold standard, and the massive increase in government borrowing marked an abrupt break with the norms that had permitted the global City to flourish. During the interwar period, attempts were made to reconstruct the pre-war golden age (most notably in the return to a gold standard in 1926), but these failed in the face of global economic instability and the rise of collectivist (democratic and non-democratic) political movements opposed to, or incompatible with, the liberal order. These factors did not bring the City's international role to an end, but they did impose unprecedented constraints that were to last until the final quarter of the twentieth century (see Chapter 4).

So far we have sketched the development of London as a specialized financial centre over four centuries. However, for the purpose of this book it is necessary to provide a more specific description of the City's position in the British financial system following the Second World War and during the 1950s. Though the City was characterized by a wide diversity of activities, for the purposes of this book it is necessary to focus on the three main activities most relevant to the British economy as a whole, and to post-war economic policymaking—the capital market, the banking system, and the foreign-exchange market.

The Capital Market

Capital markets perform an essential economic function in serving to channel savings into investment. These markets are segmented into primary and secondary markets; equity and debt markets; and corporate and government markets. Equity markets trade in shares (claims of ownership in companies); debt markets trade in bonds (fixed-period loans). Private corporations issue both equity and bonds to raise funds (for example, to purchase plant/machinery); governments issue bonds to fund budgetary deficits. Both are first issued in a primary market, but they are then traded

---

[78] Ibid. 84–8. [79] Ibid. 98–100.

in a secondary market. The liquidity of the secondary market not only reduces the risk of purchasing new issues of equity and debt (as they can be sold on if necessary), but also offers investors the opportunity to profit from their changing value determined on the secondary market. In post-war Britain, capital market investors consisted of a mix of individuals and financial institutions (for example, pension funds, insurance companies, unit trusts, investment trusts). Like the companies and governments seeking to raise investment funds, their access to the capital markets was not direct but achieved through a set of specialized intermediaries who operated those markets. In the City's primary market it was principally the role of merchant banks to arrange initial public offerings for corporate clients.[80] Following the collapse of the international trading order in the 1930s, and with the subsequent imposition of exchange controls, making public offerings for British firms became the most important component of the merchants' business. A firm looking to access funds would approach such a merchant bank and request that it assist in the sale of the shares. Under the formal aegis of the 'Accepting Houses Committee' (of which membership was obligatory), the merchant banks (alternatively known as 'accepting houses' or 'issuing houses') would analyse the share offering and then advise the client on the method, type, price, and terms of the shares offered. Using a variety of techniques, they would also take responsibility for ensuring that the public offering was sold in full.[81] The role of the bank was to ensure that investors were secured in advance of the new issue. The Bank of England was solely responsible for the raising of funds for the British government through the so-called gilt-edged market. On the purchasing side, a wide range of investment managers and advisors were responsible for making investments on behalf of their clients, most notably stock-broking firms. Equities and bonds were then traded, via these intermediaries, on the Stock Exchange. The London Stock Exchange was subject to a strict rulebook, the most significant of which was the formal divide between stockbrokers, who acted on behalf of investing clients; and jobbers, who dealt with brokers on the Stock Exchange floor. The stockbrokers were the intermediaries between the investing public and

---

[80] David Chambers, 'Gentlemanly Capitalism Revisited: A Case Study of the Under-pricing of Initial Public Offerings on the London Stock Exchange, 1946–86', *Economic History Review*, 62/1 (2009), 31–2.

[81] The interchangeability of the terms 'merchant bank', 'accepting house', and 'issuing house' are discussed in Richard Roberts, 'What's in a Name? Merchants, Merchant Bankers, Accepting Houses, Issuing Houses, Industrial Bankers and Investment Bankers', *Business History*, 35/3 (1993), 22–38; Chambers, 'Gentlemanly Capitalism Revisited', 31–2.

the jobbers.[82] These rules were enforced until the 'Big Bang' reform of the Stock Exchange imposed by the Conservative government in 1986.[83]

The Banking System

The characteristics of the British banking system at the end of the 1950s had their origins at the turn of the nineteenth century. The widespread adoption of limited liability in the 1880s evolved into a process of banking amalgamation over the follow forty years. In this period a group of 'big five' banks emerged to dominate the market—Barclays, Lloyds, Midland, National Provincial, and Westminster. Up until the end of the 1950s, they held a roughly consistent 80 per cent of all deposits.[84] In addition to the 'big five' were the 'little six'—the three independent banks of Martins, District, and National; and three subsidiaries: Williams Deacon's Bank and Glyn, Mills & Co. were owned by the Royal Bank of Scotland, and Coutts & Co. owned by National Provincial. Scotland and Northern Ireland also had their own deposit banks, yet London's clearers remained most significant.[85]

The clearing banks, headquartered in the City of London, but with a branch structure throughout the country, offered a narrow set of banking functions to the public. The key banking service offered by the clearers was the current account, which provided depositors with a secure place where their money could be held, and permitted savers to access their funds immediately without prior notice. They also allowed depositors to transfer money securely through cheque and other methods of payment. The current account paid no interest to depositors. The benefits of the account were in the services of security and easy access to funds. If depositors wished to accumulate interest on their deposits, they were required to open a 'time deposit' account. For such accounts, the depositor would not be able to access their funds immediately—instead a seven-day period of notice would have to be given. The inability to withdraw cash immediately was compensated by the capacity to earn interest on deposits, as well as qualified access to transfer and payment facilities.

[82] Philip Augar, *The Death of Gentlemanly Capitalism* (London: Penguin, 2000), 8–17.
[83] Christopher Bellringer and Ranald Michie, 'Big Bang in the City of London: An Intentional Revolution or an Accident?', *Financial History Review*, 21/2 (2014), 111–37.
[84] Forrest Capie and Mark Billings, 'Evidence on Competition in English Commercial Banking, 1920–1970', *Financial History Review*, 11/1 (2004), 69.
[85] Central Office of Information, *British Banking and Other Financial Institutions* (London: HMSO, 1974), 27–9.

As a function of the banks' short-term liabilities—having to allow depositors access to their deposits at short notice—clearing-bank lending was short term. Prudence dictated that to tie up deposits in medium or long-term lending (to make loans that would not be repaid for a number of years), or equity investment, would endanger bank stability. Lending therefore took a specific form of short-term advances to individuals and firms in the form of loans or overdrafts. The latter allowed a bank's existing depositors to borrow from their bank by withdrawing more than they had deposited—having agreed upon such a facility with the bank in advance.[86] Banks did engage in investment, but overwhelmingly in highly liquid and safe assets—primarily in British government securities, or those backed by the government, which could be sold easily on the London money market.[87] Agreements to limit competition between banks emerged in the mid-nineteenth century and had been cemented through the oligopoly of the 'big five' in the twentieth century. Though there was some competition over rates of interest offered for deposits during the interwar period, this was eradicated by the onset of war in 1939, as the clearing banks agreed that all 'ordinary competition' between them would 'cease entirely.' This arrangement was maintained after the war, as the banks agreed not to compete for deposits by offering higher rates of interest on time deposits than a figure agreed among them. The rate of interest would be set at 2 per cent less than bank rate.[88] This cartel agreement was given official sanction by the authorities—the government and the Bank of England (see Chapter 2).

The clearing banks were dependent on the London money market to provide the liquidity necessary for their operation. The market in money, which had historically characterized the City of London's operations, was known as the 'Discount Market'. Made up of a number of 'discount houses' operating under the formal organization of the 'London Discount Market Association', the market was one that allowed for the 'orderly flow of short-term funds'.[89] The houses operated by borrowing money 'at call' (meaning that the funds could be recalled at any time by the lenders) from the clearing banks (and some other financial institutions) and lending it on to another institution at a price. They provided a service to the banks by allowing them to earn interest on their liquid funds while not hindering their ability to pay their depositors on demand. Alternatively, if a bank found itself short of cash at the end of the day, it could temporarily borrow

---

[86] Edward T. Nevin and E. W. Davies, *The London Clearing Banks* (London: Elek Books, 1970), 174.
[87] Ibid. 159.   [88] Capie and Billings, 'Evidence on Competition', 81–4.
[89] Central Office of Information, *British Banking and Other Financial Institutions*, 22–6.

from the discount market to fill the gap. The discount houses were backed by the Bank of England as the lender of last resort, ensuring that a liquidity crisis did not occur in the event that one or more of the houses was unable to repay 'on call'. The discount houses would also purchase Treasury bills (short-term government debts) issued by the Bank, alongside commercial bills, to trade in the discount market. Banks could purchase these securities in the discount market. This was the traditional money market that operated in the City, and, because of its vital role in allowing the Bank of England to engage in open market operations, it was also permitted to operate as a cartel.[90]

Foreign-Exchange Market

A market in foreign exchange is one in which it is possible to buy or sell currencies. Though the market's primary purpose is to enable trade and investment between nations using different currencies, it is possible to profit by speculating on fluctuations in exchange rates. The market consists of buyers and sellers (including individuals in need of foreign currency for foreign travel; banks and other financial institutions; and large and small companies investing and trading across borders), and brokers who earn commissions and seek profit through arbitrage. In a free foreign-exchange market, the relative value of currencies is determined by a range of factors relating to the currency's host nation or currency union. These include the rate of inflation; interest rate differentials between nations; the balance of trade; and other political factors.

Sterling's position as the dominant global trading and reserve currency had ensured that, prior to the First World War, foreign-exchange dealing was not one of London's most significant activities. It was not until the post-1918 ascendance of the US dollar as a currency to rival sterling, and interwar currency instability in Europe, that the market began to increase in size—although, despite its flourishing in the 1920s, the global depression limited its growth in the 1930s. The demands of fighting the Second World War meant that the market was closed in 1939, and the Bank of England was appointed the sole dealer in foreign currency in order to secure and maintain the national reserves.[91] Although this rigid wartime set-up was loosened slightly under the Labour government, it was not

---

[90] Ibid.
[91] John Atkin, *The Foreign Exchange Market: Development since 1900* (Routledge: Abingdon, 2005), 2.

until the end of 1951 that the foreign-exchange market was reopened in London. Yet this was by no means a complete liberalization. The Bank of England continued to play a significant role in the management and control of the market over the following decades. The Bank was responsible for deciding which banks were allowed to operate in the market as 'authorized dealers', and also decided which firms could act as brokers. The market was subject to a number of restrictive practices that were condoned by the Bank—notably the agreement between brokers of a fixed brokerage rate.[92] The market was also limited by the system of post-war exchange controls. These controls, which were first established during the war but later codified in the Labour government's 1947 Exchange Control Act, prevented the free movement of currency in and out of Britain. Their purpose was to prevent the return of destabilizing flows of 'hot money', which had led to chronic exchange-rate instability during the interwar period. Furthermore, controls sought to insulate national economic policies from restive capital seeking to avoid the costs of policies designed to achieve full employment (for example, preventing investors fleeing low interest rates). For most of the period in which exchange controls were in place, their purpose was to conserve the nation's external reserves and balance of payments for the purpose of maintaining the fixed exchange-rate parity of sterling. Controls sought to prevent the erosion of the reserves by strictly limiting overseas investment—a policy that was further bolstered by a desire to maintain investment and employment within Britain, rather than allowing capital to be exported abroad.[93] Under the Conservative governments of the 1950s, there were gradual reductions to exchange controls that benefited the foreign-exchange market—most notably in 1958, when non-UK residents were given permission to convert sterling into foreign currency in London.[94] These liberalizations created the conditions that were to allow London's foreign-exchange market to grow over the following decades.

Historiography of the City of London

There is an extensive literature on the history of the City of London. David Kynaston's four-volume history stands out as the most significant

---

[92] Ibid. 109–35.

[93] For a brief, though not unbiased, account of post-war exchange controls, see Robert Miller and John B. Wood, *Exchange Control for Ever?*, IEA Research Monograph, 33 (London: IEA, 1979).

[94] Atkin, *The Foreign Exchange Market*, 114–17.

contribution, alongside the extensive work of Ranald Michie.[95] In the broader context of modern British history, the role and position of the City of London within the British economy, and in British economic management, have been a source of intense debate since the onset of relative economic decline during the final quarter of the nineteenth century.[96] The emergence of rapid economic growth in the United States and Germany after 1870 had served to undermine Britain's position as the pre-eminent industrialized nation.[97] Average growth rates in Germany and the USA outstripped those of Britain, and the nation's share of world trade was squeezed by new, more advanced industries in foreign countries. Contemporary economic, political, and cultural commentators, used to Britain's global pre-eminence, were shocked. Explanations of such failure abounded, and the issue continues to engage the energies of economic historians today.[98] From the narratives of national economic decline emerged a claim that blamed the City of London, arguing that 'investor biases and institutional rigidities' misallocated capital in such a way that was deeply harmful to the industrial base of the domestic economy.[99] The structure and behaviour of the City ensured a failure to invest in and support efforts to head off foreign

[95] David Kynaston, *The City of London*, i. *A World of its Own 1815–1890* (London: Chatto & Windus, 1994); David Kynaston, *The City of London*, ii. *Golden Years 1890–1914* (London: Chatto & Windus, 1995); David Kynaston, *The City of London*, iii. *Illusions of Gold 1914–1945* (London: Chatto & Windus, 2000); David Kynaston, *The City of London*, iv. *A Club No More 1945–2000* (London: Chatto & Windus, 2002); Michie, *The City of London*; Ranald Michie, *The London Stock Exchange: A History* (Oxford: Oxford University Press, 1999).

[96] Jim Tomlinson, 'Thrice Denied: "Declinism" as a Recurrent Theme in British History in the Long Twentieth Century', *Twentieth Century British History*, 20/2 (2009), 229–32.

[97] N. F. R. Crafts, 'Long-Run Growth', in R. Floud and P. Johnson (eds), *The Cambridge Economic History of Modern Britain*, ii. *Economic Maturity, 1860–1939* (Cambridge: Cambridge University Press, 2003), 1–24; Barry Supple, 'Official Economic Inquiry and Britain's Industrial Decline: The First Fifty Years', in M. Furner and B. Supple (eds), *The State and Economic Knowledge: The American and British Experiences* (Cambridge: Cambridge University Press, 1990), 330–7.

[98] D. C. Coleman, 'Gentlemen and Players', *Economic History Review*, 26/1 (1973), 92–116; N. F. R. Crafts, 'Forging Ahead and Falling Behind: The Rise and Relative Decline of the First Industrial Nation', *Journal of Economic Perspectives*, 12 (1998), 193–210; Bernard Elbaum and William Lazonick, 'The Decline of the British Economy: An Institutional Perspective', *Journal of Economic History*, 44/2 (1984), 567–83; W. P. Kennedy, *Industrial Structure, Capital Markets, and the Origins of British Economic Decline* (Cambridge: Cambridge University Press, 1987); David S. Landes, *The Unbound Prometheus* (Cambridge: Cambridge University Press, 1969), 326–58; Donald McCloskey, 'Did Victorian Britain Fail?', *Economic History Review*, 23/3 (1971), 446–59.

[99] Sidney Pollard, 'Capital Exports, 1870–1914: Harmful or Beneficial?', *Economic History Review*, 38/4 (1985) 489–514; Michael Dintenfass, *The Decline of Industrial Britain, 1870–1990* (London: Routledge, 1992), 41.

competitors, and condemned Britain to (what would become perceived as) a century of relative economic decline.[100]

The primary, and earliest, criticism of the City's capital markets was that investors and financial intermediaries were primarily geared towards the vast export of domestic savings. Rentiers in the City, indifferent to the health and development of the industrial home economy, sought larger returns on investment abroad, rather than ploughing capital into expanding and regenerating British industry. This perspective found its most influential expression in J. A. Hobson's *Imperialism* (1902), which saw under-consumption at home and subsequent vast capital exports as the driving force behind Britain's global empire.[101] Writing on *Riches and Poverty* in 1905, the economist Leo Chiozza Money pronounced: 'While capital has gone overseas in a never-ending stream, the people whose united activities produced the commodities embodied in that capital have remained poor for the lack of proper investment at home.'[102] Despite having a savings rate roughly equal to the United States and Germany (11–15 per cent of Gross National Product (GNP)), British domestic investment rates averaged a mere 7 per cent compared with the 12 per cent rate prevalent in the competitor nations.[103] The effect of foreign investment on the British economy has been debated extensively by economists and historians, with the debate generally dividing between critics who cite its damaging effects, and neoclassical defenders who argue for the contribution to national welfare generated by higher rates of return earned abroad.[104]

The critique of international bias in the capital market was matched by a condemnation of the inadequacy of the British banking system to meet the demands of modern industrial competition. In a lecture to the Royal Institution in 1917, the economist Herbert S. Foxwell deplored the structural and behavioural faults of banks based in London, which he compared unfavourably to the banking model prevalent in Germany. These competitor banks were highly organized, cartelized, and more capable of dealing with large financial propositions. As a result, the German banking system was perceived as being more able to manage risk than the British banking system, as it could be spread more widely and was supported by a high liability ratio. Most importantly, German banks

---

[100] Barry Supple, 'Fear of Failing: Economic History and the Decline of Britain', *Economic History Review*, 47 (1994), 441–58; Tomlinson, 'Thrice Denied'.

[101] J. A. Hobson, *Imperialism: A Study* (London: John Atkins, 1902).

[102] Quoted in Avner Offer, 'Empire and Social Reform: British Overseas Investment and Domestic Politics, 1908–1914', *Historical Journal*, 26/1 (1983), 120.

[103] Pollard, 'Capital Exports, 1870–1914', 489.

[104] McCloskey, 'Did Victorian Britain Fail?'.

were understood to be much more integrated with industrial concerns—often as 'controlling partners'.[105] In his lecture, Foxwell quoted at length W. R. Lawson's comparison of the two banking systems made in a 1906 edition of *Bankers' Magazine*. Lawson argued:

> German banking does not stand aloof from industry and commerce as ours does... The German banker has a finger in everything that is going on. He is represented directly or indirectly on the boards of manufacturing, trading, shipping, and mining companies. He has his eye on all the staple markets... Underwriting is one of his recognised functions, and Germany is thereby spared many of the scandals of British company promoting... What have our London banks to set against them? Simply the old Lancashire maxim of 'Every man to his own job.'[106]

The advantages of universal banking in supporting trade and the development of the German economy compared favourably with London, which, despite being 'unrivalled' in financial resources, had 'carried specialization to an extreme'.[107] The result was that the City lacked a 'natural basis in an intimate connection with the national industries', and failed to understand that a 'proper foundation of overseas finance is well-financed home industry'.[108] The City is alleged to have permitted the industrial base of the British economy to stagnate, failing to take on the responsibilities of coordinating industrial reconstruction, reorganization, and rationalization needed to transform British industry away from a model dominated by small-scale, competitive firms unable to reap the economies of scale and scope necessary to head off foreign challengers.[109] Furthermore, it was deemed that Britain's banks were excessively conservative in their lending and unduly preoccupied with short-term liquidity at the expense of industrial lending.

This criticism of the relationship between the City and British industry was developed further during the interwar period. The inability of London's financial institutions to forge a close integration between themselves and domestic industry was viewed by many as a key impediment preventing the British economy from escaping its interwar malaise. The demand for amalgamations in the staple industries as a scheme for industry-wide rationalization became a predominant theme of economic and industrial discourse during the 1920s. The Committee on Industry and Trade (Balfour Committee) in 1929 represented the high point of this

---

[105] Herbert S. Foxwell, 'The Financing of Industry and Trade', *Economic Journal*, 27/108 (1917), 511–17.
[106] Ibid. 513.   [107] Ibid. 517.   [108] Ibid. 518.
[109] Alfred. D. Chandler Jr, *Scale and Scope: The Dynamics of Industrial Capitalism* (Cambridge, MA: Belknap Press, 1990).

campaign. Its findings reasserted the failure of British banks to coordinate amalgamations, in contrast with their continental peers.[110] This criticism was matched in the same year by the findings of the Committee on Finance and Industry (Macmillan Committee), which alleged that Britain's capital markets left gaps in their provision of finance to 'smaller and medium sized businesses' unable to raise sufficient capital, and called for the establishment of an institution that could serve this un-met demand.[111] For economic historians, the extent to which British banks and other financial institutions could be deemed to have failed domestic industries in this period has been hotly contested.[112]

Sociologists and social historians have attempted to examine the reasons for the supposed disjuncture between the City and industry in a long-term historical perspective. Those working within a Marxist framework of analysis have attempted to comprehend why British 'Capital' was supposedly fractured along financial and industrial lines.[113] Perplexingly, why did capitalism in Britain not escape its liberal, competitive shape and evolve into the centralized model of 'Finance Capital' in the form described by the Marxist theorist of finance Rudolf Hilferding?[114] When, in 1964, Perry Anderson sought to explain the root cause of the 'secular decline of the British economy' in the pages of the *New Left Review*, he provided a structural analysis based on a 'totalizing' history of modern British society. In this assessment he alleged that Britain had not witnessed a full bourgeois revolution, as in other nations, and that aristocratic norms and institutional practices had been unfortunately retained at the expense of bourgeois cultural ascendancy. The landed classes had retained power through the previous three centuries by co-opting industrialists into their ranks and inculcating them with 'traditionalist' ideology.

---

[110] Cmd 3282, *The Final Report of the Committee on Trade and Industry* (London: HMSO, 1929).

[111] Cmd 3897, *The Report of the Committee on Finance and Industry* (London: HMSO, 1931), para. 404.

[112] M. H. Best and Jane Humphries, 'The City and Industrial Decline', in Bernard Elbaum and Willam Lazonick (eds), *The Decline of the British Economy* (Oxford: Clarendon Press, 1978), 223–39; Steven Tolliday, *Business, Banking, and Politics: The Case of British Steel, 1918–1939* (Cambridge, MA: Harvard University Press, 1987); Forrest Capie and Michael Collins, *Have the Banks Failed British Industry?: An Historical Survey of Bank/ Industry Relations in Britain, 1870–1990* (London: Institute of Economic Affairs, 1992); Youssef Cassis, 'British Finance: Success and Controversy', in Jean Jacques van Helten and Youssef Cassis (eds), *Capitalism in a Mature Economy* (Aldershot: Edward Elgar, 1990), 1–22.

[113] David Nicholls, 'Fractions of Capital: The Aristocracy, the City and Industry in the Development of Modern British Capitalism', *Social History*, 13/1 (1988), 71–83.

[114] Rudolf Hilferding, *Finance Capital: A Study of the Latest Phase of Capitalist Development*, ed. Tom Bottomore, trans. Morris Watnick and Sam Gordon (1910; London: Routledge, 2006).

In the nineteenth century the aristocratic class forged a new social and political bloc with commercial and financial elites in the City, which cemented the subordination of industry and captured the machinery of the state to assert policies amenable to an 'externally orientated commercial capitalism' based on the fundamental principles of free trade and the maintenance of the gold standard.[115] Despite E. P. Thompson's attack on Anderson's thesis, it has remained highly influential and the source of ongoing debate.[116] With its cultural connotations of blunting the bourgeois entrepreneurial spirit, it has been characterized as the triumph of 'gentlemanly capitalism'—a source of Britain's global pre-eminence in commerce and trading and the root cause of its long-term industrial decline.[117] When foreign nations caught up with Britain's industrial leadership, the gentlemanly capitalists were supposedly content to live off their foreign investments and unwilling to prevent national economic deterioration.

The notion that the City's institutional and cultural practices have damaged the long-term health of the British economy by imposing a check on its industrial development is joined by a concurrent argument that claims that the City and its representatives have been able to determine and dictate the economic policies of the British state to the benefit of international financial and commercial interests at the expense of domestic industry. This is most substantively expressed in the historical work of Cain and Hopkins, in which, building on Hobson's earlier analysis, it is argued that the financial 'gentlemanly capitalists' of the City drove the expansion of the British Empire. Imperial advance was motivated by the desire to secure returns on capital investments abroad on behalf of moneyed commercial and financial interests that were socially, culturally, and geographically close to the political and administrative classes in Westminster.[118] This City dominance is alleged to have continued

[115] Perry Anderson, 'Origins of the Present Crisis', *New Left Review*, 23 (1964), 26–53; Ingham, *Capitalism Divided?*, 15–39.

[116] E. P. Thompson, 'The Peculiarities of the English', *Socialist Register* (1965), 311–62; Perry Anderson, 'Figures of Descent', *New Left Review*, 161 (1987), 20–77; W. D. Rubinstein, *Men of Property: The Very Wealthy in Britain since the Industrial Revolution* (London: Croom Helm, 1981); Nicholls, 'Fractions of Capital'; Ingham, *Capitalism Divided?*; Youssef Cassis, *City Bankers, 1890–1914* (Cambridge: Cambridge University Press, 1995); Martin J. Wiener, *English Culture and the Decline of the Industrial Spirit, 1850–1980* (Cambridge: Cambridge University Press, 1981), 128–9.

[117] P. J. Cain and A. G. Hopkins, 'Gentlemanly Capitalism and British Expansion Overseas II: New Imperialism, 1850–1945', *Economic History Review*, 40/1 (1987), 1–26; this view has been sceptically evaluated by Martin J. Daunton, '"Gentlemanly Capitalism" and British Industry, 1820–1914', *Past and Present*, 122 (1989), 119–58.

[118] P. J. Cain and A. G. Hopkins, *British Imperialism, 1688–2000* (London: Longman, 2002).

throughout the twentieth century. In 1979 Frank Longstreth charged that
the City had 'largely set the parameters of economic policy and its interests
have generally predominated since the late nineteenth century'.[119] The
Bank of England and the Treasury have been viewed as instruments of the
City in pursuing its goals, regardless of the impact on the domestic
economy. This idea was developed further by the sociologist Geoffrey
Ingham in his argument that a Bank–City–Treasury nexus was based on a
shared interest in preserving 'stable money forms'.[120] Newton and Porter
allege that this relationship and its determination of economic policy
norms were a key reason why Britain was unable to modernize its
industrial base in the twentieth century as the policies required for
doing so were constrained by the biases of Whitehall and the Square
Mile. They claim that 'the central feature of the political economy of
twentieth-century Britain [was] the dominance of City-based finance
capital and the subordination of the interests of production'.[121]

The return to gold in 1925 at its pre-war parity is often cited as the
most vivid example of the City's dominant ideology, with its apparent
costs to industry and employment seen as a sacrifice to the demands of
the City and its international role.[122] E. H. H. Green has argued that in
the late nineteenth century this commitment to the gold standard by the
British state represented the power and influence of the City, which
derived from the structural relationship between Whitehall and the Square
Mile, at the expense of domestic productive interests.[123] In the post-war
decades the commitment to maintain a high and stable sterling exchange
rate is often viewed as a further example of this (see Chapters 4 and 5).

PLAN AND ARGUMENT

This book does not contain a systematic coverage of all aspects of the
financial system in the period, but focuses on areas that were most

---

[119] Frank Longstreth, 'The City, Industry and the State', in Colin Crouch (ed.), *State
and Economy in Contemporary Capitalism* (London: Croom Helm, 1979), 157–90.

[120] Ingham, *Capitalism Divided?*, 9–11.

[121] Scott Newton and Dilwyn Porter, *Modernization Frustrated: The Politics of Industrial
Decline since 1900* (London: Unwin Hyman, 1988), pp. xi–xii.

[122] Sidney Pollard, 'Introduction', to Sidney Pollard (ed.), *The Gold Standard and Employment Policies between the Wars* (London: Methuen, 1970), 1–26.

[123] E. H. H. Green, 'Rentiers versus Producers? The Political Economy of the Bimetallic
Controversy, c.1880–1898', *English Historical Review*, 103/408 (1988), 588–612;
E. H. H. Green, 'The Influence of the City over British Economic Policy, c.1880–1960',
in Youssef Cassis (ed.), *Finance and Financiers in European History, 1880–1960* (Cambridge: Cambridge University Press, 1992), 193–218.

pertinent to social democratic political economy. It is not exhaustive in this sense, but it does highlight a number of important aspects of economic politics in this period that might provide a more detailed and complex understanding of the apparent transition from social democracy to 'neoliberalism'. In the incipient historiography of this transition there has so far been no in-depth study of the role played by the financial sector. This is unusual, given the significant material success of the City of London as an international financial centre, which has accompanied the late-twentieth-century 'neoliberal' consensus. Furthermore, the wider literature on neoliberalism often cites finance capital, and 'financialization', as critical to its emergence.[124]

Chapter 1 focuses on the growth of institutional saving and investment in the post-war decades, and the impact of this on efforts to manage and shape the domestic industrial economy. Throughout the post-war period individual share ownership was progressively displaced by institutional investors. The most significant of these institutional investors managed the pooled savings of millions of individuals in the form of pension and insurance funds. The radical change in the nature of investment and ownership entailed by this process was underappreciated in political and public discourse in the 1950s and 1960s. It was only in response to the acceleration of industrial decline in the 1970s that institutional investors, and their influence on the performance and well-being of the national economy, was finally recognized. Edward Heath's Conservative government, perturbed by the divorce between ownership and control engendered by institutionalization, and the failure of the institutions to support Britain's struggling industries, unsuccessfully attempted to establish a mechanism by which institutional investors could meet their obligations as owners of capitalist firms. Meanwhile, within the Labour Party and trade-union movement, a more thoroughgoing critique of the institutions and proposals for their reform was developed, which argued not only that investors should meet their proprietary obligations, but that they should also channel a greater proportion of the nation's savings into long-term investment in domestic industry. Furthermore, it was argued that they should be brought under a greater degree of public and worker control to ensure that their investment practices were efficient, accountable, and in line with the requirements of national economic development—contrary to the apparent short-termism prevalent on the London Stock Exchange. In the crisis decade of the 1970s, these attempted reforms represented a struggle to adapt and reformulate

---

[124] Gérard Duménil and Dominique Lévy, *Capital Resurgent: Roots of the Neoliberal Revolution* (Cambridge, MA: Harvard University Press, 2004).

social democracy to the changing patterns of ownership and investment that had challenged the fundamental structure of the post-war settlement.

Chapter 2 concerns the politics of managing the domestic banking system. It focuses on the breakdown in the post-war settlement model of voluntary cooperation between the state and an oligopoly of cartelized banks in the 1960s, and the implication of this for managing the domestic economy. It highlights the political pressure to abolish the banking cartel in the late 1960s, in addition to material changes to the banking sector, which resulted in the adoption of liberal policies designed to encourage competition in banking under the Heath government in 1971. The property bubble, and subsequent secondary banking crisis of 1974, demonstrated to many on the left that a liberalized banking system was incapable of rational and efficient credit provision that served the needs of the domestic industrial economy. In addition, the permission to compete freely for deposits was deemed to have failed customers, as the retail banking sector remained dominated by an oligopoly of major banks that were uncompetitive on price and services. It is in this context, and against the background of the decade's industrial crisis, that the left wing of the Labour Party revived its pre-war policy of nationalizing the banking system in order to recapture the state's capacity to create and allocate credit in accordance with the needs of national economic development. This was driven by a desire to revive the ailing industrial economy, but was also an attempt to rationalize and make more efficient the provision of banking services to the public.

Chapter 3 focuses on the failure of the labour movement to generate any significant reform of the financial system during the 1970s. It highlights a variety of political factors that limited the scope for change, yet argues that these were rooted in the more fundamental failure of the left to garner support for reforms from non-financial industrial economic interests. Despite apparent tensions between 'industry' and 'finance' at the start of the decade, and the collapse of the stock market in 1974, which starved firms of investment capital, the left was unable to build a 'producer's alliance' against an intransigent City establishment. Instead, financial and industrial interests, having increasingly integrated in the post-war decades, developed a political and ideological alliance in response to the mid-decade economic crisis. This alliance was forged by the severe crisis of profitability after 1973, which saw the rate of return on investment, and the share of national income accruing to profits, decline sharply. The means to achieve the restoration of profits amounted to a simple set of proposed solutions: cut taxation on capital and personal income, eradicate inflation, and reduce government interference in the operation of the economy. These proposals for government economic retrenchment as the solution to industrial decline were an outright rejection of the state-coordinated financial strategy offered by the left. Furthermore, they were a direct challenge to the fundamental premises of post-war social democracy.

Chapter 4 considers the resurgence of the City of London as an international financial centre in the post-war decades. It challenges the notion that this process was simply a material one in which the regulatory and institutional changes permitted the revival of the City's financial entrepôt position in the world economy. Instead it asserts the additional importance of a distinct political and public-relations campaign that promoted the revival of the City as a post-sterling international financial centre. The Committee on Invisible Exports campaigned for the recognition of the City's positive contribution to Britain's balance of payments through its 'invisible earnings', and argued that this contribution could be increased by reducing impediments on its activities (primarily by removing exchange controls and cutting taxation). The campaign sought to build a broad-based alliance between invisible exporters, but existed primarily to promote the interests of the City. The invisibles campaign was a distinct product of the post-war preoccupation with the balance of payments, which challenged the fundamental belief, embedded in economic policy since the war, that the route to national prosperity could be found in expanding industrial production. The campaign sought to reconceptualize Britain as a historic commercial and financial, rather than industrial, economy. In doing so it undercut a core principle on which the social democratic political–economic project was based.

Chapter 5 considers the widespread claim that the City of London was capable of dictating and determining British macroeconomic policy in the twentieth century. This has been explored in great depth with regards to the sterling crises of the 1960s, but historians have not considered the role of the City in the transition from 'Keynesian' demand management to 'monetarist' policy norms during the 1970s. The chapter argues that investors in the markets for government debt and currency were central to the emergence of British monetarism. It describes the post-devaluation valorization of the 'money supply', which led investors to realign their expectations with the behaviour of monetary aggregates. The collapse of the global fixed exchange-rate regime, coupled with vast domestic inflationary pressures after 1973, determined that investors came to employ the 'money supply' as a convenient new measure with which to assess the soundness of British economic management. The critical juncture of the 1976 sterling crisis forced the Labour government into a reluctant adoption of monetary targets as part of a desperate attempt to regain market confidence. The result was to impose significant constraints on the government's economic policymaking freedom, as attempts to retain favourable money supply figures were exposed to the short-term volatility of increasingly globalized and highly capitalized financial markets. The undermining of the social democratic norms of macroeconomic management was not the result of government capture by 'gentlemanly capitalists',[125] nor was it a simple conspiracy, but it was the product of new financial pressures being brought to bear on the state in response to a set of material and institutional changes.

The concluding chapter will reflect on the implications of the research presented in this book for the wider debate concerning the transition from social democracy to neoliberalism in Britain during the final third of the twentieth century.

---

[125] Cain and Hopkins, *British Imperialism.*

1

'Pension Fund Socialism'

Institutional Investment and Social Democracy

The British financial system underwent a fundamental and radical restructuring in the post-war era—the institutionalization of ownership and investment. A 'financial institution' is any organization responsible for holding and managing the savings of individuals and firms. Such institutions aggregate these separate savings into a fund that is then invested on behalf of those individuals and firms. Financial institutions (also referred to as 'institutional investors') may take on a variety of forms, such as insurance companies, pension funds, merchant banks, and investment trusts.[1] In terms of size and impact, insurance company and pension funds were the most significant institutional investors in the post-war period. Insurance funds collected and held the contributions of millions of individuals, companies, and organizations. The purpose of such contributions was to insure against the uncertainties of life, as well as retirement and death. Although insurance companies provided private pension coverage to some individuals, employers were the primary provider of non-state pensions in post-war Britain. Occupational pensions are private arrangements between an employer and employee, in which the former is responsible for the creation of a fund into which both the employer and the employee contribute a percentage of the employee's salary. The accumulated pension fund is controlled by a board of trustees (drawn primarily from management, although employees and outside experts (such as actuaries and economists) are also often represented). Among larger pension funds, the task of investing the fund on behalf of the trustees is usually carried out by an in-house fund manager. Most pension schemes delegate this role to an external professional fund manager, such as an insurance company, a merchant bank, or a stockbroking firm. On

---

[1] Richard J. Briston and Richard Dobbins, *The Growth and Impact of Institutional Investor: A Report to the Research Committee of the Institute of Chartered Accountants in England and Wales* (London: Institute of Chartered Accountants, 1978), 9.

retirement, each employee is entitled to draw money from the fund in the form of a pension. In the post-war period, the size of the pension entitlement would, in almost all cases, be related to salary at the time of retirement—the 'final salary'—plus the time spent contributing to the scheme.

The growth of private and occupational pension saving in the post-war decades was a function of the specific context in which state pension provision had been established under the 1945 Labour government.[2] The creation of a basic state pension in 1948 offered only a subsistence level upon which it was expected that other voluntary insurance would be made. Individuals and their employers were expected to save in order to ensure a comfortable retirement beyond the minimum. This form of saving was given encouragement through the state in the form of tax reliefs on employer and employee contributions to schemes, as well as exemptions from taxation on interest, dividends, and capital gains that arose from the investment of funds.[3] Superannuation schemes were at the heart of the post-war settlement in pension policy, although the extent to which the state should provide earnings-related pensions was hotly contested between an enthusiastic Labour Party and a reluctant Conservative Party.[4]

The number of people enrolled in private/occupational pension schemes rose rapidly throughout the post-war decades, from 6.2 million in 1953 to 11.8 million in 1979. This amounted to an increase from 28.9 per cent of the total workforce to 51.1 per cent.[5] Subsequently, the total funds held by these institutional funds increased from an estimated total nominal market value of £2,000 million in 1957 to £31,000 million in 1978 (Fig. 1.1). The management of such funds, which held the savings of millions of individuals, was delegated either to in-house fund managers of pension funds, or to an elite group of London merchant banks and stockbrokers. In 1980, Richard Minns estimated that three-quarters of all externally managed funds were controlled by just twenty City firms.[6]

---

[2] Hugh Pemberton, 'Politics and Pensions in Post-War Britain', in Hugh Pemberton, Pat Thane, and Noel Whiteside (eds), *Britain's Pensions Crisis: History and Policy* (Oxford: Oxford University Press, 2006), 39–63.

[3] Richard Minns, *Pension Funds and British Capitalism: The Ownership and Control of Shareholdings* (London: Heinemann, 1980), 3–4.

[4] Steven Nesbitt, *British Pensions Policy Making in the 1980s: The Rise and Fall of a Policy Community* (Aldershot: Avebury, 1995), 9; Hugh Pemberton, ' "What Matters is what Works": Labour's Journey from "Superannuation" to "Personal Accounts"', *British Politics*, 5/1 (2010), 41–64.

[5] Joan C. Brown and Stephen Small, *Occupational Benefits as Social Security* (London: Policy Studies Institute, 1985), 138, 153.

[6] Minns, *Pension Funds and British Capitalism*, 32.

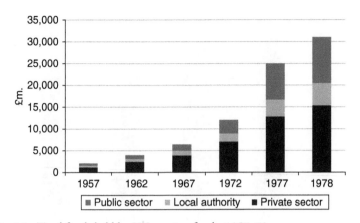

Fig. 1.1. Total funds held by UK pension funds, 1957–78

Source: Committee to Review the Functioning of Financial Institutions: Evidence on the Financing of Industry and Trade, appendix (1980), table 3.50.

The growth of institutional funds radically changed the nature of the equity market as the funds sought out investment opportunities that could provide adequate retirement benefits to savers. The result was the sustained colonization of private shareholding by institutions at the expense of personal investors. At the start of the Second World War private individuals were estimated to own over 80 per cent of the ordinary shares listed on the London Stock Exchange. By the end of the 1970s the percentage of shares held by individuals was estimated to have fallen to roughly one-third of the Stock Exchange listings (see Fig. 1.2). In a hostile tax environment, rich individuals divested themselves of stock, while tax incentives generated a 'wall of money' for institutions that could be invested in equity.[7] Writing in 1982, the financial journalist John Plender observed that in each year since the war the collective savings institutions had 'quietly absorbed an average 1%–1½% of the share capital of quoted companies, thereby establishing a growing hold on the means of production in Britain'.[8] By 1981 pension funds and insurance companies were recorded as the nominal owners of almost half of all shareholdings on the London Stock Exchange. This was as much a function of the growth of the funds as it was a cultural shift in the practices of investment managers, who, following the success of Imperial Tobacco's highly prominent

---

[7] Brian R. Cheffins, *Corporate Ownership and Control: British Business Transformed* (Oxford: Oxford University Press, 2008), 344–81.

[8] John Plender, *That's the Way the Money Goes: Financial Institutions and your Savings* (London: André Deutsch, 1982), 13.

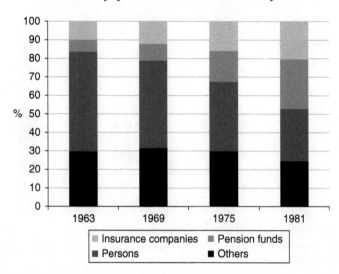

Fig. 1.2. Distribution of share ownership on the London Stock Exchange, 1963–81
Source: Stock Exchange Survey of Share Ownership, (London: London Stock Exchange, 1983), table 2.1b.

pension fund manager George Ross Goobey, signed up to the 'cult of equity' in pursuit of inflation-beating returns.[9]

The growth of pension funds and their takeover of the nation's equity markets was, according to Harold Wilson, 'the biggest revolution in the financial scene this century'.[10] The rise of the institutions revolutionized the political economy of British capitalism by establishing and expanding a form a collective ownership of the means of production that was distinct from the pursuit of 'public ownership', which had been at the heart of the political debate since the war. Peter F. Drucker, a Professor of Management at New York University, described the similar process that had occurred in the United States during the same period as the emergence of 'pension fund socialism'.[11] Yet, despite the significance of the institutions' ascent, the change went largely unnoticed outside the financial world until the mid-1970s. In his 1977 memoirs Harold Wilson observed that 'surprisingly it was totally unperceived by political or even financial

---

[9] Ibid. 40–2; Yally Avrahampour, '"Cult of Equity": Actuaries and the Transformation of Pension Fund Investing, 1948–1960', *Business History Review*, 89/2 (2015), 281–304.

[10] Harold Wilson, *Final Term: The Labour Government, 1974–1976* (London: Weidenfeld & Nicolson, 1977), 146–50.

[11] Peter F. Drucker, *The Unseen Revolution: How Pension Fund Socialism Came to America* (London: Heineman, 1976); see also Gordon Clark, *Pension Fund Capitalism* (Oxford: Oxford University Press, 2000).

commentators until very recently'.[12] Historians of Britain's post-war
political economy have subsequently paid little attention to this phenomenon.[13] Where the issue of nationalization has dominated historical
studies of the politics of ownership and control, little has been said
about the position of institutional investment.[14]

This chapter attempts to remedy this deficiency. It argues that the
emergence of institutional investment and ownership undermined the
foundations upon which the social democratic settlement had been
built. The spread of beneficial ownership to millions of individuals
through the collective savings managed by the institutions fundamentally
changed a number of the key economic and political relationships of
British society. The tools by which social democracy had been pursued
in the 1940s and 1950s—particularly the disaggregated, profits-based
mechanism employed for managing investment—were far less relevant
and efficacious by the 1970s. On the left and right of politics, attempts
were made to bring the institutions within the framework of national
economic management, and to knit the long-term savings of the community within the requirements of the domestic industrial economy. Edward
Heath's Conservative government, perturbed by the divorce between
ownership and control engendered by institutionalization, unsuccessfully
attempted to establish a mechanism by which institutional investors could
meet their obligations as owners of capitalist firms. Meanwhile, within the
Labour Party and trade-union movement, a more thoroughgoing critique
of the institutions and proposals for their reform was developed that argued
not only that investors should meet their proprietary obligations, but that
they should channel a greater proportion of the nation's savings into long-
term investment in domestic industry. Furthermore, it was argued that
they should be brought under a greater degree of public control to ensure
that their investment practices were efficient, accountable, and in line
with the requirements of national economic development—contrary to
the apparent short-termism prevalent on the London Stock Exchange.

---

[12] Wilson, *Final Term*, 146–50.
[13] The notable exceptions are Robin Blackburn's *Banking on Death: Or, Investing in
Life: The History and Future of Pensions* (London: Verso, 2002); Robin Blackburn, *Age
Shock: How Finance is Failing us* (London: Verso, 2006); Pemberton, 'What Matters is what
Works'; Hugh Pemberton, 'The Failure of "Nationalization by Attraction": Britain's Cross-
Class Alliance against Earnings Related Pensions in the 1950s', *Economic History Review*,
65/4 (2012), 1428–49; Pemberton, 'Politics and Pensions in Post-War Britain'.
[14] e.g. Leslie Hannah, 'A Failed Experiment: The State Ownership of Industry', in
Roderick Floud and Paul Johnson (eds), *The Cambridge Economic History of Modern
Britain*, iii. *Structural Change and Growth, 1939–2000* (Cambridge: Cambridge University
Press, 2004), 84–111; Jim Tomlinson, '"A Failed Experiment"? Public Ownership and the
Narratives of Post-War Britain', *Labour History Review*, 73/ 2 (2008), 228–43.

In the crisis decade of the 1970s these attempted reforms represented a struggle to adapt and reformulate social democracy in response to fundamental material changes to the British economy that had taken place over the post-war decades.

THE HEATH GOVERNMENT AND THE INSTITUTIONAL INVESTORS

The shock election of Edward Heath's Conservative government in 1970 marked a significant moment in the post-war administration and management of the national economy. For the six previous years the Labour government, under the leadership of Harold Wilson, had been engaged in an economic strategy that had sought to harness the scale and scope of the state to expand and modernize the industrial sectors of the economy. The 'purposive economic planning' of the National Plan had attempted to use the state to work with industries operating in the market economy to cooperate, coordinate, and plan economic development.[15] Alongside the macroeconomic goals of the Department of Economic Affairs (DEA) a host of interventionist state institutions were created, including the National Board for Price and Incomes (NBPI) in 1965, a Ministry of Technology (Mintech), and the Industrial Reorganization Corporation (IRC) in 1966. As a government body, the IRC was designed to work with industry to identify opportunities for reorganization, concentration, and rationalization that could bring about greater efficiency and make British industry more internationally competitive. The idea was built upon the well-established belief that the fragmented nature of industrial organization in Britain prevented the benefits of scale and sectoral rationalization from being realized, which was to the detriment of national economic performance. In addition it attempted to provide a means by which inefficient management, pursuing outdated practices, could be reformed.[16] The IRC was established on the assumption that only the state could supposedly oversee such a transformation. The election of the Heath government signalled an explicit attempt to break with the approach of the Wilson governments. Its main objective was to abandon all that had gone before, and, under the mythical new guise of

---

[15] Cmd 2764, *The National Plan*, 395.

[16] Jim Tomlinson, *The Labour Governments, 1964–70*, iii. *Economic Policy* (Manchester: Manchester University Press, 2004), 109–12; C. Pass, 'The Industrial Reorganization Corporation—a Positive Approach to the Structure of Industry', *Long Range Planning*, 4/1 (1971), 63–70; Cheffins, *Corporate Ownership and Control*, 338–40.

the hard-edged, business-minded 'Selsdon Man', it threw the interventionist framework on a 'bonfire of Wilsonism' and pursued a deliberate policy of disengagement.[17] Heath sought to achieve the same goals as the Wilson government—a more rational, coordinated, internationally competitive industrial economy that could overcome national 'decline'. Yet the approach differed—the power of market competition and business efficiency was to be harnessed, rather than that of the state.[18]

The IRC was one of the first of the Wilson initiatives to be scrapped by the incoming Tory government. It was condemned as a wasteful means of channelling public subsidies into failing 'lame duck' firms. Speaking at the twenty-fifth anniversary dinner of the Industrial and Commercial Finance Corporation in 1970, John Davies, the Secretary of State for Trade and Industry, condemned the IRC for its reliance on public funds 'in order to bring about changes of structure in industry which apparently others could not see profit in achieving.' The government believed that private investors, operating through the mechanisms of the City's financial markets, could do the job of creating a profitable, rational, and efficient industrial sector far more effectively. Yet Davies clearly felt that the City needed some prodding in the right direction. At the same dinner he asked his City audience to consider

> whether the City of London has sufficiently modernized its structures and its facilities to meet the present day needs of industry. Is it fully ready to meet the increased responsibilities which will devolve upon it following the disengagement of the Government from intervention in industry?...the City is justly proud of its experience and its history. It is also proud of its traditions and tends to preserve the traditional relationships both within the City and between City institutions and their industrial clients.[19]

Davies's critique drew on the long-standing notion of the City's detachment from the domestic industrial economy. He was, in the spirit of cooperation rather than direction, asking the City to equip itself to meet the national interest and to abandon some of its more conservative traditions. With the possible ascension to the EEC in mind, Davies advised the institutions to 'look more closely at what is now going on in

---

[17] Dilwyn Porter, 'Government and the Economy', in Richard Coopey and N. Woodward (eds), *Britain in the 1970s: The Troubled Economy* (London: University College London Press, 1996), 36.

[18] Alec Cairncross, 'The Heath Government and the British Economy', in Stuart Ball and Anthony Seldon (eds), *The Heath Government, 1970–1974: A Reappraisal* (London: Longman, 1996), 107–38.

[19] Public Record Office, The National Archives, Kew [henceforward TNA]: T 326/ 1236. Department of Trade and Industry Press Notice, 'Finance for Small Companies', 5 November 1970.

Europe', where investors were 'prepared to acquire technical expertise to enable them to assess and advise on proposals for new investment put to them by industry'. Furthermore, they were 'increasingly prepared to exercise their powers to influence and, if necessary, effect changes in management and companies in which they have an interest'.[20] The mechanism of the national capital market, operated through the City of London, would have to modernize in order to ensure that investors could meet their responsibilities as custodians of British industry. Where the state had retreated, the City had to engage.[21]

Willingness on behalf of the government to wait for the City firms and investing institutions to self-organize was short-lived. In early 1971 the engineering firm Rolls Royce went bankrupt, and the government was forced to take it into public ownership. In the mid-1960s the firm had been highly successful, with increasing profits and rising dividends. When the firm signed a contract with the American aerospace contractor Lockheed Aircraft Corporation in March 1968 to deliver a technologically advanced engine, the RB 211, it was widely celebrated as a great achievement for British industry. However, the project did not go to plan, as technical problems emerged, and costs rose precipitously.[22] Rolls Royce's bankruptcy, and subsequent nationalization, were a great embarrassment for the government, which had so publicly professed its pro-market, anti-state agenda. In a speech to the Young Conservatives shortly afterwards, Heath declared it as the final eclipse of Britain's economic and industrial 'illusions'—no less than a fundamental reappraisal of the nation's economy, society, and politics was required.[23] Moreover, it signalled to Heath that something needed to be done immediately to ensure that the financial institutions, and the City mechanisms for managing industrial investment, became more engaged with the firms in which they owned shares. The affair had demonstrated that there was some inherent flaw in the capacity of the investors to ensure that firms were effectively monitored and supported. Writing in the *Financial Times*, the business consultants Dr G. Tugendhat and A. Kennaway observed that the collapse had 'thrown a glaring light on one of the most serious deficiencies of the City . . . its lack of knowledge of the technologies employed by the companies it is dealing with', and the willingness of investors to place too

---

[20] Ibid.
[21] S. McLachlan, 'Davies Questions Ability of City to Meet Needs of Modern Industry', *Financial Times*, 6 November 1970.
[22] Sue M. Bowden, 'Ownership Responsibilities and Corporate Governance: The Crisis at Rolls Royce, 1968–71', *Business History*, 44/3 (2002), 36–40.
[23] David Thompson, 'Premier Lashes out at "Britain's Great Illusions"', *Daily Mirror*, 8 February 1971.

much trust in the expertise of industrial managements without any detailed evaluation of their plans. In the case of Rolls Royce there had apparently been a 'curious lack of co-ordination between the engineering and financial side'.[24] In 1968, although 50,742 private individuals held 45 per cent of the company's shares, pension and insurance companies alone held 26 per cent.[25] Many of these investors, to the frustration of Heath and others, did not take any active responsibility for the firm's difficulties and had made no significant attempt to assist Rolls Royce. Instead they treated their shareholdings simply as investments in which they had the right to sell at any time in order to transfer ownership. When difficulties arose, some (for example, the Prudential) exited the company completely.[26]

For the modernizing and liberalizing Heath administration, private ownership was key to coordinating industrial development. The under-performance of British industrial management could be resolved only through the external force of shareholders. Yet, in the case of Rolls Royce, its shareholders had failed miserably to live up to this task. The response from a purely liberal perspective might be to assert the right of shareholders to exit when faced with the possibility of making a loss, and perhaps argue that such behaviour is the most effective discipline on firms. Yet, for the Heath government, accepting the collapse of a major industrial firm and the concomitant loss of jobs, export trade, and national prestige, was beyond the realms of acceptability. In this sense the government remained constrained by the expectations of the industrial social democratic settlement. Heath and critics of the institutions were frustrated that the shareholders had exercised no custodial responsibilities for the firm and made no attempt to support it when in trouble. This assumed that ownership came with duties beyond immediate financial gain. Indeed, the post-war Conservative ideal of a property-owning democracy was embedded in a set of values and norms that associated ownership with obligation. In a 1953 document produced by Michael Fraser of the Conservative Research Department (Deputy Chair of the Party between 1964 and 1975), it was argued that property not only provided the 'historical basis of liberty and status' but also offered an 'educative and stabilizing force' that could 'preserve moral values'. The spread of private ownership in society was 'just as concerned to spread responsibility as to

---

[24] G. Tugendhat and A. Kennaway, 'Harsh Lessons for the City', *Financial Times*, 12 February 1971.
[25] Bowden, 'Ownership Responsibilities and Corporate Governance', 42.
[26] Ibid. 43–6.

spread wealth'.[27] What was required in the age of institutionalized owner-ship and a liquid secondary market in company shares was a mechanism by which this responsibility could be exercised.

ATTEMPTED INSTITUTIONAL COORDINATION

Shortly after the Rolls Royce affair, Heath met the Governor of the Bank of England, Leslie O'Brien, to discuss a solution. The Prime Minister began by asking O'Brien whether the Bank of England could redevelop its industrial interventionist role of the 1930s.[28] The Governor thought that this would be too simplistic, but promised that something would be arranged once the 'immediate aftermath of the Rolls-Royce collapse' had subsided.[29] The Bank had already been considering the creation of some sort of mechanism for improving the relationship between financial insti-tutions and industry since the election. Following the abolition of the IRC, the Bank had been concerned that a replacement would have to be found. The Bank, and many in the City, are recorded as expressing disquiet at the disappearance of the IRC, which many believed had actually served a useful purpose in saving some industries from failure through reconstruction and reorganization. Heath's rhetoric that the body existed only to bail out inefficient industries with public money was not completely accurate. John Fforde, the Bank's executive director for Home Finance, was a vocal supporter of the IRC's role. Writing to the board of governors at the time of the collapse, he praised the IRC's role in supporting industries and firms in difficulty—contrary to the current government's criticisms. Although it was not 'the Great Rescuer' that some Labour supporters claimed (it would not have been able to save Rolls Royce), he was firmly committed to the value of the IRC as a

---

[27] Conservative Party Archive, Bodleian Library, Oxford [henceforward CPA]: ACP 3/3, Michael Fraser, 'The Ownership of Property', 1 May 1953; Ben Jackson, 'Property-Owning Democracy: A Short History', in Martin O'Neill and Thad Williamson (eds), *Property-Owning Democracy: Rawls and Beyond* (Oxford: Wiley-Blackwell, 2012), 33–52.

[28] TNA: T 326/1236, letter from Robert Armstrong to W. S. Ryrie, 12 February 1971; see Carol E. Heim, 'Limits to Intervention: The Bank of England and Industrial Diversi-fication in the Depressed Areas', *Economic History Review*, 37/4 (1984), 533–50; Sue M. Bowden and Michael Collins, 'The Bank of England, Industrial Regeneration, and Hire Purchase between the War', *Economic History Review*, 44 (1991), 120–36; William Garside and Julian Greaves, 'The Bank of England and Industrial Intervention in Interwar Britain', *Financial History Review*, 3/1 (1996), 69–86.

[29] TNA: T 326/1236, W. S. Ryrie, 'Note for the Record: The Bank of England and Industrial Financing', 23 February 1971.

'rather brilliant improvisation' for dealing with industrial problems.[30] By the end of 1971 even Heath had privately agreed that abolishing the IRC had been 'over hasty' and some sort of replacement (with a different name) was needed.[31]

It fell to the Governor, in his role as both an arm of the state and a representative of the City, to draw the investing institutions into some sort of organization that could meet the demands of the government for greater institutional intervention in industry on a 'voluntary' basis. Unlike the banks and other organizations that 'operated' the City's markets, the pension and insurance funds themselves were not conventionally part of the City structure. Their relationship with the Bank was not well developed, which made negotiations difficult. In a short memo written to gather opinion and try to bring the institutions together, O'Brien wrote:

> Both in Government and in the City there has long been deep concern about the serious and widespread defects in the management of British industry. The Labour Government sought to alleviate the problem by creating the IRC and placing large funds at its disposal. The present Government are not willing to use public money for such a purpose . . . Certainly money alone is not the answer to the problem. The need is for closer contact between those who invest in industry and those who run it. If, in this way, industrial management could be made subject to more informed and continuous scrutiny there seems good prospect of its efficiency being improved and private investment capital being more wisely used.[32]

The Governor believed that the responsibility fell on the institutional investors, because any attempt to mobilize individual shareholders would be worthless, as 'the weight of inertia was too great'. He needed to persuade the institutions to take an active interest and involvement in the companies in which they had invested; to limit their preference for selling shares in response to bad news; and to encourage them to use their power and influence as a direct discipline on British industry. Furthermore, it was intended that the institutions should work together to meet the operations previously fulfilled by the IRC in making firms and sectors more efficient through amalgamation and rationalization. The institutions needed to develop some way of providing capital for such operations, enforce necessary changes where managements refused, and prevent firms in prospective or actual financial difficulty from going unnecessarily bankrupt.

---

[30] Bank of England Archive, Bank of England [henceforward BOE]: 7A19/2, J. Fforde, 'Industrial Management and the Institutional Investor', 12 November 1971.
[31] BOE: 7A19/2, L. O'Brien, 'Governor's Note: Industrial Efficiency and Finance', 25 November 1971.
[32] BOE: 7A19/1, L. O'Brien, 'The Finance of Industry', 1 March 1971.

The Governor suggested setting up a 'highly expert organization' in which the individual institutions, working in collaboration with each other, would achieve these ends. Due to its expertise, and its backing by the institutional investors, he believed that it would have the full confidence of both industry and finance.[33]

The response, from generally supportive advisors to the Governor, was not wholly positive. Leopold de Rothschild, like so many others, expressed disappointment in a meeting with O'Brien that the IRC had been abandoned, but thought that the City was 'cautious to the point of cynicism' of the Governor's proposed venture. He suggested that an alternative would be to create a working party to handle such cases directly through the Bank of England.[34] Despite various ideas, such as using the existing merchant banks to meet the need, expanding the FCI, or starting an 'investors' club', which would 'watch the interests of members in the field of industrial investment', the only idea that had any real traction was the notion of a 'focal point'.[35] This would simply be a management-consultancy-type body that would assist in improving the management of poorly performing companies. There would be no special financial provisions available. Writing to Fforde in October, O'Brien acknowledged that a 'focal point' would be 'a body of enormous political power'. This was good insofar as the problem of inadequate management in industry was 'not going to be taken in hand with a feather duster'. However, 'outright war' on management was not what the Governor intended. He continued: 'We want quietly but effectively to make management in industry realize that shareholder opinion has a mobilization centre from which it can, if need be, make its power felt.'[36] However, the various types of financial institution, each with different investment strategies and obligations, made coordination difficult. When Fforde visited the Holborn offices of the Prudential (the nation's largest life-insurance firm) in October, its Director, Kenneth Usherwood, informed him that there were differences between the attitudes of investment trusts and the life offices. The former were 'closed-end funds which grew relatively slowly and did not have the function of investing the current savings of the populace'. Additionally, the life offices were not keen on publicity and 'preferred doing good by stealth', whereas the Association of Investment Trusts was much more eager to promote and improve public relations. The Prudential was

---

[33] Ibid.

[34] BOE: 7A19/1, L. O'Brien, 'Governor's Note: The Finance of Industry', 25 March 1971.

[35] BOE: 7A19/1, 'Industry and the Institutional Investor', 11 July 1971.

[36] BOE: 7A19/2, letter from L. O'Brien to J. Fforde, 27 October 1971.

sympathetic to the 'focal point' ideal, which could overcome some of the weaknesses in the organization and staffing of individual pension funds (particularly in the nationalized industries).[37] Yet on the whole pension and insurance fund investors were largely unenthusiastic, as they did not see it as their responsibility to intervene in industry. The investment manager of the British Petroleum pension fund, Jack Butterworth, told Fforde that he knew 'very little about industrial management' and expected that other fund managers knew just as little. His concern, if he was to be 'stuck with a bad investment', was to attempt to offset the losses elsewhere in the portfolio. He invested only in the largest firms and never committed more than 5 per cent of the equity of one company. Furthermore, Butterworth did not think it was his responsibility to provide small or unquoted companies with equity.[38]

While most institutions were willing to accept that 'something' be done regarding the relationship between industrial management and external investors, there was widespread resistance to any organization that might impinge upon the sovereignty of the funds or individual companies by a newly created body. The British Insurance Association (BIA), having consulted with its twelve largest members, expressed concern that they might be expected to decide which firms were or were not 'lame ducks', and might even be expected to rescue them in response to political pressure. Furthermore, the BIA believed that individual funds should concern themselves only with companies in which they had invested— not the entirety of British industry.[39] The National Association of Pension Funds (NAPF) was more supportive of the Bank's efforts, but the extent to which the body represented the interests of individual funds is questionable. Butterworth, for example, told Fforde that the NAPF was merely a representative body and did not express his viewpoint on matters of investment.[40] David Clement, finance member of the National Coal Board fund, thought the association was 'a bit young and brash'.[41] This was a view held by a number of other independently managed pension funds.[42] Clement expressed support for developing some kind of 'focal point' organization but was 'fearful of overdoing things and becoming

[37] BOE: 7A19/2, J. Fforde, 'City Initiative: Talk with the Prudential', 13 October 1971.
[38] BOE: 7A19/2, J. Fforde, 'City Initiative: Pension Funds', 26 November 1971.
[39] BOE: 7A19/3, letter from K. N. Bevins (Chairman of British Insurance Association) to L. O'Brien, 'Industrial Management and the Institutional Investor', 14 February 1972.
[40] BOE: 7A19/2, J. Fforde, 'City Initiative: Pension Funds', 26 November 1971.
[41] BOE: 7A19/4, J. Fforde, 'Initiative', 10 April 1972.
[42] BOE: 7A19/3, J. Fforde, 'The Initiative', 29 February 1972.

"the absentee landlords of the 20th century"—oppressively harassing the unfortunate tenantry'.[43]

In March 1972 a working party was established to look into 'whether it was possible and useful to develop more effective relationships between institutional investors and the public companies in which they have an interest'.[44] The working party consisted of all the major City organizations and representative bodies, as well as the Confederation of British Industry (CBI). At the first meeting Kenneth Bevins, the chairman of the BIA, reasserted that the insurance associations would not get involved in companies in which they had not invested, and would not undertake a more general responsibility for 'policing industry'.[45] Subsequently, of the twenty-two members of the BIA, seven were completely opposed to changing their arrangements and were unwilling to become integrated into a scheme. The remaining fifteen expressed support for the initiative, but remained very conservative in what they thought would be appropriate. Most were against any visible public body with a standing committee. All but one felt that any interventions could be agreed upon only if they were accepted by the individual constituent associations. As the Governor noted, these qualifications were 'so far-reaching as to effectively destroy the basic idea'. O'Brien thought their objectives were 'understandable' but 'out of date'. If the institutions would not take responsibility, he told Bevins, he could not prevent the government from stepping in.[46] The merchant banks, managers of many of the investments made by the funds, were also opposed for the different reason that they were often financial advisors to industrial companies, and were concerned not to be put in an embarrassing conflict of interest or to dictate a course of action to their clients.[47] Eventually, following months of wrangling over the formation of such a body, an agreement was settled to establish an Institutional Shareholders Committee (ISC). Backed by the Association of Unit Trust Managers, the National Association of Pension Funds, the Association of Investment Trust Companies, and the British Insurance Association, its conservative purpose was 'to co-ordinate and extend existing investment protection activities of institutional investors with a view, where this is judged necessary, to stimulating action by industrial and commercial

---

[43] BOE: 7A19/4, J. Fforde, 'Initiative', 10 April 1972.

[44] BOE: 7A19/3, 'Bank of England Press Announcement', 15 March 1972.

[45] BOE: 7A19/4, minutes of a meeting held at the Bank of England, 4 April 1972.

[46] BOE: 7A19/5, 'Note for the Record: Industrial Management and the Institutional Investor', 24 October 1972; S. Fleming, 'Bank and City talks on Industry Hits BIA Snags', *Guardian*, 11 November 1972.

[47] BOE: 7A19/5, D. Malbert, ' "Prod the Sluggish" Move Has City Split', *Evening Standard*, 14 December 1972.

companies to improve efficiency'. The body was made up of individual representatives from each of the above bodies, with an annually alternated chairperson.[48] The BIA originally refused to join; however, the 'very bad' press it received for its resistance, in which it faced charges of being 'antediluvian and...unhelpful', had persuaded the body eventually to involve itself.[49]

The ISC was not a success. As the financial editor of *The Times* noted a mere six months after the decision for the BIA to join, the committee was a 'profound disappointment to the Bank'. As the product of cajoling and compromise on behalf of O'Brien, it was alleged by cynics to be 'a dead letter before it was ever launched'. The fact that the committee had met 'from time to time', and had a complete aversion to any publicity, ensured that public confidence in the ISC could not be developed.[50] John Fforde, writing to the Governors of the Bank in response to this editorial, was in agreement. More substantially, he argued that the continued reticence of the institutions to engage with industry in any meaningful sense posed a deeper challenge to the ethical and moral underpinnings of the public company. The owners of firms should bear responsibility for their operation and performance. If the shareholder could not, or would not, be 'resuscitated', he believed that they would undermine the basis of their own existence.[51] Against the background of a growing economic crisis, and the increasingly loud voices of left-wing radicalism from within the Labour Party, the future of liberal capitalism seemed genuinely imperilled. The obstinacy of the institutions would only increase this danger further.

The Heath government's attempts to improve the relationship between institutional investors and British industry were a distinct product of its unique economic strategy. The government sought to rid itself of the interventionist overhang of 'Wilsonism' and to harness the power of the competitive business to regenerate, and make more dynamic, British industry. Where the previous Labour government had sought to fix the problem of industrial management failure through the IRC, Heath believed that the owners of industry, the financial institutions themselves, were duty-bound and capable of taking up the mantle. In this sense the

---

[48] BOE: 7A19/6, 'Draft: Institutional Shareholders Committee', 26 February 1973; 'Press Release: Institutional Shareholders' Committee', 16 April 1973.

[49] BOE: 7A19/6, J. S. Beverly, 'Note for the Record', 5 April 1973; C. Wilkins, 'Bank Hails BIA Decision to Join City Investors' "Ginger Group"', *Financial Times*, 17 April 1973.

[50] BOE: 7A19/6, 'Whatever Happened to the City Ginger Man?' *The Times*, 22 October 1973.

[51] BOE: 7A19/6, J. Fforde, 'Institutional Shareholders' Committee: Comment by the Financial Editor of "The Times"', 30 October 1973.

Heath government was attempting to realign the relationship between ownership and control of capitalist firms, which had become increasingly divorced in the post-war decades.[52] The collapse of Rolls Royce provoked the government, through the Bank of England, to try to create a mechanism by which this could be achieved. The government's political objectives of averting industrial decline by modernizing and making industry more competitive ensured that it was unable to stand aside fully from management of industry. The Heath government was not ready to accept, despite some of its rhetoric, the hard-headed approach that underperforming firms should be allowed to fail in the name of efficiency and competition. Thus it remained constrained by the expectations and norms of the social democratic industrial 'consensus' in which the state had a responsibility for maintaining the national industrial economy. Yet Heath's approach was restrained. It did not challenge the fundamental relationship between the institutions, the capital market, and industrial firms. Meanwhile, many in the Labour Party and broader labour movement were developing a more radical and thoroughgoing critique of the role of the financial institutions.

THE CITY'S CAPITAL MARKETS:
SHORT-TERMISM AND GREED?

As described in the Introduction, the economic strategy of social democracy in post-war Britain had two primary aims. The first was to ensure that there was no return to the mass unemployment experienced during the interwar years. The second was to avert national decline, so that the British economy could retain its international significance, despite the costs of the war effort. These goals were tied together throughout the three decades after 1945 in a broad political commitment to developing and promoting an explicitly industrial economy in which the physical export of goods and manufactures were at the heart of post-war economic revival. Key to this strategy was a belief that British industrial expansion could be achieved only through an increase in the rate of domestic investment. The approach taken by the Attlee government had relied on encouraging investment from retained profits. This was continued in modified form by the Wilson governments in the 1960s.[53] This may explain why, as Tomlinson has

---

[52] R. Dobbins, B. Lowes, and C. L. Pass, 'Financial Institutions and the Ownership and Control of British Industry', *Managerial and Decision Economics*, 2/1 (1981), 16–24.
[53] See Introduction.

argued, there was no great emphasis in the Labour Party on an alleged 'supply-side' failure of the capital markets during the 1950s and 1960s. The interwar concern with planning the financial system in order to direct credit and investment had faded to meet the realities of Britain's decentralized capitalist economy. Tomlinson claims that any concern with City failings was peripheral to Labour's economic analysis in the twenty-five years after the war. Where the City was singled out for blame, it was only in its outdated commitment to sterling, which, by imposing stop–go macroeconomic policies, undercut long-term domestic investment (see Chapter 4).[54] Yet it is clear that, with changes to the financial system in the post-war decades, Labour attitudes towards the City's capital markets did begin to shift back to interwar concerns about their negative impact on the nation's economic development.

In the 1940s, domestic industry had been in a position of great liquidity, allowing for the continuation of self-generated funds for investment as the primary means of business recovery.[55] Yet by the 1950s, with controls on domestic investment relaxed by Conservative governments, the demand for external capital increased, heralding the emergence of a vibrant new issue market for industrial securities. This did not completely supplant the traditional model of reinvested profits as the most important means of funding investment; however, by the 1960s, external capital accounted for over half of total industrial investment.[56] This capital was accessed through the issue of securities on the London market, coordinated and managed by an elite group of merchant banks. The change in the ownership of industry, and in the character of the investment process, was not ignored by Labour. The separation of ownership and control was a key concern for Labour revisionists and their opponents in the 1950s and 1960s. However, the changes also brought the capital market in the City back into focus, particularly following the emergence of corporate takeovers at the end of the 1950s. The so-called Aluminium War of 1959, in which British Aluminium was aggressively taken over by Tube Investments on the advice of the merchant bank S. G. Warburg, brought the practice to public prominence.[57] For the Labour Shadow Chancellor, Harold Wilson, the fractious takeover process was illustrative of a •

---

[54] Jim Tomlinson, 'The Labour Party and the City, 1945–1970', in Ranald Michie and Philip Williamson (eds), *The British Government and the City of London in the Twentieth Century* (Cambridge: Cambridge University Press, 2004), 190–1.
[55] John F. Wilson, *British Business History, 1720–1994* (Manchester: Manchester University Press, 1995), 189.
[56] Ibid.
[57] For a full account of this episode, see Niall Ferguson, *High Financier: The Lives and Time and Siegmund Warburg* (London: Penguin, 2011), 183–99.

fundamental flaw in the national economic model. In the House of Commons in June 1959, with a general election looming, he requested:

> in view of undesirable developments in private industry, including take-over bids, excessive speculation in share and property values and practices designed to avoid taxes . . . Her Majesty's Government . . . take steps to prevent these and other abuses and to ensure that private industry is carried on in accordance with the national interest.[58]

For Wilson, in keeping with the contemporary concern for Britain's international competitiveness, the challenge was to keep pace with Russia, China, and Germany, which were 'far outstripping [Britain] in quantitative measures of industrial advance and productive investment'—countries whose 'industrial systems . . . [were] more purposively directed'. Britain was unable to maintain parity with such advancing nations when 'the City and the boardrooms of some of our big companies' had 'been infected more and more by get-rich-quick attitudes'. He continued:

> during the past few weeks the City has been more concerned to justify Lord Keynes's description of it as a 'casino'. If we turn to the City columns of any newspaper over the past few weeks what will we find? Take-over bids and rumours of bids; erratic movements of share values, where those who are euphemistically called 'investors' are paying less and less regard to the inherent earning power of particular shares and more and more regard to short-run capital gains.[59]

This theme of the City's alleged short-term profit motive was embedded in a wider critique of national inefficiencies. In the month following the 1959 Conservative election victory he asked the Commons:

> are we really to counter the Soviet industrial developments with an economic system the higher manifestations of which are the take-over bid and a Stock Exchange behaving like a casino run mad? Are we to counter their educational achievements with a system which still creates this artificial educational apartheid at the age of 11? Are we to counter their technological challenge with the frivolities of our so-called Western civilization? The Soviets have photographed the reverse side of the moon. The summit of Western competitive achievement is an aspiration to photograph the reverse side of Miss Jayne Mansfield.[60]

---

[58] Harold Wilson, *Parliamentary Debates, Commons*, vol. 608, cols 34–174 (29 June 1959).

[59] Ibid.

[60] Harold Wilson, *Parliamentary Debates, Commons*, vol. 612, cols 242–364 (28 October 1959).

The 'casino' idea drew directly on Harold Macmillan's arguments made during the interwar period—something Wilson made great efforts to remind the Prime Minister of by often quoting at length from *The Middle Way* about the need to regulate and direct credit and investment in accordance with the needs of the productive economy rather than 'irrational and anti-social speculation'.[61] Wilson believed that the pressure for immediate dividends—in order to stave off the threat of an aggressive takeover—prevented healthy investment strategies by firms that would, in the long run, be more advantageous to the nation. When the Chancellor requested dividend restraint in July 1961, Wilson asserted the difficulties facing

> far-sighted managements who want to plough back their profits in further expansion are forced into uneconomic dividends because of the fears of predatory take-over bidders...We cannot make the national appeal we need in an economic society dominated by the take-over bidder. We cannot appeal for restraint in productive industry when the Stock Exchange behaves like a casino.[62]

More broadly, and in keeping with the themes of his famed 'White Heat' speech at the Scarborough Conference in 1963, Wilson decried the subordination of 'genuine hardworking business men, executives, scientists and salesmen ... under a system which exalts the take-over bidder, the tycoon, the financier, share-pusher, speculator and property racketeer'.[63] The 'commanding position' of the Stock Exchange had 'a totally unjustified and often harmful influence over productive industry'. Wilson asserted, in his rhetorical attempt to paint the Tories as representatives of establishment principles of laissez-faire, that 'for hon. Gentlemen opposite the commanding heights of the economy are and should be in the City, and in private hands. In our view, they should be within the control of the community and accountable to it.'[64]

It is clear then, at least in senior Labour rhetoric at the start of the 1960s, the City's alleged short-term speculative preferences divided it

---

[61] Harold Wilson, *Parliamentary Debates, Commons*, vol. 621, cols 204–326 (5 April 1960); Harold Macmillan, *The Middle Way* (1938; London: Pickering & Chatto, 1994), 240–65.

[62] Harold Wilson, *Parliamentary Debates, Commons*, vol. 645, cols 433–563 (26 July 1961).

[63] Harold Wilson, *Parliamentary Debates, Commons*, vol. 644, cols 1068–1199 (18 July 1961); Steven Fielding, *The Labour Governments 1964–70, i. Labour and Cultural Change* (Manchester: Manchester University Press, 2003), 76–8.

[64] Harold Wilson, *Parliamentary Debates, Commons*, vol. 621, cols 242–364 (5 April 1960).

from the long-term goals of legitimate productive economic activities, which, in turn, threatened the competitive capacities of the British nation. However, this did not translate into an attempt to reforms of the City once Wilson had moved into Downing Street in 1964.[65] Instead, as already described, the power of the state in the form of the IRC was deployed to rationalize industry where the market was incapable.

LABOUR, THE CITY, AND THE INDUSTRIAL CRISIS

The concern with the City's alleged corrosive effect on the whole British economy was revived once more at the end of the decade. The City's role in derailing Labour's economic strategy through its pressure on sterling, and the subsequent humiliation of devaluation in 1967, had once again cast financiers in a villainous role—as had been the case in 1931 (this is discussed further in Chapter 5). George Brown's famous allusion to the 'Gnomes of Zurich', and his 1965 speech to the Lancashire Miners' Gala in which he claimed that a 'sinister conspiracy' in the City was at the root of sterling's problems, exemplified this.[66] For many in the Labour Party, and on the political left more broadly, the failure to challenge the orthodoxy of maintaining the sterling parity embodied a wider failure of the Wilson government to alter Britain's economy and society.[67] Its willingness to prioritize the typical deflationary preferences of the City, promoted and supported by the Governor of the Bank of England, failed to place the national economy ahead of the sectional and self-interested desires of financiers. Furthermore, in the early years of the 1970s, the City experienced a number of high-profile scandals that once again seemed to confirm the greedy and selfish agenda of financiers and their scant regard for national economic well-being or decency. The most notable of these scandals was an affair in which the financier 'Tiny' Rowland engaged in a fractious legal battle with other chairmen of the firm Lonrho, and in doing so revealed a variety of illegal activities and measures of tax avoidance that Heath subsequently, and famously, described as 'the unacceptable face of capitalism'.[68] This scandal was particularly popular in the Labour ranks because the senior Conservative

---

[65] Tomlinson, 'Labour Party and the City', 190–1.
[66] Kynaston, *City of London*, iv. 312.
[67] Thompson, *Political Economy and the Labour Party*, 197.
[68] 'Mr Heath Calls Lonrho Affair "the Unpleasant and Unacceptable Face of Capitalism"', *The Times*, 15 May 1973.

MP Duncan Sandys was a Lonrho Chairman.[69] Such scandals were met with the emergence of a new financial practice of 'asset-stripping'— corporate raids on companies designed to increase short-term share values—in the late 1960s. Made famous by the financier Jim Slater, they exemplified to left-wing critics the City's apparent selfishness, greed, and overriding concern with rapid returns regardless of economic impact.[70] This pursuit of immediate financial gratification was condemned passionately by Cliff Rice, a delegate to the Labour conference in 1972. He denounced the 'pirates of industry' as 'flesh eaters' who

> take over manufacturing firms, sell up their assets and leave the bones of industry, the workers, to stagnate in the idleness and wastefulness of unemployment and the dole queue . . .

According to Rice, there was 'scarcely an area of Britain that [had] not been affected by take-overs and asset-stripping as we know it, and suffered unemployment as a result'.[71]

The influence of such scandals and practices encouraged the Heath government to produce a White Paper on the reform of company law— although no legislation was introduced.[72] More broadly, the early 1970s saw a general preoccupation with an apparent institutional and cultural divide between the City and domestic industry. John Davies's attempts to cajole the City into integrating with industry formed part of this consensus position at the start of the decade. The supposed division between the financial and industrial sectors in Britain was routinely contrasted with the financial systems abroad, particularly in West Germany and France, in which integration and strong working relationships between finance and industry were the norm—and were seemingly one of the root sources of their post-war miracle in economic growth.[73] The most exhaustive comparisons between national financial systems was made in a *Political and*

---

[69] Labour Party Archive, People's History Museum, Manchester [henceforward LPA]: Martin Linton, 'What they've All Got out of Lonrho: Nearest Thing to a British Watergate', *Labour Weekly*, 18 May 1973; 'Lessons of Lonrho', *Labour Weekly*, 25 May 1973; John Grant, 'How Corrupt Are our Financial Institutions?', *Labour Weekly*, 8 June 1973; 'Scandals in the City', *Labour Weekly*, 25 January 1974.

[70] Charles Raw, *Slater Walker: An Investigation of a Financial Phenomenon* (London: Deutsch, 1977); LPA: 'Scandals in the City', *Labour Weekly*, 25 January 1974.

[71] *Report of the Annual Conference of the Labour Party* (London: Labour Party, 1972), 268–70.

[72] Cmd 5391, *Company Law Reform* (London: HMSO, 1973); LPA: Basil Jeuda, 'Reform?—Oh, Mr Walker, what a Big Whitewash', *Labour Weekly*, 3 August 1973.

[73] LPA: Re. 17, 'Financial Institutions Group: A Note on Institutions and Investment Policy', November 1974.

Economic Planning publication by Yao Hu-Su. This influential pamphlet published in 1975 demonstrated that the London stock market provided less new equity finance than its continental competitors.[74] Many on the left particularly admired the active interventionism of both private banks and the state on the Continent.[75] Tom Jackson, general secretary of the Union of Post Office Workers, praised the interest taken by universal bankers in raising industrial capital, but also in having a closer identification between banks and the companies in which they invested. Jackson argued: 'We demand a similar commitment from the City. It must forge closer links with industry and try to meet the need for greater long-term investment in British industry.'[76]

This concern was a function of the increased significance of external financing, and financial institutions, in the overall investment process, which had emerged during the previous two decades. This had resulted in a change to the fundamental nature of the largest firms in British business, with control of the boardroom wrested away from personal and family-tied directorships, and into the hands of external investors in company equity whose involvement in the firm was simply financial. Where the divorce between ownership and control had been apparent in only a small number of the largest firms at the time of the Second World War, in 1972 it was estimated that in only 14 of the top 100 non-financial companies did directors hold more than 10 per cent of total equity, and in 56 companies held less than 0.5 per cent.[77] Merchant banks were central to the process of industrial takeovers and mergers that characterized the 1960s and 1970s, and much of the equity of British industrial concerns was absorbed by the emerging institutional investors. The result of these changes was to place strains on the established approach to managing domestic investment.

The changing nature of British capitalism, in addition to the processes of firm concentration and 'multinationalization', presented social democrats with a set of challenges to their fundamental political economy. As described in the Introduction, this provoked a shift towards a more far-reaching, interventionist approach within the Labour movement. This

[74] Yao Su-Hu, *National Attitudes and the Financing of Industry* (London: Political and Economic Planning, 1975).
[75] Trades Union Congress Papers, Modern Records Centre, University of Warwick [henceforward TUC]: MSS 2920/463/2, Tom Jackson, 'A Trade Unionist's View of the Role of the City', 25 February 1976.
[76] Ibid.
[77] Wilson, *British Business History*, 190; S. J. Prais, *The Evolution of Giant Firms: A Study of the Growth of Concentration in Manufacturing Industry in Britain* (Cambridge: Cambridge University Press, 1976), 89; for a survey of the separation of the ownership and control in post-war Britain see Cheffins, *Corporate Ownership and Control*, 301–36.

was also catalysed by the specific experience of the Wilson governments after 1964 in which attempts to raise the rate of manufacturing fixed investment to 7 per cent per annum under the National Plan had proved ineffective. Policies, such as the attempted creation of a National Enterprise Board, exemplified both the willingness and desire of many in the Labour movement to find a means of pursuing economic modernization and expansionism in a more direct manner than had previously been attempted. It was a break with the apparent timidity and weakness of Wilson's approach, and represented an attempt to give a greater role to the state in the planning and control of the national investment process, which was more akin to interwar proposals. As Ian Mikardo, a leading member of the Tribune-left recalled in his memoirs, frustration had developed on behalf of industrial expansionists that investment would not increase despite favourable tax and grant incentives in the 1960s. He wrote:

> Past governments had offered and provided—sometimes over-generous— grants and loans for investment, especially in development areas and special development areas, with results that were only marginal. Our research groups [those of the Labour party in post-1970 opposition] . . . were proposing not to weep over this diagnosis of the British disease but to prescribe some effective remedies for it. Since industrialists couldn't be induced by honey or money to invest adequately, the Government would have to do it for them.[78]

Labour's approach was given a sense of urgency, as economic difficulties and a crisis of the industrial economy unfolded over the 1970s. The Rolls Royce crisis, and the increase in the number of unemployed to over one million at the start of 1972, suggested that the British industrial economy was experiencing a fundamental set of challenges to its existing form.[79] The following decade was to be characterized by the onset of global economic turmoil following the oil price shocks, a vast rise in inflation, a concurrent rising rate of unemployment, and the onset of an unprecedented rate of deindustrialization. In the decade after 1970, 1.5 million manufacturing jobs were lost, and Britain's share of world trade in manufactures declined to a mere 9 per cent.[80] Manufacturing exports had exceeded imports by 59 per cent in 1970, but this was eroded to only 10 per cent in 1979.[81] The material basis upon which post-war social

---

[78] Ian Mikardo, *Back Bencher* (London: Weidenfeld & Nicolson, 1988), 187.
[79] 'Commons Sitting Suspendedi Uproar after Clash over Million Unemployed', *The Times*, 21 January 1972.
[80] Tomlinson, 'Economic Policy', 56.
[81] Tweedale, 'Industry and De-industrialization in the 1970s', 253–5.

democracy had been built, the industrialized economy, was seemingly threatened with extinction.

A number of interpretations and criticisms of this apparent failure emerged in response—for the 'Thatcherite' right wing, which came to political power at the end of the decade, the blame could be assigned to the deadening effects of a cozy and consensual corporatist economic strategy, and an unwillingness to challenge the obstructive practices and sectional interests of the trade-union movement. Unsurprisingly, this was not the diagnosis reached within the Labour movement, which instead placed the blame on chronic underinvestment. Indeed, investment in manufacturing was comparatively low in Britain. Tweedale notes that, even at the start of the decade, a time in which technological innovation and foreign competition was intensifying, net capital spending in manufacturing accounted for only 2.5 per cent of net national domestic product. By the end of the decade it had fallen further to 1 per cent.[82] In 1975, Tony Benn (Secretary of State for Industry), Frances Morrell, and Francis Cripps wrote 'A Ten Year Industry Strategy for Britain'. These senior members of the Labour left, who were concurrently developing policies associated with the Alternative Economic Strategy (AES), claimed:

> British manufacturing industry, the primary source of our national income is trapped in a spiral of decline, and after 30 years of low investment is contracting under its own momentum . . . the trend to contraction of British manufacturing industry has gathered force in the last 4 years. If this trend is allowed to continue, we will have closed down 15% of our entire manufacturing capacity and nearly 2,000,000 industrial workers will have been made redundant between 1970 and 1980.

They argued that, in order to provide a sufficient flow of new industrial employment, and to modernize 'low-wage, low-productivity' jobs, it was necessary to double the rate of annual new investment from £3 billion per annum to £6 billion per annum.[83] The left-wing Labour MP Frank Allaun told the *Bankers' Magazine* in September 1976 that there had been an 'abject failure' in the previous half-century to develop the domestic industrial base of the British economy owing to a severe lack of investment in new plant and machinery. Allaun asserted that British investment rates as a share of GDP were half that of their continental competitors in France and West Germany.[84] In its written evidence to the Committee to Review the Functioning of Financial Institutions (described

---

[82] Ibid. 255.

[83] TUC: MSS.2920/450/2, Tony Benn, Frances Morrell, and Francis Cripps, 'A Ten Year Industry Strategy for Britain', April 1975.

[84] Frank Allaun, 'Socialise the Profits', *Bankers' Magazine*, September 1976.

later in this chapter) in 1977, the Trades Union Congress (TUC) shared this analysis, citing the 'insufficient quantity' and 'poor quality' of investment, which had resulted in an outdated manufacturing sector unable to produce goods at competitive prices. Echoing Benn et al., the TUC called for a doubling of the amount of gross fixed domestic capital by 1988— equivalent to an annual increase of 7–8 per cent a year.[85]

LABOUR'S RESPONSE TO
INSTITUTIONALIZATION

The crisis of industrial underinvestment, combined with a reappraisal of Labour's economic strategy in the light of the 'failure' of the Wilson government, brought the capital market and the institutional funds into focus for the left. In November 1966, the Finance and Economic Affairs Advisory Committee of the Labour Party decided to arrange a weekend conference on the subject of 'Private Financial Institutions'. The purpose of the conference was to consider the influence and effect of the financial system on the economic policy of government and the 'general performance of the economy'. At the heart of this reappraisal was the fact that 'the Government's capital investment plans [were] deeply bound up in the operation and attitudes of these institutions', and a recognition that economic planning required financial-sector intervention in addition to planning of the industrial sector. The Labour Party had, in the post-war era, 'traditionally stood aside from detached studies of the machinery of private finance', but, perhaps in response to the recent battles with the City over sterling devaluation, the time was 'more than ripe to instruct [themselves] in the technicalities of this field'.[86] A report of the findings of the conference was subsequently produced in February 1970. In the relationship between the capital market and the 'home economy', the report identified the two major structural changes that had taken place in the economy and capital market since the war. First, the growth of large-scale firms through mergers and reorganization, which had important implications for any future planning of capital flows. Secondly, the 'growth in the power of the institutional investors', which had witnessed an increased domination of the supply of capital by a network of life assurance and pension funds. Despite their dominance in managing the

---

[85] Trades Union Congress, *The Role of Financial Institutions: TUC Evidence to the Committee to Review the Functioning of Financial Institutions* (London, 1979), 15.

[86] LPA: Re. 74, Finance and Economic Affairs Subcommittee, 'Future Weekend Conference—Private Financial Institutions', January 1967.

lion's share of public savings, and the colonization of the provision of investable funds, the institutions were 'free of any significant degree of public accountability', and analysis of their investment criteria was 'impossible', despite their importance to national and regional economic planning. The allocation of funds in the capital market was determined by 'the best return available' which, despite offering the benefits of increased productivity and a higher savings rate, neglected wider 'social priorities'.[87]

Such a conclusion had been reached almost a decade earlier by Richard Titmuss. In a 1959 Fabian pamphlet entitled *The Irresponsible Society*, the Professor of Social Administration at the London School of Economics described the 'explosion in the accumulation of immense funds in the hands of private insurance companies and pensions funds'. An ex-clerk in a county fire insurance office, Titmuss was concerned that the large institutions were not exposed to the public interest, despite the fact that as the insurance companies grew they would 'increasingly become the arbiters of welfare and amenity for larger sections of the community'. He claimed that

> their directors, managers and professionally trained advisors will be making, in their own eyes and in the eyes of many other people, sober, profitable and responsible decisions. But ultimately and in aggregate they will not lead to a more rational and balanced disposition of social resources in relation to the needs of the nation... one of the most important problems of the future will centre round the socially effective use of rising national incomes... a wrong sense of the proportion in attitudes to the 'economic surplus'—to the savings of the community—for example, may well be one of the more serious dangers to public morality in the 1960s.[88]

In this pamphlet Titmuss identified a number of themes that left-wing critics of the institutions were to develop into the 1970s. In 1957, he, alongside Brian Abel-Smith and Peter Townsend, had shaped the Labour Party proposals on pension fund reform (*National Superannuation: Labour's Policy of Security in Old Age*), which had proposed that earnings-related contributions to a state pension fund could be 'boldly invested' through the stock market in order to modernize British industry.[89] At the same time, in Sweden, the Confederation of Swedish Trade Unions had successfully pressured for the creation of a 'Supplementary Pension Programme' (in

[87] LPA: Re. 582, Labour Party Research Department, 'The Role of Financial Institutions in Britain's Economy: A Report of a Conference Organised by the National Executive Committee of the Labour Party on 8/9 June, 1968 (Preliminary Draft)', February 1970.

[88] Richard Titmuss, *The Irresponsible Society* (London: George Allen & Unwin, 1958), 1–2.

[89] Pemberton, 'What Matters is what Works', 46–7.

addition to the flat-rate basic state pension), which used its accumulated funds to lend to the public sector. Most of the savings managed by the funds went into public-sector investment projects, particularly the modernization of the nation's housing stock in the 1960s. Yet, when profit margins began to erode at the end of that decade, and self-financing of investment by private firms could not meet the nation's requirements, the Swedish trade-union movement pushed for sources of collective capital to be used for equity investment and the provision of credit to industry.[90] In Britain, outside the confines of policies for pension reform (which focused primarily on pension provision rather than fund investment), the key debate over political economy in the Labour Party during the late 1950s concerned the purported existence of a separation of ownership and control. For Crosland this was a fact—and an amenable one for the purposes of advancing his version of social democracy.[91] Yet his critics on the 'new left' denied that there was such a division, and sought to expose the concentration of wealth and power that continued to characterize post-war British capitalism.[92] The capacity for expanding collective ownership through institutional investment did not feature to any significant extent in the discourse of left political economy during the 1950s and 1960s.[93]

It was not until the 1970s that the trade-union movement began to drive the public case for critically assessing the role of the institutions in investing in industry, arguing that their investment policies, combined with the flawed mechanisms of the capital market operating in the City, hindered long-term economic development. In written evidence given to the House of Commons Committee on Expenditure in 1971 regarding aid to private industry, the TUC, as part of a broader assault on the 'disengagement' policies of the Heath government, observed that the 'increasing domination of shareholdings, including new issue holdings, by large financial institutions, [had] led to capital markets becoming inert and not performing a dynamic reallocative function...this is the nature of institutional forms which control the flow of private finance'. Echoing John Davies, the TUC argued that the inability of 'the City' to understand changes to technology and industrial practice blocked

---

[90] Henry Milner, *Sweden: Social Democracy in Practice* (Oxford: Oxford University Press, 1989), 126–8.

[91] Jackson, *Equality and the British Left*, 155–7; Tomlinson, 'Labour Party and the Capitalist Firm', 692–5.

[92] Wickham-Jones, 'The New Left's Economic Model', 24–31.

[93] For Labour Party ideas about collective ownership other than nationalization, see Jackson, 'Revisionism Reconsidered', 433–7.

economic development. Furthermore, the unwillingness of the government to intervene in the capital market had 'led to a severe malfunction of the system, and inhibited worthwhile long term investment'. Expressing regret over the abolition of the IRC, the TUC proposed that the government should take a more active role in the capital market. The solution was to create a large public agency that could 'effectively achieve the desirable reallocation of resources that the private sector had failed to perform'.[94] Vic Feather, general secretary of the TUC, told the conference of the National Union of Furniture Trade Operatives in Blackpool that such a public agency would direct funds into 'worthwhile long term industrial and social investments'.[95] This theme was developed further in oral evidence provided to the committee in July. The TUC argued that the financial institutions were failing to provide long-term capital for firms operating in areas of 'advanced technology', and that the capital market took a short-term approach to investment owing in large part to the lack of effective communication between industry and the investing institutions. The TUC also expressed concern that the institutions were responsible for the savings of ordinary people, yet their concentrated management tended to exclude those savers from decisions about how those funds were used. A public agency could link the financial institutions more effectively with industry, and provide an overall framework for the reallocation of resources to companies and entire sectors with the view to meet social and economic need.[96]

One of the left's most important figures in the appraisal of the role played by the financial institutions was John Hughes. A tutor in economics and industrial relations at Ruskin College in Oxford, Hughes was the college's Vice-Principal between 1970 and 1979 (he subsequently became its Principal in 1980) and a founder of the Trade Union Research Unit based there. Hughes was also a key figure in the 'new left' of the late 1950s and early 1960s, in which his most significant work had been a 'socialist wages plan' developed with the economist Ken Alexander in 1959.[97] From the late

[94] TUC: MSS.2920/450/1, Trades Union Congress, 'Aid to Private Industry: Evidence to the House of Commons Committee on Expenditure', 12 May 1971.

[95] TNA: T 326/1236, 'TUC Wants Inquiry on Value of City', *Guardian*, 18 June 1971.

[96] TUC: MSS.2920/450/1, 'Aid to Private Industry Oral Evidence: Summary of TUC Memorandum', July 1971.

[97] John Hughes, 'New Left Economic Policy', in Oxford University Socialist Discussion Group (ed.), *Out of Apathy: Voices of the New Left Thirty Years on* (London: Verso, 1989), 95–103; Michael Kenny, *The First New Left: British Intellectuals after Stalin* (London: Lawrence & Wishart, 1995); Ken Alexander and John Hughes, *A Socialist Wages Plan: The*

1960s, and throughout the 1970s, Hughes switched his focus to a critical analysis of the relationship between investing institutions and the real economy, and developed proposals for reform that would bring them within the operation of the planned, mixed, economy. Having contributed a paper on 'gaps' in the capital market to the Labour Party conference on financial institutions, Hughes produced a variety of papers and policy documents on these matters throughout the following decade.[98] In a paper for the party's 'Banking and Insurance Working Party' in 1972, he assessed the relative merits of public intervention in the financial sector. As will be described in Chapter 2, this was an issue being debated by the working party in the wake of the Labour conference passing a motion in favour of nationalizing 'all the banks, insurance companies and building societies'. Hughes's paper focused on the operation of the capital market and the institutional investors' role within it. It was notable in the first instance for its rejection, contrary to the preference of many within the group, of the notion that 'pure' public control of finance was immediately relevant to the party's approach. Instead, some form of mixed economy (with a predominately private or public ownership) was, according to Hughes, the only realistic option. Regardless, Hughes believed that there was 'much to be said for the Labour Party attempting a coordinated policy approach' to the financial sector. The issue at hand was the extent to which the financial system as a whole was able to fulfil its role in allocating investment funds in an 'efficient' way. In particular, the purpose and incentives of the financial system were often out of line with those of society as a whole to such a degree that

> allocation may be efficient in terms of private costs and surpluses, but defective in terms of the 'total sum' of social costs and benefits. This is particularly important when the economic system generates cumulative dynamic processes, since the financial system may reinforce processes creating a serious imbalance in the economy. An outstanding example is the channelling of funds into property speculation and development in the last 15 years, which has not only reinforced regional imbalance but generated a violent inflation of property values.[99]

Politics of the Pay Packet (London: Universities and Left Review/New Reasoner, 1959); Mark Wickham-Jones, 'The Debate about Wages: The New Left, the Labour Party and Incomes Policy', *Journal of Political Ideologies*, 18/1 (2013), 83–105.

[98] LPA: Re. 291, Conference on Financial Institutions, J. Hughes, 'A Note on "Gaps" in the Capital Market, and the Role of Public Agencies', April 1968.

[99] LPA: Rd. 343, Finance and Economic Affairs Sub-Committee, Banking and Insurance Working Party, John Hughes, 'Public Ownership and Control: The Financial Sector. Why Intervene?', April 1972.

From this analysis Hughes began to flesh out an idea in which the investment funds of pension and life assurance companies would be compulsorily channelled through a 'state investment agency'—similar to that which had earlier been suggested by the TUC. The purpose of doing so would be to ensure that 'the main part of the savings of members of the community . . . could be used in a coordinated way to finance the main part of the physical investment programme that is key to the future real wealth of the community', thus achieving a pattern of economy-wide investment that 'would be economically logical and organisationally coherent'. Hughes concluded that

> what is being done with immediate information through a great variety of intermediaries and with a narrow view of private costs and benefits could be done on the basis of detailed knowledge and continuing study, in a coherent and unified way, and in the light of the 'total sum' of costs and benefits involved in the community.[100]

The imposition of this compulsory direction of funds would probably be achieved by removing the favourable fiscal and tax advantages afforded to long-term savings institutions unless they consented to the practice. No public ownership would be involved. Instead, something similar to the approach of incentivizing the within-firm reinvestment of profits would be replicated for the institutions. According to Hughes, channelling funds in this way would not only achieve a more efficient outcome, but would serve to bring the financial system under the control of the 'community'. The present system ensured that private managers of the investment process could not be held accountable for either their motives, the 'efficiency of their participation', or whether effective analysis was taking place. Through the state agency the 'community' would be able to 'conserve strategically its role in the planning and financing of the country's major investment programme and to use the power of its holdings to exercise a positive and persistent influence on the enterprises it channelled funds into'. It is worth noting that Hughes did not explore the possible tension between democratic control by the community and economic efficiency.[101] He celebrated his proposed approach as an effective nationalization of the investment process, which strengthened public accountability without the 'cumbersome problems of compensation' and the 'time-consuming process of large-scale administrative

---

[100] Ibid.
[101] It is not difficult to imagine a situation in which a national agency could invest in certain industries or sectors to placate interest groups that might be contrary to the long-term benefit of the community as a whole.

reorganization in the insurance field', which could come with a purely public ownership approach.

In 1974 international stock markets collapsed, triggered by government efforts to control inflation through interest rate hikes. With money increasingly difficult to obtain, there was less opportunity to invest in assets, and what was available was more sensibly directed into fixed interest securities or high-interest bank accounts. Equity values declined, due, in part, to the belief that equity holdings would not hold their value in the face of inflation compared with other assets such as property and land. This pessimism was made worse once the bubble in property investment was dramatically burst by a drop in prices and the subsequent collapse of a number of 'fringe' or 'secondary' banks. By autumn of 1974, inflation-adjusted share prices on the London Stock Exchange were equivalent in value to the mid-1920s. In this environment, it became increasingly difficult for firms to obtain new equity investment.[102] The frozen market in equity capital prompted Hughes to argue for a co-option of the institutional funds as a source of massive investment to fill the gap. The severe crisis of confidence diminished both the supply of, and demand for, investment—thus preventing economic recovery. For many on the left, the only solution appeared to be that the state should provide risk capital to firms, thus extending the state's ownership of the economy. A related proposal made by Tony Benn was to make a proportion of institutional funds available for use by the state-run NEB.[103] Hughes, however, observed that many firms would probably have been reluctant to accept government part-ownership. Instead, he said, the solution was to look to the pension and insurance funds as an alternative source of investment. Defenders of the institutions argued that their duty was to the immediate interests of their savers, and could not be expected to meet the vague demands of the national interest. Writing in the *Investors' Chronicle* in the months following the abrupt halt to Anthony Barber's 'boom', Tony Benn challenged this narrow focus, asking:

> What does it really profit a fund if it puts the money into something advantageous in the short term but contributes in that process to a denial of investment that British industry needs, so that the whole fund operates in a country going downhill?'[104]

---

[102] Frances Cairncross and Hamish McRae, *The Second Great Crash: How the Oil Crisis Could Destroy the World's Economy* (London: Methuen, 1975), 80–5.
[103] 'Wilson Disowns Pension Funds Plan', *Financial Times*, 28 April 1975.
[104] Quoted in Kynaston, *The City of London*, iv. 532.

Hughes supported this view, arguing:

> 'they [institutional funds] must recognize that their medium to long-term
> financial interests and responsibilities cannot be divorced from the success or
> otherwise of the UK economy in generating key investment decisions that
> ensure industrial modernization and expansion and consequently the basis
> for future real income and employment prospects ... There should ... be no
> conflict of interest if the funds were to work out ways for positive cooper-
> ation in the necessary process of supporting new industrial investment.

The solution would therefore be to pursue a form of semi-voluntary
'consortium action' between the pension funds and other interest groups
(including the state), the purpose of which would be to mobilize large-
scale funds as available risk capital to give firms, trapped by low confidence, access to funds that would sustain and expand their investment
plans. Though Hughes believed that the 'intelligent backing of coherent
corporate development returns should provide better than average
returns', he argued that that the state should guarantee a proportion of
any funds invested. The mobilizing of such resources would encourage a
greater degree of accountability and public monitoring of company
planning—in line with many of the ideals of the NEB. More profoundly,
Hughes argued that the revival of the economy could be achieved in the
middle of the decade not by the market alone, nor solely by the direct
control and intervention of the state. The investment gap 'may be better
filled by making intelligent use, alongside governmental aid and capital, of
that other form of "social" ownership—the cooperative deployment of the
institutional saving (or deferred pay) of the country's labour force'.[105]
This proposal was reworked for a paper produced on behalf of the
Transport and General Workers Union in August 1975 that proposed
that all financial institutions (not only pension and insurance funds, but
banks and unit trusts also) should nominate a proportion of their inflow of
funds for the acquisition of private equities or government stock. These
funds would be managed through the 'consortia' described above.[106]

Hughes developed his position further in a pamphlet published by
the Fabian Society in March 1976, entitled 'Funds for Investment'.
He challenged some of the preoccupations of the Labour left, which was
demanding full-scale nationalization of insurance funds, by stating:

---

[105] LPA: Re. 90, Industrial Policy Subcommittee, John Hughes, 'The "Institutions",
Risk Capital, and UK Real Investment', March 1975.
[106] TNA: T 386/80: 'Schemes to Increase the Level of Productive Investment',
15 December 1975.

some socialists seem to assume that because new [state] instruments have been developed for stimulating economic development... these can substitute for the capital market and for the development responsibilities at present in the hands of private sector companies. But given the scale of the development crisis of the British economy... it may be argued that the Labour movement should be giving attention also to the private sector's management of funds that could be channelled into productive investment.

What was required was a solution to the challenge posed by the institutionalization of investment, and the weaknesses of the private capital market, which 'shad[ed] the distinction' between voluntary and compelled action. This solution would need to meet the demands of an economic system that 'in its mixed form is becoming more concerned with effective management of corporate development and planned investment programme that will ensure the competitive viability of the UK industrial base'. Hughes argued that institutional investors should be made more 'specifically concerned with the provision of long-term capital to industry as a primary market activity', not as secondary to their operations, and that they should develop much greater industrial expertise and accountability. Furthermore, the institutions needed to become 'more genuinely accountable to the people whose funds they handle'. With the exception perhaps of the latter point, there was nothing in Hughes's desiderata that would have stood out significantly from the Heath government's efforts to bring the institutions into greater engagement with industrial economy. He reasserted the need to initiate and establish consortia of 'voluntary groupings', which would be large enough to provide significant funding, spread risk, and develop a high degree of investment specialization, but which would not override the 'effective autonomy and choice of each institution'. He claimed that, even if the institutions were only to devote between 15 and 20 per cent of the annual inflow to such consortia, the private primary capital market would be strengthened by around £500 million–£600 million per annum.[107]

Hughes's analysis and proposed reforms highlights a number of the preoccupations within the Labour movement with regards to the financial system and the financial institutions. Although there is no evidence to link Hughes directly to the TUC proposals cited earlier, it seems likely that his position of influence as the founder of the Trade Union Research Unit at Ruskin probably contributed in some way to the case being proposed. More generally, Hughes's critique of the financial institutions must be seen as part of the broader frustrations with the apparent short-termism and irrationality that had so exercised many in both the Labour and the Conservative parties.

---

[107] John Hughes, 'Funds for Investment', *Fabian Research Series*, 325 (1976).

Many of the funds employed by the secondary banks in the lending boom after 1971 were on behalf on institutional funds, and a number of those funds were even equity holders in the doomed secondary banks (see Chapter 2).[108] The rush into speculative investments demonstrated the fundamental myopia of the institutions and banks. A draft statement on industrial policy for the 1975 Labour conference observed that, given the City's apparent preference for socially useless investment, the evidence suggested that

> the free market in funds in this country has not helped to ensure that industry is provided with the funds it needs, at the right price and maturity. Indeed, financial institutions—and even the industrial companies themselves—have shown a distinct preference, especially in recent years, for investing in property or in profitable short-term securities . . .

The problem with this myopia was that it 'tended to undermine the value of the institutions' own substantial holdings [in Britain], since the companies in which they invest are now in no position to meet international competition'.[109]

HAROLD WILSON, THE TUC, AND THE INSTITUTIONS

The proponents of employing the institutional funds for increased industrial investment, without the necessity of nationalization, were able to gain a more public airing of their views in the latter years of the decade. The vote by the Labour Party conference in favour of the 'Banking and Finance' motion for widespread nationalization of the financial sector was met with scant enthusiasm by the party leadership (this is discussed further in Chapters 2 and 3). To placate the demands, the Prime Minister, Jim Callaghan, established a committee on the functioning of financial institutions, which would look at their operation and effect on the economy. The committee was chaired by the recently retired Prime Minister, Harold Wilson, and drew together members from the City, industry, academia, and the trade unions.[110] At the behest of Wilson, and

---

[108] Plender, *That's the Way the Money Goes*, 49–51.
[109] TUC: MSS 2920/450/2, 'Labour Party Draft Industrial Statement: 1975 Annual Conference—Labour and Industry: The Next Steps (Home Policy Committee)', August 1975.
[110] LPA: LP/RD/9/21, 'Statement Made by James Callaghan at a Meeting of the NEC in Blackpool', 24 September 1976; LP/RD/48/4, Norman Stagg (Deputy General Secretary of Post Office Workers), 'Union of Post Office Workers: The Development of the Giro

with the support of the trade-union members, the emphasis of the committee was placed on the provision of funds for industry and trade.[111] The formal evidence provided by the TUC to the committee was predicated on the arguments that had been developed by Hughes and others since the beginning of the decade. It was reiterated that the failure of the nation's industrial sectors could be attributed to 'an insufficient quantity' and 'poor quality' of investment. Out-of-date machinery produced poor quality and expensive goods, which domestic and international consumers did not want to buy. A tendency for capital to be exported (the book value of net assets abroad attributable to the UK increased from £3.4 billion in 1962 to £10.1 billion in 1974, with capital export to other West European nations increasing from £455 million to £2.8 billion over the same period) was deemed to be a major cause; as was the continuing balance of payments constraint, which restricted aggregate demand and prevented sustained investment growth.[112] What was required was a doubling of the rate of gross fixed capital investment in manufacturing over the following decade.

Furthermore, the TUC argued, as Hughes had done before, that the pursuit of short-term returns often led to defective long-term outcomes for the British economy. The question remained whether narrow 'profitability' alone was the most efficient and effective incentive for investment. Its written evidence quoted approvingly from chapter twelve of Keynes' *General Theory*:

> I expect to see the state, which is in a position to calculate the marginal efficiency of capital goods on long views and on the basis of the general social advantage, taking an ever greater responsibility for directly organising investments...[113]

The TUC believed that, working within the framework of the mixed economy, the financial institutions should direct their funds into companies and projects with 'an adequate rate of return in the long run, to companies' investment at home rather than abroad, and to projects which help[ed] raise the growth rate of the UK economy and therefore help[ed]

Service, the National Savings Bank, and the Work of the Paymaster General's Department into a Common State Banking Service', 21 April 1977.

[111] Committee to Review the Functioning of Financial Institutions Papers, British Library of Political and Economic Science, London School of Economics [henceforward FI]: 1/1, 'Meeting No. 1—Minutes', 18 January 1977; 1/2, FI (77) 7, 'The Committee's Work Programme and Priorities within it: Note by the TUC Members of the Committee', 3 February 1977.

[112] Trades Union Congress, *The Role of Financial Institutions*, 13–15.

[113] Ibid. 19; John Maynard Keynes, *The General Theory of Employment, Interest and Money* (London: Macmillan, 1936), 164.

restore full employment'. This would not be out of step with the custodial duty to protect savers from losses, but would be in line with the long-term needs of the national community from which those savings were produced. The future ability, it was argued, to pay adequate pensions, or bonuses on life insurance policies, was dependent on a stable rate of growth for the economy until the end of the century. If this was not assured, opportunities for any profitable investment would disappear. This argument was predicated on the idea that investment would be constrained within national boundaries by exchange and capital controls—an irrelevant assumption after 1979. The main TUC proposal was for the creation of a new lending facility to industry, which would be funded by both the private and public sectors. In addition to the institutional funds, the public tranche would be financed by the funds generated by North Sea Oil reserves, and the proposed facility would be a massive extension of Equity Capital for Industry.[114] A new scheme (possibly entitled 'North Sea Oil Bonds') could be set up directly to draw public savings into the facility. Additionally, the TUC proposed a new standing committee regarding finance for investment, which, 'on a strict tripartite basis', would serve to transmit to private institutions the priorities of the industrial strategy.

The non-trade-union members of the Wilson committee disagreed with the notion that there was any shortage of funding for industry, and asserted that no new mechanism for directing funds was required (see Chapter 3 for more detail). Yet Harold Wilson supported the trade-union members in the publication of a 'Note of Dissent', which proposed the need for such an institution. Wilson, writing in his memoirs about 'the pension funds revolution', was not a virulent critic of the institutional funds. He was a strong advocate of the custodial obligation of the institutions to their savers. He believed that their investment strategies should be

> dictated by one single duty—ensuring in maximising the inflation proofed pension which that young 16 year old, who left school this summer, will receive on retiring from work in the middle twenties of the next century. Any other consideration would be a breach of a very solemn legal trust and a betrayal of the duties of the trustees.[115]

Yet this did not mean, for Wilson, that the institutions did not have a sensible role to play in industrial renewal. In dissenting from the financiers and industrialists on the committee, Wilson and the trade unionists put

---

[114] Trades Union Congress, *The Role of Financial Institutions*, 25; Kynaston, *City of London*, iv. 537–8.
[115] Wilson, *Final Term*, 146–50.

the case for a public/institutional fund. The new investment facility, jointly funded by the public sector and the institutional investors, would advance loan and equity capital. Policyholders would be safeguarded by a guarantee of a fixed rate of minimum of return equal to that received by investment in government gilt-edged stock. Wilson did, however, diverge from the trade unionists in believing that a £1 billion fund would suffice, whereas they argued for £2 billion. The facility would be administered by a 'tripartite steering committee' comprising employer and employee representatives from finance and industry, as well as government departments. This was based on the assumption that 'government, employers and trade unions are permanent and responsible centres of power in the economy'.[116] As Michael Lisle-Williams observed a few years later, this was 'less a step towards the Alternative Economic Strategy', and more of an attempt to bring the financial institutions within the tripartite model of economic planning.[117]

The eventual publication of the Wilson committee's report in 1980 meant that such a policy was never to be initiated. The Thatcher government, committed to dismantling the excesses of the social democratic settlement, and opposed in principle to state intervention, had no interest in pursuing such a policy. Policy groups within the trade unions and the Labour Party debated the issues into the mid-1980s, yet the dominance of the Conservative Party throughout the decade blocked any prospect of possible reform along the lines desired. Hughes continued to argue that pension funds were unable to 'handle efficiently their long-run responsibilities in managing what are essentially social funds'.[118] In 1982 the TUC produced a report on pension fund investment and trusteeship that argued that the investment policies of the funds were 'reinforcing the long-term decline in UK industry'.[119] Following the abolition of exchange controls in 1979, this process had been exacerbated by a significant increase in pension funds investing overseas 'at the expense of UK equities and other investments'.[120] By 1986 it asserted that the City 'cannot isolate itself

---

[116] 'A Note of Dissent by the Chairman, Lord Allen, Mr Jenkins, Mr Mills and the Rt Hon. Lionel Murray, "The Institutions and the Industrial Challenge of the Eighties: The Need for a New Investment Facility"', in Cmd 7937, *Report: Committee to Review the Functioning of Financial Institutions* (1980), 274–87.

[117] Michael Lisle-Williams, 'The State, Finance and Industry in Britain', in Andrew W. Cox (ed.), *State, Finance and Industry: A Comparative Analysis of Post-War Trends in Six Advanced Industrial Economies* (Brighton: Wheatsheaf, 1986), 238.

[118] LPA: LP/RD/120/2, 'Financial Institutions Study Group Minutes', 15 December 1981.

[119] LPA: LP/RD/120/3, 'TUC Conference: Report on Pension Fund Investment and Trusteeship', 11 November 1982.

[120] Ibid.

from the rest of the economy. It cannot be an island of affluence in an industrial desert.'[121] Yet the opportunity to bring the savings of the national community to bear on the underperforming industrial economy had gone, and the industrial desert grew while the City prospered as an international financial centre free from the shackles of state intervention.

CONCLUSION

The post-war rise of institutional investment went largely unnoticed in British political and economic policy discussions until the onset of severe industrial crisis in the 1970s. The size and influence of the investing institutions offered both an opportunity and a challenge to the operation of industrial social democracy in Britain. Critics on the political left, and within the trade-union movement, believed that the institutions were failing to support industry by underinvesting, or investing in wasteful ventures. The Heath government sought to strengthen and improve the industrial economy—in keeping with the established norms of post-war economic strategy—by harnessing the power of the institutions to oversee industrial improvement. The institutions on their own, however, were incapable of doing so—pushing the Heath government back towards the interventionism that it had been attempting to escape. More advanced analysis and proposals for reform sought to align the priorities of the institutions with the requirements of industrial expansionism in order to support the economic well-being of the nation as a whole. These proposals maintained that the long-term contractual savings of the community should be used to secure future economic prosperity. This conceptualization of the pension funds fitted within an adapted form of social democracy that met the changing nature and requirements of the British economy. It represented an attempt not merely to uphold the pillars of the social democratic settlement, but to advance it further by bring the investment process within a more rational, and democratic, frame.

This chapter has focused on the attempt to reconcile the institutionalization of ownership and investment with the social democratic strategy for managing investment that had prevailed since the war. Chapter 2 broadens our analysis to look at how changes to the domestic banking system affected the social democratic settlement in credit creation and allocation, and will again assess how social democrats responded to these changes.

---

[121] TUC: MSS.2920/461/2, *The Financial World: Today and Tomorrow: A TUC Report*, June 1986.

2

The Politics of Banking and Social Democracy

The political economy of banking during the British social democratic 'moment' has been studied to only a limited degree in the historiography of post-war Britain. Financial and economic historians have undertaken extensive research on the performance and activities of the banking sector, and assessed its impact on the economy as a whole.[1] Descriptions of the operation of post-war monetary policy are also well covered—most exhaustively in Forrest Capie's recent history of the Bank of England.[2] Yet what is missing from the historiography is the place of banks in British politics in the period. Much of the literature focuses its attention on the seemingly apolitical policymaking of elites in the Bank of England, and to a lesser extent the Treasury. This tends to exclude the more contested areas of political and public debate, and assumes that the politics of banking was solely the preserve of technocratic administrators and expert financiers. There is also a tendency not to enquire into the political and economic assumptions that underpinned the operation of monetary policy. Undeniably the arcane nature of financial matters, and the technicalities of monetary policy, ultimately determined that banking issues were often

---

[1] Mae Baker and Michael Collins, 'English Commercial Banks and Business Client Distress, 1946–63', *European Review of Economic History*, 7 (2003), 365–88; Mae Baker and Michael Collins, 'English Commercial Banks and Organization Inertia: The Financing of SMEs, 1944–1960', *Enterprise and Society*, 11/1 (2009), 65–97; Mae Baker and Michael Collins, 'English Bank Business Loans,1920–1968: Transaction Bank Characteristics and Small Firm Discrimination', *Financial History Review*, 12 (2005), 135–71; Mark Billings and Forrest Capie, 'Capital in British Banking, 1920–1970', *Business History*, 49/2 (2007), 139–62; Alan Booth, 'Technical Change in Branch Banking at the Midland Bank, 1945–75', *Accounting, Business & Financial History*, 14/3 (2004), 277–300; Capie and Billings, 'Evidence on Competition; Forrest Capie and Mark Billings, 'Profitability in English Banking in the Twentieth Century', *European Review of Economic History*, 5/3 (2001), 367–401.

[2] Forrest Capie, *The Bank of England, 1950s to 1979* (Cambridge: Cambridge University Press, 2010); Duncan M. Ross, 'Domestic Monetary Policy and the Banking System in Britain 1945–1971', in Michie and Williamson (eds), *The British Government and the City of London*, 298–321.

insulated from politics in contemporary discourse. The lay public and political activists were largely ignorant of, or perhaps intimidated by, the apparent complexities of banking. Yet this should not deter us from trying to bring politics back into the history of banking in this period, as it is clear that banks were subject to a great deal of public attention in Westminster and beyond—especially during the crisis decades of the 1970s. Furthermore, it is important for historians to avoid falling into the trap of assuming that banking can be treated separately from other contemporary issues of political economy. The banking system is at the heart of any advanced economy, and as such it should not be isolated from the broader study of politics and the economy in the age of social democracy.

This chapter argues that the politics of banking in post-war social democratic Britain consisted of a set of fundamental tensions that translated into broader political frictions whenever attempts were made to reconcile them. The tension between the private ownership of the banks and their centrality to the functioning and management of the economy as a whole was at the heart of this. The extent to which the banking system, as the primary means by which credit was created and allocated, should be brought under the control or direction of the state was the fundamental fault line. Within this were embedded a set of related conflicts, between the demand for control over credit creation and the desire for a competitive banking sector; and between the need for competition and the ideal of a rationalized, and more efficient, 'universal' banking system.

The first part of the chapter discusses the relationship between the state and the banking system as it had evolved by the end of the 1950s. The settlement between the banks and the state consisted of the latter accepting private ownership and cartelization in exchange for the former implementing the credit control strictures necessary to fulfil the policies of demand management. In the 1960s the conditions that enabled this settlement were eroded. The growth of secondary banks and credit creating institutions outside the purview of the banking settlement was a key factor here, but so too was the growing political pressure to abolish the restrictive practices of the clearing banks. Frustration with their secrecy, profitability, lack of competition, and poor customer service fuelled this demand. The clearing banks also grew frustrated at aspects of the settlement. The implementation of new techniques of monetary control in 1971, which abolished the cartel agreements and restricted the influence of the state, was an attempt to resolve these pressures for change. The second part of the chapter considers how the abandonment of existing practices impacted on the place of banking in politics in the 1970s. The resurgence of the Labour Party's left wing, spurred by the accelerating decline of the nation's industrial base, revived pre-1945 attempts to bring the banking system within the ownership and direction of the state. The loss of control over credit allocation engendered by the Heath government's new approach after 1971 spurred interventionists to argue for a reassertion of the right of the state to direct credit according to national economic need. This was supported by a desire to use the state to modernize and rationalize the inefficient provision of banking services to the public.

THE POST-WAR BANKING SETTLEMENT

In the years following the war British clearing banks and the state settled on a relationship of voluntary cooperation.[3] This relationship was one built upon the material conditions of the British domestic banking system, which was characterized by oligopoly, cartelization, and relative stability. These conditions permitted the state to control the creation and general allocation of credit in the economy effectively without taking the banks into public ownership. The post-war settlement in monetary policy was one in which the state, operating through the nationalized Bank of England, sought to control the creation of, and to a lesser extent allocation of, credit by the banking system for the purposes of demand management. As described in the Introduction, the macroeconomic strategy of the social democratic settlement was an attempt to expand the domestic economy, strengthen the balance of payments, and resist pressure on sterling. Monetary policy was dedicated to meeting these often contradictory demands. In the two and a half decades following 1945 this goal was pursued through three separate mechanisms. First, the clearing banks were required to hold minimum ratios of cash and liquid assets to ensure the banks' stability and consistency of lending. Secondly, the Bank of England engaged in a set of 'market' techniques designed to manipulate the general cost of lending. The most prominent of these techniques was the traditional method of altering the bank rate (the rate at which the Bank of England would lend to other banks). This was supported by 'open market operations' (intervening in the discount market to buy and sell government liabilities in order to manipulate bank balance sheets) and 'special deposits' (which required that banks hold a certain percentage of deposits with the Bank of England). Thirdly, physical controls on bank lending were often imposed when the balance of payments fell into deficit owing

---

[3] The structure of the British banking system is described in the Introduction.

to excessive domestic consumption. Ceilings on the amount of lending banks could undertake were designed to choke off such consumption, and were often specifically designed to direct credit into industry or activities that would support exports.[4] The Radcliffe Committee on monetary policy agreed in the late 1950s that such controls should be employed only as emergency measures, yet throughout the 1960s they were heavily relied upon to bolster the parity of sterling.[5] The clearing bank cartel (described in the Introduction) enabled the state to implement its monetary policy with greater ease and effect. Non-competition on deposit rates ensured that lending rates were kept low and stable, but also ensured that policy changes fed through into the real economy in a quick and uniform manner. Yet the implementation of this policy was not backed by formal legislation or agreement, but structured around a set of voluntary agreements between the government, the Bank of England, and the clearing banks.[6]

Monetary policy involved constant negotiations with the banks. Although the Bank of England had some limited official powers to direct lending entrusted by the 1946 Act of Nationalization, it was unwilling to impose itself, with force, upon the banks. Instead, the Bank preferred to use its 'moral suasion' in which the Governor requested, rather than commanded, the banks to meet the demands incumbent upon them as a result of the government's economic policies. In exchange for meeting such demands, the banks were allowed to retain their freedom as privately owned firms, and to engage in uncompetitive and oligopolistic practices. A Bank of England note, produced in June 1964, described the methods of credit control used over the banks:

> Our existing methods of credit control rely essentially on persuasion, and on the banks' willingness to be persuaded even when what we ask requires them to refrain from doing business that would be attractive to them; the methods used must therefore be acceptable to the banks. If statutory compulsion were to be applied at any point the element of voluntary co-operation could well be destroyed over a wide field; and statutory definitions and rules would then

---

[4] For a chronology of post-war monetary policy, see Ross, 'Domestic Monetary Policy', 301–7.

[5] The Committee on the Working of the Monetary System (Radcliffe Committee) was established by the Chancellor, Peter Thorneycroft, in 1957 to inquire into operation of monetary policy: Cmnd 827, *Report: Committee on the Working of the Monetary System*, (London: HMSO, 1959), 129–88.

[6] TNA: T 230/814, 'Treasury Historical Memorandum No. 21: Control of Credit in the Private Sector, 1965–1971', January 1975; for a detailed description of the operation of monetary policy until the end of the 1950s, see Cmnd 827, *Report: Committee on the Working of the Monetary System*, 129–88.

at once be needed to enforce the restrictions and, subsequently, to preserve or replace many other existing voluntary arrangements.[7]

This negotiated settlement had evolved followed the war. Yet during the interwar period the 'progressive' agenda for the banking system had proposed to go much further in bringing it within the control of the state. 'Progressives' from each of the main political parties saw the need for greater government intervention in the financial system if the economy was to be rationally and efficiently planned. These reforming proposals were embedded more widely in the increased prevalence and popularity of 'planning' as a model of economic management.[8] The input of Tory moderates was led by Harold Macmillan, who accepted the part failure of the existing financial system and championed the creation of new institutions—notably proposing in *The Middle Way* (1938) the creation of a National Investment Board, and the establishment of a 'more rational financial mechanism' that could manage and direct productive investment.[9] The Liberal Party also expressed some support for the creation of an investment board.[10] Yet it was the Labour Party that ultimately took the lead in this area. The apparent failure of the free capital market to organize and assist the domestic industrial base efficiently, contributing to the vast scale of interwar unemployment, emphasized to the party that planning and interventionism on behalf of the state was vital for economic modernization and recovery. This imperative took place against the wider background of intra-party debates over the merits and relative importance of nationalization and other methods for obtaining economic control designed to implement a socialist economic strategy. As early as 1918 the Labour Advisory Committee on Trade and Finance had argued for the 'immediate reorganization of the banking system', in which the Bank of England would be nationalized and its activities widened to included branch banking in the form of a 'National Bank' and a 'Post Office Savings Bank'. The purpose was sixfold: (1) to control or displace the 'capitalist system'; (2) to obtain greater security for depositors; (3) to cut administration costs; (4) to direct credit—'having regard for the estimated social utility of the subject of the loan' rather than 'private or immediate gains'; (5) to control prices, production, and employment where attributable to finance; and (6) to reduce the cost of having to bail out the banking

[7] TNA: T 230/710, 'Control of Bank Credit', 3 June 1964.

[8] D. Ritschel, *The Politics of Planning: The Debate on Economic Planning in Britain in the 1930s* (Oxford: Clarendon Press, 1997).

[9] E. H. H. Green, 'The Conservatives and the City', in Michie and Williamson (eds), *The British Government and the City of London*, 156–66.

[10] Tomlinson, 'Attlee's Inheritance, 142–3.

system in periods of crisis.[11] Having adopted 'Clause IV' in its constitution, which committed the party to common ownership of production as well as the 'means of distribution and exchange', the party's desire to intervene in the banking system was spurred by the animosity generated by the perceived 'Bankers' Ramp' in 1931, which had derailed and split the Labour government.[12] The 1932 conference carried a resolution condemning the deflation and unemployment 'engineered' by City institutions that wielded 'unacceptable powers', and stated that public control was needed over finance so that national development could be effectively planned and so that socialist policies would not be 'sabotaged by the banks'.[13] Ernest Bevin, general secretary of the Transport and General Workers' Union (TGWU), famously declared in 1931 that 'you can talk about socializing the railways and other things. Socialise credit and the rest is comparatively easy.'[14]

There was a general consensus by the end of the 1930s on the vital need for the Bank of England to be brought into state ownership as a means of controlling and managing credit. The issue of wider nationalization— namely, the expansion of public ownership to include the joint-stock banks—was more controversial. Following the emotive events of 1931, the party conference voted overwhelmingly in favour of adopting this policy—supported by leading Labour figures such as Attlee and Cripps, as well as Evan Durbin and Hugh Gaitskell. In 1933 Attlee and Cripps submitted a memorandum to the party's national executive stating that it was vital to nationalize the banks immediately with such speed that 'the blow struck must be a fatal one and not merely designed to wound'.[15] State control over the joint-stock banks would ensure that, while the nationalized central bank would create credit, it could be directed in a rational and efficient manner. The policy was included in the 1935 manifesto, yet there were opponents of the idea—notably Bevin, Dalton, and Morrison—who considered it electorally damaging and not particularly necessary given the capacity of a publicly owned Bank of England to

[11] Sidney Pollard, 'The Nationalisation of the Banks: The Chequered History of a Socialist Proposal', in David E. Martin and Martin Rubinstein (eds), *Ideology and the Labour Movement: Essays Presented to John Saville* (London: Croom Helm, 1979), 169.

[12] Philip Williamson, 'A "Bankers' Ramp"? Financiers and the British Political Crisis of August 1931', *English Historical Review*, 99/393 (1984), 770–806.

[13] Ibid. 175.

[14] Toye, *The Labour Party and the Planned Economy*, 61; for a fuller account of the development of Labour's policy towards the banks in the 1930s, see ibid. 34–64; Durbin, *New Jerusalems*, 162–7.

[15] Edmund Dell, *A Strange and Eventful History: Democratic Socialism in Britain*, (London: Harper Collins, 2000), 40–1.

regulate the banks 'without improper disturbance'.[16] It was this latter view that was to win out. *Labour's Immediate Programme* in 1937, while resolutely stating that 'no nation can plan its economic life unless it can control both its finance and financiers', dropped joint-stock bank nationalization in favour of the efficacy of the Bank of England in managing the overall provision of credit.[17] The post-1945 Labour government successfully brought the Bank of England into public ownership, and left the allocation of credit to the privately owned banks. The interwar proposals for planning and directing credit were abandoned and gave way in the post-war decades to a Keynesian monetary policy in which domestic demand could be manipulated in aggregate through the tools described in the Introduction to this book. Credit had been semi-socialized. The banks retained their freedom as privately owned firms, but they were constrained by the demands of the social democratic economic agenda pursued by the state. They could have their freedom so long as they met their obligations to the national economy by adhering to government requests.

CHALLENGES TO THE BANKING SETTLEMENT

The settlement between banking and the state was underpinned by a set of material conditions in the banking system—the oligopoly of large banks, which overwhelmingly dominated deposit-taking and lending. Over the course of the 1950s and (with increasing speed) the 1960s, these conditions were eroded by the emergence of new credit-creating institutions, which offered banking and credit services in direct competition with the clearing banks. The effect of this was to place pressure on the clearers to compete on price with the new institutions, and to challenge the existing methods for controlling credit, as the non-clearing banks came outside the influence of the state and the Bank of England. However, these material changes were matched by widespread demand for a more competitive banking sector, and a general demand on both the political left and right for the existing cartel arrangements of the clearing banks to be abolished.

Through the 1960s the clearing banks' market share of deposits was eroded. In 1951 clearing bank deposits comprised almost 80 per cent of total bank deposits. By the end of 1967 this had been almost halved.[18] Among the major beneficiaries were the building societies, whose deposits increased significantly over the post-war decades as a result of the expansion

---

[16] Pollard, 'The Nationalisation of the Banks', 178.   [17] Ibid.
[18] Nevin and Davies, *The London Clearing Banks*, 214.

of owner-occupation. Another reason was the emergence of alternative financial institutions that could compete for deposits outside the clearing bank cartel—foreign banks, British overseas banks, merchant banks, and other specialized financial institutions. From the beginning of the 1950s, the merchant, overseas, and foreign banks based in the City had broken away from interest-rate agreements of the clearing banks and begun to offer higher rates of interest for short-term depositors. When restrictions on hire-purchase companies and non-clearing bank lending were removed in 1958, competition for funds intensified. From this situation two banking systems emerged.[19] The clearing banks at the centre of the 'primary' market; and a parallel market consisting of 'secondary' banks. The latter were far less restrained by the strictures of the authorities, or the 'self-denying ordinances' of the conservative practices of the 'big five'.

The traditional London money market—known as the discount market—was central to the operation of monetary policy.[20] However, from the late 1950s, its centrality was challenged by a collection of 'parallel money markets' that emerged alongside the existing discount market. In these markets money was bought and sold at a price between the non-clearing bank financial institutions. These secondary markets were divided into those that traded in sterling-denominated inter-bank deposits, certificates of deposits, local authority and finance house deposits, and inter-company loans; and those that traded in non-sterling deposits—known as the 'Eurocurrency' or 'Eurodollar' market (discussed further in Chapter 4). The sterling inter-bank market allowed for non-clearing banks operating in London to lend their funds at higher rates than would be obtainable on the discount market. Lending between institutions could be very short term (overnight) or for a number of years. These funds could be lent profitably to local authorities (now encouraged by government policy to borrow), hire-purchase companies, industrial and commercial firms, property companies, and so on. Unlike the clearing banks, they were not subject to official requirements that they maintain a fixed liquidity ratio. The clearing banks engaged with these new opportunities, but not directly. While retaining the cartel agreements on non-competition, the banks obtained ownership of a number of hire-purchase companies outside the agreement. This allowed the banks to engage in the expanding area of consumer finance, and permitted them to engage in profitable lending that the banks themselves could not undertake directly. Additionally, the clearers' involvement became more significant when

[19] Ibid. 215.
[20] The structure of the mid-century London money market is described in the Introduction.

they began to establish their own subsidiaries, which could operate in the secondary markets.[21]

The effect of the changes to the banking system described above were twofold. First, it brought the existing mechanisms for controlling credit under stress. Credit creation was no longer narrowly the preserve of the clearing banks, but was increasingly the product of a variety of competing financial institutions, of which the state had far less ability to keep control. The Treasury was not unaware of the effect that 'other' banks could have upon its conventional approach to monetary policy; however, it originally thought little of the threat. In a paper written at the end of 1963, John F. Slater, the Assistant Secretary to the Treasury, claimed that such new institutions were not displacing the clearing banks, and did not pose any 'special or novel problems' for monetary policy. The fact that they were subject to the same requests to limit advances and bill finance as the clearers was enough.[22] This was reiterated in a Treasury study a year later.[23] Yet by 1965 Slater had come around to thinking that the 'other' banks and financial intermediaries posed a more significant challenge than he had previously concluded. Although the clearing banks still accounted for 85 per cent of all credit granted by financial institutions, the rapidly growing importance of the accepting houses, overseas banks, and hire-purchase finance companies was eroding this dominance. The credit provided by the last of these was controlled only through the requests of voluntary cooperation to the 'finance houses' and 'industrial bankers' by the Governor. There was no recourse to official sanction if they did not obey. The flexibility of credit providers outside the usual channels constantly undermined attempts to control its growth. For example, despite attempts to rein in credit in July 1968, R. T. Armstrong, Under-Secretary for Home Finance, observed how 'awfully easy' it was 'to find a way around credit restrictions'.[24] Comprehensive reform was needed, as persuasion was not effective—'it makes for bad feeling on the part of the banks [who felt that they were being forced to carry the burden of the government's policies alone], for a progressive loss of business during times of tight money, and so to a gradual weakening of the apparatus of credit control'.[25] It was necessary for banks and other intermediaries to be put on a shared and equal footing with uniform liquidity controls on

---

[21] Nevin and Davies, *The London Clearing Banks*, 217.

[22] TNA: T 326/236, J. F. Slater, 'Clearing Banks and "Other" Banks', 28 October 1963.

[23] TNA: T 326/478, J. F. Slater and C. H. Harvie, 'The Money Supply and Liabilities of Financial Intermediaries', 26 November 1964.

[24] TNA: T 326/969, R. T. Armstrong to Lovell, 5 July 1968.

[25] TNA: T 230/761, 'Credit Control', 17 May 1965.

both.[26] This concern was mirrored in a note produced by the governments' economic advisor, Frank Cassell, in September 1966, in which he stated the need for the Treasury to consider applying liquidity controls to the non-clearers. This had been 'ducked' by the Radcliffe Committee, but since then the importance of the 'outside banks [had] grown phenomenally':

> In consequence, we find ourselves in the unhappy position of being unable to exert effective control over what has in recent years been the most dynamic component of money supply or over what has become the most internationally significant for short-term interest rates... The possibility of enforcing some form of liquidity control over the accepting houses and overseas banks should, I submit, be explored before we fall back on tightening the controls on the clearing banks just because they happen to be the most accessible.[27]

Secondly, it created new pressures for the clearing banks to change their deposit and lending policies to be able to compete with the new institutions. In 1963 the Governor of the Bank of England, Lord Cromer, called for the clearers to engage in competition with the newcomers. He hinted that the banks might consider abandoning the cartel and compete for deposits by offering different interest rates. The reaction of the Treasury, and the Conservative Chancellor, was one of trepidation. Shortly after the speech, Treasury Under-Secretary Italo de Lisle Radice told the Bank of England's chief cashier, Jasper Hollom, that 'ministers would be very excited if there were any suggestion that the banks might start increasing the rates of interest charged on advances'.[28] There was no great need for the government to worry that the cartel would be abandoned, as the clearing banks had no inclination to engage directly in such competitive practices. When Alec Cairncross, at that time an economic advisor to the Conservative government, visited the Midland Bank shortly afterwards, he was informed that competition was not going to happen—deposits rates would be forced up and costs would increase, thus leading to an increase in lending rates. The banks would not countenance this.[29] Furthermore, the banks did not consider themselves to be a true cartel anyway, citing the 'non-price' competition that took place between themselves and with other financial institutions. In a memorandum produced for the Treasury by the Committee of London Clearing Bankers (CLCB) at the start of

---

[26] TNA: T 326/128, J. F. Slater, 'The Position of the Clearing Banks in the National Economy', 1 November 1963.

[27] TNA: T 230/710, F. Cassell, 'Controlling the Parallel Markets', 8 September 1966.

[28] TNA: T 326/128, note from I. de L. Radice, 5 June 1963.

[29] TNA: T 326/128, note from A. K. Cairncross, 4 July 1963.

1964, it was stated that they had 'always sought to maintain a reasonable and proper margin between Deposit Rate and Lending Rates' and that 'almost all financial centres find it necessary to have some agreement on rating structure, if only to preserve an orderly market'.[30] In other words, their agreements were simply prudent and helped to maintain financial stability. As the Governor pointed out in his discussion with Armstrong in October 1963, the breakdown of the cartel would have 'serious consequence for the authorities' as they relied upon it to 'enable their monetary policy to work'.[31] The Janus-faced Bank of England, led by the liberal Cromer but with responsibilities of the state, recognized the inherent tensions of the existing settlement and clearly did not feel comfortable in placing too great a strain on them.

In response to another suggestion by the Governor in the same April speech, the clearing banks did, however, propose to increase their overdraft rate of interest by 0.5 per cent and introduce a new special savings deposits scheme with an interest rate of 3.5 per cent. Such a change would help to restore their contracting profit margins and competitive power in the face of other financial intermediaries. At the Treasury, Armstrong was perturbed by this proposal to increase the cost of lending, as the government was 'set on a policy of steady expansion', and it was 'particularly concerned to see that bank credit was available for those who needed it as activity expanded'. Such a collective increase in overdraft rates would act as a check on this expansion, if not by actually changing the likelihood of borrowers taking further advances but in sending a psychological message that the government was thinking of enacting some form of demand restraint if it was allowed to go ahead.[32] The significance of such a proposal to the Treasury is demonstrated by the fact that the Conservative Chancellor, who was in Washington at the time, was immediately sent an emergency telegram to ask for a response. Reginald Maudling and Cromer both agreed that the timing for the proposal was 'most unfortunate' and that the latter would 'represent to them [the clearing banks] in the strongest terms that this change should not be announced at the present time'.[33] Even the Prime Minster, Harold Macmillan, was consulted, and he expressed deep concern about the 'political and economic consequences of any such move by the Clearing Banks at this time, but also

---

[30] TNA: T 326/236, the Committee of London Clearing Bankers, 'Memorandum', 2 January 1964.

[31] TNA: T 326/128, W. Armstrong, 'Clearing Banks' Proposals', 18 October 1963.

[32] TNA: T 326/128, W. Armstrong, 'Clearing Banks: Interest Rates', 2 October 1963.

[33] TNA: T 326/128, telegram to Mitchell, Private Secretary to the Chancellor of the Exchequer, 3 October 1963; telegram to Sir William Armstrong, 3 October 1963.

on the longer term relations between the Government and the Banks'.[34] When the CLCB acquiesced to the Governor's request, and agreed to postpone their decision, the Prime Minster joked: 'Many thanks. This is better. I suppose we could send Thompson [Sir Edward, Deputy Chairman of the CLCB] to the Tower, if necessary.'[35]

It is clear that the banking system was, therefore, held tightly within the mechanism of macroeconomic policymaking. The pressure to meet the new financial environment came up against the needs of the social democratic state to maintain control over the price of credit. This exacerbated the key tension at the heart of the post-war settlement on banking—how far were the banks independent commercial institutions with autonomy over their activities; and how far were they agents of the government in its macroeconomic interventionism? In the subsequent negotiations over the overdraft rate increase, it was noted by Radice that the banks were opposed to the 'doctrine that the level of overdraft rates is entirely a matter for the Government's monetary policy'.[36] As the debate continued over whether overdraft rates could be increased in December, the Economic Secretary to the Treasury, Maurice Macmillan, argued that the bank rate could not be separated from the needs of manufacturing and commercial firms. He wrote: 'There is a social (and political) point to be considered here. It is not easy for small and medium sized businesses to finance their expansion except on overdraft.'[37] Two years later, in 1965, Slater was 'startled' when the Chairman of Midland announced to the bank's shareholders that they were 'free to fix their rates' so long as they were not 'out of accord with the Government's view of the needs of the economy at a particular juncture'. This liberal attitude was not government policy as far as Slater was aware.[38] Cairncross agreed that it was a surprise that the banks should have been able to go ahead with plans for differentiation in overdraft charges without the Treasury being consulted. As he put it:

> I daresay that the banks are 'free' to fix their rates, but they can hardly pretend that the matter is of no interest to the Government or that the Government is without powers to make it very difficult to persevere if their policies are out of line with the wishes of the Government...there is no reason why the banks should now regard themselves as free to obtain higher

[34] TNA: T 326/128: from John Boyd-Carpenter to The Earl of Cromer, 4 October 1963.
[35] TNA: T 326/128: 'Minute to the Prime Minster from the Chief Secretary of the Treasury about Clearing Banks Proposals', 7 October 1963.
[36] TNA: T 326/128, note by I. de L. Radice, 24 October 1963.
[37] TNA: T 326/236, 'Clearing Banks' Proposals', 6 December 1963.
[38] TNA: T 326/478, J. F. Slater, 'Bank Lending Rates', 21 January 1965.

returns on advances in relation to current bank rate independently of the general economic situation.[39]

In response to being prevented from increasing the rates, the banks decided instead to introduce a broader spectrum of lending rates, in which the basic rate remained unchanged for high-security borrowers but increased for hire purchase, property development, and some other types of personal and professional borrowers. They also raised the minimum rate for industrial and commercial borrowers by 1 per cent, and intended to increase the lending rates to public-sector borrowers. In a memorandum on the subject, an Assistant Secretary to the Treasury, John McKinnon Rhodes, described the change as not 'self-evidently necessary' but not 'wholly unreasonable'.[40] However, there was little sympathy for the clearing banks from the Labour Chancellor. Exposed as he was at that time to endless speculation against the pound, the desire of the banks to restore their profits at the expense of the public sector was never going to get an easy hearing from Jim Callaghan. He responded sarcastically and angrily to Rhodes's note:

> My heart bleeds for the Clearing Banks. Of course we cannot agree to this. Will you let me see how their profits this year compare with recent years? I believe we are awaiting their Statements now, are we not? . . . If not, I will see the Governor—but it might be more diplomatic if I didn't.[41]

A few weeks later, he continued:

> irrespective of its merits, surely the Clearing Banks must see that this is the wrong timing!! And as to merits, would it be a good idea for us to suggest that they opened up their accounts to us so that we can examine with the aid of accountants how far their claim is justified?[42]

When the Chancellor and the CLCB chairmen met to discuss the proposals, he was more conciliatory, and explained that he was not opposed to the proposals 'in substance', but that he wanted to discuss the timing and presentation further. Given that bank profits had risen considerably in 1965, and that the local authorities were in the process of deciding their 'rates' (for which the banks may be blamed if they were to increase),

---

[39] TNA: T 326/478, A. K. Cairncross to Mr Goldman, 25 January 1965.

[40] TNA: T 326/478, J. I. McK. Rhodes, 'Clearing Banks' Lending Rates', 8 December 1965.

[41] TNA: T 326/478, I. P. Bancroft, 'Clearing Banks' Lending Rates', 20 December 1965.

[42] TNA: T 326/478, I. P. Bancroft, 'Clearing Banks' Lending Rates', 10 January 1966.

it was not the correct time.[43] This was evidently the typical Treasury approach—never to deny the banks' requests outright but to delay until the time was more appropriate.

The changes to the banking system in the 1960s applied great strain to the post-war settlement in this area as credit creation spilled outside the framework in which the clearing banks operated. The clearers were not keen to alter radically their practices in response to this challenge and held tightly to the cartel agreements, engaging with the new possibilities only at arm's length. However, pressure to allow the clearing banks to compete collectively for deposits grew, as did the hope that the new institutions would be equally exposed to the demands of government policy. For the Conservative and Labour governments of the 1960s, committed to retaining control over bank lending for the purposes of national economic development, the challenge from outside financial institutions pushed them to assert their commitment to the existing settlement. Yet a popular belief was simultaneously emerging, across the political spectrum, that the cartel agreement in banking was no longer acceptable, and that a more competitive banking sector was necessary.

THE NATIONAL BOARD OF PRICES AND INCOMES REVIEW

The battle to retain the parity of sterling following Harold Wilson's election victory in 1964 brought the banks back into focus for the Labour movement. Having been condemned in the 1930s for imposing deflation and derailing the democratically elected plans of the Labour government, City financiers re-emerged as the villains who, through constant speculation against sterling, were destroying the government's grand plans for economic modernization and social equity. Under pressure to take action, and probably keen to exact some form of revenge, George Brown at the Department of Economic Affairs requested in June 1966 that the National Board for Prices and Incomes (NBPI) review the system and level of bank charges for clearing bank customers 'in the light of their profit and dividend record', in which both had increased substantially 'in recent years'. The decision to ask the NBPI to inquire into the banks appears to have been explicitly, and simplistically, 'political'—a genuflection to the Labour government's critics within its own party, who claimed that it was subservient to the banking community in sacrificing its political

---

[43] TNA: T 326/478, 'Note of a Meeting Held...in the Chancellor of the Exchequer's Room, H.M. Treasury', 18 January 1966.

and economic plans. *The Economist* recorded that many in the City suspected as much, and the newspaper alleged that the inquiry was motivated by the 'diffuse feeling that this is somehow a bankers' recession, and that the bankers should not be allowed to emerge from it without scars'.[44] Indeed, the Governor of the Bank of England, in his ongoing fractious relationship with Wilson's government, wrote to the Chancellor to describe the move as 'an attack' on the City.[45] The reference to bank profits highlights the tension once more between whether the banking system was part of the private economy or a public service. Bank profits were legitimate targets for public interest—if they were too high, it was suggested that the public interest was not being served by the banking oligopoly.

The NBPI inquiry went ahead and published its report in May 1967. The members of the board, under the chairmanship of the ex-Conservative minister and businessmen Aubrey Jones, took it upon themselves to query the charges by examining the way in which banks acquired and employed their resources; as well as considering the charges themselves and their effect on profits. The explicit assumption that underpinned the report was that the clearing banks were 'commercial institutions, evolving in a changing commercial environment, and that the techniques of monetary control have to evolve in correspondence with the evolution of the banks'. There was a degree of 'mission creep' in the scope of the inquiry—to the frustration of the Bank of England, the clearing banks, and the Treasury.[46] The report concluded that the banks had not been guilty of overcharging their customers—yet this was the least interesting and impactful aspect of the board's findings. More importantly, the report proposed a variety of far-reaching reforms: banks should move into new fields (such as mortgage lending); should rationalize their branch networks; and should offer more flexible opening hours. Most significantly, it argued that the clearing banks should abandon their cartel agreements and start competing for deposits by offering different interest rates. The board acknowledged that the banks were already doing so through their subsidiaries, but it would be better to do this directly.[47]

The clearing banks came out in strong and unequivocal rejection of the proposals.[48] In his presidential address to the Institute of Bankers in 1969, the Director of Barclays, Sir Cuthbert Clegg, spoke at length on the

---

[44] 'Bank Charges in Britain', *The Economist*, 26 November 1966.
[45] Capie, *The Bank of England*, 441.   [46] Ibid. 442–3.
[47] Cmd 3292, *National Board for Prices and Incomes. Report No. 34: Bank Charges* (London, 1967).
[48] Keith Payne, 'Counter Attack by Banks on PIB Report Criticisms', *The Times*, 25 May 1967.

inherent dangers of competition in this area. He claimed that intense competition for deposits in the third quarter of the nineteenth century had resulted in a series of crises. Fierce competition weakened the traditional security of banks, thus risking monetary and financial instability. Clegg asked his audience:'Would it not be unwise to abandon all forms of mutual restraint?' He concluded:

> The banks believe, in the light of their experience, that in more fundamental ways they serve the country's interests best by removing deposit interest rates from the areas in which they compete...the 'widening of the area of competition' between banks, to include interest rates, could prove to be at the expense of a potential loss of stability; the desirability which the Price and Incomes Board claimed for such a course is not apparent from experience of history in this country; nor, judging by current practice, does it find support in many other countries either.[49]

R. J. Clark of the National Westminster, speaking at a conference to mark ten years since the Radcliffe Report in 1969, argued that bringing subsidiaries that did compete within the main activities of the bank would be a bad idea as they did not fit within the stringent requirements of a clearing bank's balance sheet. Furthermore, despite the fact the banks might 'present a better public image' by abandoning the cartel, actual rates would be unlikely to differ. Advertising to make each bank look unique would increase—'and that would surely benefit no one'.[50] As Capie notes, the report was disapproved of in the Bank and the Treasury. The new Governor, O'Brien, referred to the report as 'thought-provoking' in his October Mansion House speech, but its findings were quickly forgotten.[51] Yet, despite the reluctance of the banks and the authorities, there was significant support for greater competition from across the political spectrum, in both conventional politics and in the media. When the NBPI began its investigation, *The Economist* expressed hope that the banks—renowned for their 'cumbersome indecisiveness'—would begin to compete genuinely on price because 'ultimately, there is no substitute for...direct and full-blooded competition'.[52] Another renowned economic liberal, the economist Harry Johnson, praised the report for breathing fresh air into the economic analysis of the banking system,

---

[49] Sir Cuthbert B. Clegg, 'Competing for Deposits', *Journal of the Institute of Bankers*, 90/3 (1969), 163–78.

[50] R. J. Clark, 'The Evolution of Monetary and Financial Institutions', in David R. Croome and Harry G. Johnson (eds.), *Money in Britain: 1959–1969* (Oxford: Oxford University Press, 1970), 131–49.

[51] Capie, *The Bank of England*, 442–3.

[52] 'No Substitute for Competition', *The Economist*, 18 June 1966.

and forcing a public debate on issues 'that so far have been kept closed by gentlemen's agreement'.[53]

The unique position of the Labour Party in this matter is worth considering further. In the first place, the report was seemingly commissioned as a political, and largely futile, manoeuvre against the banks at a time of crisis. Yet the findings of the report, and the party's response to it, went deeper, exposing the tensions inherent within its political economy in the period. In their report on the NBPI findings, *The Economist* noted the 'supreme irony in the prospect of the gentle oligopolies of Lombard Street finally being propelled into all this capitalistic rough stuff by a socialist government: it is like having the anti-blood sports people breathe fire into Ferdinand the Bull, who just wanted to sit and smell the flowers'.[54] However, Labour's commitment to breaking up monopolies when they were against the interests of the public was well established, particularly following the introduction of the Monopolies and Mergers bill in 1965. This had attempted to juggle the Labour government's desire to break up monopolistic industries where necessary, and to oversee the streamlining of sectors where it would improve efficiency and overall economic performance. As the President of the Board of Trade, Douglas Jay, told the Commons during the second reading of the Bill, it was 'conceived in the belief... that neither monopolies nor mergers are always bad. Sometimes they are and sometimes they are not.'[55] Noel Thompson has thus argued that, when placed in relation to the policies of the Industrial Reorganization Committee (IRC), the government was attempting simultaneously to 'reap the economies of scale associated with industrial concentration' and 'prevent the abuse of monopoly power that a concentration of ownership bestowed'.[56] The contradictory nature of this often pulled the party in two directions, although in banking during the 1960s the preference increasingly lay with competition over mergers.

Following a rise in bank charges across the banks in 1970, Dr John Gilbert, the Labour Member of Parliament for Dudley, denounced it as only 'the latest manifestation in a whole series of manifestations of the cosy little cartel that has been operated by the clearing banks in this country over many years'. Gilbert, an economist, expressed anger at the 'open cartel... a brazen, self-flaunting cartel', such that, if there was strong

---

[53] H. G. Johnson, 'The Report on Bank Charges', *Bankers' Magazine* (August 1967), 64–8.

[54] 'Revolution for the City', *The Economist*, 7 May 1967.

[55] Douglas Jay, Parliamentary Debates, Commons, vol. 709, cols 1207–55 (29 March 1965).

[56] Thompson, *Politics Economy and the Labour Party*, 187.

anti-trust legislation in Britain, it would have 'landed the board of directors of the clearing banks behind bars a long time ago'. Expressing his 'deep regret' that the Labour Party had not done anything when in office, he went on to press the new Conservative Parliamentary Under-Secretary of State at the Department of Trade and Industry, Nicholas Ridley, to 'lean on the banks' to break their cartel, and warned that, 'if... nothing further transpires, he will not expect us to be as gentle with him the next time this matter is raised in the House'.[57] Gilbert was supported in the debate by fellow Labour MP Eric Deakins, who argued that the test of the new Conservative government's commitment to promoting competition 'throughout all sectors of industry and commerce... will be seen by their attitude to competition in the monopoly position of the clearing banks'. He concluded:

> It is up to the Government tonight to show, even if they cannot promise immediate action, that they have the courage of their convictions, that they really believe in competition and that they will take the first tentative steps to enforce competition in a sphere of British financial operations which hitherto has not been subject to this very important principle.[58]

Although he preferred to see the banks pursue private enterprise on their own initiative, the Tory backbencher Sir Harmar Nicholls agreed with the principle and expressed surprise that it was Labour members who were calling for such an outcome.[59] Edmund Dell retorted that it was 'not at all surprising', as 'it is this side [of the House] which has from the beginning shown the greatest interest in promoting competition'—citing the Monopolies and Mergers Act as evidence.[60] The Conservative MP Wilfred Proudfoot had put down an early day motion a month earlier urging the government to 'break the cartel practices of the Committee of London Clearing Bankers' to 'ensure that market forces bring healthy competition'.[61] Meanwhile, a pamphlet written by Brian Griffiths and published by the free-market think tank the Institute of Economic Affairs entitled 'Competition in Banking' garnered a large degree of press attention in

[57] Dr John Gilbert, Parliamentary Debates, Commons, vol. 807, cols 1423–34 (2 December 1970).

[58] Eric Deakins, Parliamentary Debates, Commons, vol. 807, cols 1423–34 (2 December 1970).

[59] Sir Harmar Nicholls, Parliamentary Debates, Commons, vol. 807, cols 1423–34 (2 December 1970).

[60] Edmund Dell, Parliamentary Debates, Commons, vol. 807, cols 1423–34 (2 December 1970).

[61] TNA: T 326/1046, A. H. M. Hillis, 'Early Day Motion: Competition in Banking', 11 November 1970.

arguing for the end of the cartel to improve competition and simplify monetary policy to control the money supply.[62] There was then, at the turn of the 1960s, a demand for the cartel arrangement to be broken up across the political spectrum. The conventional pressure for economic liberalism met the distinctive strain of anti-trust views within the Labour Party—a party angered by the profitability of the banks at a time in which the economic plans for economic renewal had apparently been derailed by the traditional City preference for deflation.

COMPETITION AND CREDIT CONTROL

In 1971 the Bank of England, with the sanction of the Heath Conservative government, implemented a new approach to monetary control under the guise of 'Competition and Credit Control'. The aim of the new approach was 'to permit the price mechanism to function efficiently in the allocation of credit, and to free the banks from rigidities and restraints which have for too long inhibited them'.[63] Much of the edifice of the post-war settlement in banking was swept away as lending ceilings were abolished, guidance on favoured borrowers abandoned, and the cartel agreement on uniform rates of interest brought to an end. Hire-purchase controls were also removed. As Michael Moran noted, in pursuing this new approach, 'the authorities gave up three powerful instruments of credit control' and fell back on the Bank of England lending rate as the primary tool for controlling credit.[64]

The established account of how this policy came to pass (it required no new legislation) emphasizes the absolute centrality of the Bank of England, and particularly John Fforde, the Executive Director for Home Finance, in attempting to find an easier and more effective method of credit control that would bring the new credit creating institutions onto an equal footing and escape the physical controls that so irritated the banks (and the authorities responsible for implementing them). This was given greater impetus by the influence of new ideas about the importance of the

---

[62] Brian Griffiths, *Competition in Banking* (London: Institute of Economic Affairs, 1970); TNA: T 326/1046, 'Why Shouldn't Banks Compete?' *Daily Telegraph*, 14 December 1970; City Editor, 'Fresh Attack on the Banks' Cartel', *Daily Telegraph*, 14 December 1970; 'Competition among Banks', *The Times*, 14 December 1970; 'Bank Cartel "Costs £90m."', *Guardian*, 14 December 1970.

[63] Michael Moran, *The Politics of Banking: The Strange Case of Competition and Credit Control* (London: Macmillan, 1984), 30–1.

[64] Ibid.

money supply being imported from the United States at the time.[65] This story of the policy's development is undeniably accurate, yet it tends to discount the widespread political frustration with the cartel arrangements as described here. It is certainly correct to reject the notion that the policy was solely a product of the Heath government's attempted deregulation of the economy, and to emphasize the structural changes to the banking system that had taken place in the 1960s. The Labour Chancellor Roy Jenkins had been broadly committed to breaking up the cartel, yet when asked to pursue such a policy he explained to the Labour MP Robert Sheldon in the Commons that, so long as the banks were required to operate under the system of tight control that was government policy at that time (ceilings on bank lending), the abolition of the cartel would have no effect. Therefore, the public interest would not be served as the macroeconomic requirements took precedence.[66]

In May 1970, a few months before the Conservative election victory, Jenkins asked his Treasury officials whether a recent increase in personal loans being provided by banks provided an opportunity to change the official attitude on the banks' interest rate cartel. Sir Douglas Allen thought that the traditional view of the cartel as a means of keeping interest rates low was 'not altogether convincing'. Once ceilings on bank lending had been removed as the stability of sterling had been assured, the cartel could also be effectively removed—which would be a good move from a 'public point of view', and would be a way to bring an end to the cosy life of the banks.[67] Armstrong's response was that the cartel would probably break down itself, sooner or later, owing to disclosure of bank's true profits and the pressure from non-banking financial institutions. Additionally, the fact that the banks were already engaging in competition for large deposits at non-cartelized rates through their subsidiary companies meant that the cartel was diminishing in importance to the banks anyway.[68] The Conservative administration that soon replaced Roy Jenkins at the Treasury continued his tentative approach, although it was

[65] For a fuller account of the policy's development and implementation, see Capie, *The Bank of England*, 427–523; Duncan Needham, *UK Monetary Policy from Devaluation to Thatcher, 1967–82* (Cambridge: Cambridge University Press, 2014), 46–77; Peter Burnham, 'The Politicisation of Monetary Policy in Post-War Britain', *British Politics*, 2 (2007), 412–15; Peter Burnham, 'Depoliticising Monetary Policy: The Minimum Lending Rate Experiment in Britain in the 1970s', *New Political Economy*, 16/4 (2011), 465–7.

[66] TNA: T 326/1046: R. T. Armstrong, 'Joint Stock Banks' Interest Rate Cartel: Annex A', 6 May 1970.

[67] TNA: T 326/1046: W. S. Ryrie, 'Joint Stock Banks' Interest Rate Cartel', 7 May 1970.

[68] TNA: T 326/1046: R. T. Armstrong, 'Joint Stock Banks' Interest Rate Cartel', 6 May 1970.

certainly given a boost by the recently revitalized Tory belief in competition. In response to Proudfoot's proposals in the Commons to abolish the cartel, the government asserted that it was keeping the issue under review, but that tight control of credit remained central to their concerns.[69] However, in reviewing the possibility of abolishing the cartel, the Treasury minister Terence Higgins told the Chancellor that 'in this as in other areas the hallmark of Conservative policy should surely be reliance on the market mechanism, rather than quantitative controls, and a belief in competition'.[70] Yet the social democratic settlement was not so easily abandoned. The Chancellor, and a number of advisors around him, felt uneasy at the possible loss of control over credit that was so central to the established practice. Though Anthony Barber was 'in principle . . . attracted by the approach', there were fears that the transition could see a rapid increase in credit, which would enforce a significant increase in interest rates. Allen said that the risk of transitioning to the new methods was acceptable so long as the Government was 'willing to accept the consequences' of a tightening of monetary policy. Sir Donald MacDougall, the chief economic advisor to the Treasury, sounded the alarm—although the idea of getting away from ceilings on bank lending was attractive, he argued that it would 'raise very difficult problems for demand management' and 'any easing of credit . . . would probably go into consumption rather than investment'. Maurice MacMillan, now Chief Secretary to the Treasury, also expressed 'considerable reservations' that there would be 'a loss of scope for directional guidance for bank lending'.[71] Yet, despite the Chancellor's hesitancy about pursuing the policy, expressed at a meeting in March, the policy eventually went ahead.[72] The crumbling efficacy of the existing approach to monetary control, combined with a widespread dislike of the cartelized settlement, made upholding post-war arrangements extremely difficult. Rather than the established methods being strengthened, a liberalizing approach was implemented in the hope that it would make control of credit more uniform while encouraging a competitive domestic banking sector.

The pressure on the post-war settlement in banking was brought about by the material changes to the banking sector over the course of

---

[69] TNA: T 326/1046, A. H. M. Hillis, 'Early Day Motion: Competition in Banking', 11 November 1970.
[70] TNA: T 326/1242, Terence L. Higgins to the Chancellor of the Exchequer, 5 January 1971.
[71] TNA: T 326/1261, 'Record of a Meeting in the Chancellor of the Exchequer's Room: Monetary Policy', 3 March 1971.
[72] TNA: T 326/1261, 'Record of a Meeting in the Chancellor of the Exchequer's Room: Monetary Policy and Related Matters', 11 March 1971.

the 1960s, which eroded the existing mechanisms for credit control. Yet the eventual abolition of the cartel in banking should also be seen in the light of widespread political and public pressure to insert a greater degree of competition in banking. The tension, however, was over how far to pursue this strategy when control over banking was so intrinsic to the mechanism of economic management that had been practised since the war. Even the optimistic drive for greater competition under the Heath government was qualified by a concern not to lose control over credit creation. In the end, the Bank of England, and the pressure from outside, pushed the government to adopt the radical new approach. The consequences were highly significant for the economic experience of the British economy in the subsequent decade, as well as for the politics of social democracy.

LABOUR PROPOSALS FOR BANKING REFORM

As already noted, the Labour Party had begun to consider the role of the financial system in the functioning of the economy at the height of its battle to preserve the parity of sterling in 1967.[73] Yet it was at the 1971 party conference that the more radical pursuit of reform was brought to public attention when Jo Richardson, the secretary to the *Tribune* group and to one of its leading figures, Ian Mikardo MP, proposed a motion that the next Labour government should nationalize the entire banking system (as well as all insurance companies). Richardson successfully requested that a working party be set up to put forward proposals to the 1972 conference regarding this matter.[74] This radical agenda culminated in a proposal, passed with overwhelming support by party delegates at the 1976 Labour conference, that most of the City be taken into public ownership. The politics of these proposals, and their failure to be adopted by the Labour governments after 1974, is discussed in the next chapter. First, however, it is necessary to understand what drove this campaign. There is a danger that we might fall into a simple narrative of seeing the push for financial-sector nationalization solely as a function of the rise of the Labour left in the 1970s—as a reflection of the party's left–right 'civil war'.[75] This is, in large part, true, yet it is important to try to understand

[73] LPA: Re. 74, Finance and Economic Affairs Subcommittee, 'Future Weekend Conference—Private Financial Institutions', January 1967.
[74] Wickham-Jones, *Economic Strategy and the Labour Party*, 64–8.
[75] Artis et. al., 'Social Democracy in Hard Times', 54.

the motivating factors behind issues such as bank nationalization, and to avoid patronizing the large numbers of political actors and activists who supported such an aim. It is clear that there were distinct causes that underpinned the push for nationalization in addition to a more general pulling to the left by those unhappy with Wilson's supposedly restrained approach in the 1960s.

Beyond the narrow confines of the City and the financial press, the impact of the new competition and credit control policy on public consciousness was negligible, despite its significance for the financial system.[76] The abstruse nature of money and banking ensured that outsiders remained largely in the dark. Edward du Cann, the senior Conservative MP and chairman of the bank Keyser Ullman, recalls explaining the new policy to the Parliamentary Conservative Party's 1922 Committee and doubting whether more than half a dozen 'had the least idea' what he was talking about.[77] Across the political spectrum, the few campaigners for greater competition in banking were undoubtedly satisfied with the end of the cartel. Beyond that, any sense of the significance of the new approach was missing. From the social democratic left, concerns were muted. Criticism of the policy was most notably and ably expressed in a critique written by Nicholas Davenport in his weekly City column in *The Spectator*. After explaining the changes briefly and in 'non-technical' language to his readership, Davenport went on to note his two objections to the change. First, that, in the event of a reflationary boom, the banks would begin to compete more aggressively for deposits in a 'scramble for money'. This posed a threat to the building societies' share of deposits and would adversely affect housing. Secondly, and more profoundly, Davenport objected to the retrograde move on the grounds that 'under the new freedom greater power will pass to the money lenders, which, for a democratic society, is a step backwards'.[78] The democratic state would lose out to the uncontrolled lending decisions of banks. By allowing banks to compete for deposits, they would gain a greater share of the 'common pool of possible deposits and possible borrowers'. The banks would expand into all areas of finance, beyond their narrow confines under the cartel. The effect of this would be to increase the influence of bank finance, as in Germany and Japan, thus 'handing over our industrial future to the stuffy boards of the established joint stock banks'. This loss

---

[76] This remains the case today, as focus on the deregulation of banking system is most closely associated with the later changes made under the Thatcher governments.

[77] Kynaston, *The City of London*, iv. 439–40; Edward du Cann would later be declared bankrupt when Keyser Ullman was engulfed by the secondary banking crisis.

[78] Nicholas Davenport, 'The Revolution in Banking', *Spectator*, 24 September 1971.

of democratic control over the investment process and allocation of credit would lead to inefficient use of national resources:–

> It could mean that the least desirable borrowers—the purveyors of pornography, the manufacturers of luxury leisure goods, the candy-floss merchants and all—will grab too high a proportion of bank finance because they are able to pay the highest rates of interest... In a democratic society which is committed to a heavy programme of social investment in houses, schools, hospitals and roads, it is extremely antisocial to allow the capital demands of private enterprise, which includes the candy-floss as well as the productive industries, to drive up the rate of interest to heights which make the desirable social investment too expensive for the taxpayer.[79]

Davenport was certainly no member of the radical Labour left. His involvement with the Labour Party on financial matters stretched back to the interwar period, when he had been a founder member of the XYZ Club—a group that consisted of Labour-supporting City figures who provided expert knowledge of financial matters to the party—and he would later oppose the campaign for bank nationalization.[80] His solution was to develop, as other 'advanced social democracies had done', a two-tier system of interest rates—one for the 'commercial community' and the other for 'housing, hospitals and schools'.[81] What Davenport's analysis anticipated, however, was the theme upon which the campaigners for greater state control over the banking system were to build much of their case—that credit and investment could not be left to banks whose interests were not naturally aligned with national economic development and well-being.

IRRATIONAL LENDING

The few years following the implementation of the new approach to monetary policy were disastrous for the British economy. Vast inflation ensued, as oil price increases combined with the Heath government's 'dash for growth' to prevent the new monetary policy mechanism from operating

---

[79] Ibid.

[80] Nicholas Davenport, 'The Two Faces of Capitalism', *Spectator*, 29 June 1973; Peter Parker, 'Davenport, Ernest Harold [Nicholas Davenport] (1893–1979)', rev. *Oxford Dictionary of National Biography* (Oxford: Oxford University Press, 2004) <http://ezproxy.ouls.ox.ac.uk:2117/view/article/31005> (accessed 17 January 2014); Ben Pimlott, *Labour and the Left in the 1930s* (Cambridge: Cambridge University Press, 1977), 37; Durbin, *New Jerusalems*, 81–3.

[81] Nicholas Davenport, 'The Revolution in Banking', *Spectator*, 24 September 1971.

effectively in order to choke off credit expansion.[82] Furthermore, most of this expansion in the supply of credit found its way not into industrial development or the promotion of exports, but into property development through the secondary banking sector.[83] Despite exhortations from the Bank of England for banks to restrain their lending to property, the neutered methods of monetary control had no effect. The result was an inevitable bubble in the price of property, and a subsequent bust that endangered the entire banking system. The hundreds of new banking and investment institutions that had sprung up in the optimistic years of lax regulation and cheap money, many of which had close ties to the major clearing banks as subsidiaries, found themselves exposed to massive losses and threatened severe systemic risk.[84] It was clear, as Davenport had stated in 1971, that the banks could not be trusted to exercise their power responsibly. The free operation of the banking system led to a series of perverse externalities in which credit was allocated not according to national or social need, but accoding to a private dividend that did not care whether returns on lending could be obtained through 'productive' or 'non-productive' outlets. The left-wing Labour MP Frank Allaun observed in 1976 that existing mechanisms to prevent such wasteful employment of capital resources were toothless—any remaining 'moral suasion' on the part of the Governor of the Bank of England in 1972 had failed completely. Allaun claimed that the secondary banks had invested to the tune of £5,000 million at the height of the boom, matched by a further £800 million from insurance companies.[85] This 'outrageous land and property ramp' had, according to Mikardo, 'enriched the few at the expense of the whole community, not least the young couples trying to set up home'.[86] This critique mirrored, and was directly linked to, that of the institutional investors and capital market discussed in the previous chapter. The property bubble and subsequent crisis had taken place in the vacuum left by the discarded post-war settlement in banking. When the failure of the Heath government's approach became apparent at the end of 1973, Harold Wilson took the opportunity to denounce the 'organized anarchy in the City which he [Barber] set up in 1971 under the heading

[82] Duncan Needham, 'Britain's Money Supply Experiment, 1971-73', *English Historical Review*, 130/542 (2015), 89–122.

[83] Avner Offer, 'Narrow Banking, Real Estate, and Financial Stability in the UK, c.1870–2010', *University of Oxford Economic and Social History Working Papers*, 116 (2013), 14–15.

[84] Capie, *Bank of England*, 524–86; Margaret Reid, *The Secondary Banking Crisis, 1973–75* (London: Macmillan, 1982); Kynaston, *The City of London*, iv. 484–93.

[85] Frank Allaun, 'Socialise the Profits', *Bankers' Magazine*, September 1976.

[86] Ian Mikardo, 'Tomorrow you May Be a Civil Servant...', *Bankers' Magazine*, January 1974.

Competition and Credit Control', and called for the government to impose 'orderly borrowing controls based on priorities'.[87] The failure of the Competition and Credit Control experiment was to return control of monetary policy to the Treasury in the latter half of the decade, although the constraints on macroeconomic policymaking in this period did not permit the government much freedom (see Chapter 5).[88]

In a paper submitted to the post-1971 Labour working party on finance, John Hughes expressed concern at the immense power the banks had over the functioning of the entire economy. Since the Bank of England no longer provided adequate control over credit allocation, banks were left free to pursue their own ends regardless of the macroeconomic outcome. This theme tied into his broader critique of the capital market discussed in the previous chapter, and reflected a wider concern that the financial system neglected the needs of the real economy.[89] This fed into a more long-standing belief—described in the Introduction to this book—that the banks were disconnected from, and uninterested in, domestic industry, and chose to pursue conservative lending strategies that did not contribute to industrial development. Except in this instance, excessive conservatism was not the only problem, but risky and competitive lending strategies focused on gaining large and immediate returns. A Labour Party working party paper in 1973 stated:

> it is certainly true that British financial institutions have been very slow to take a really deep interest in the affairs of their corporate customers, to the extent of becoming involved in the long-term planning in a way that, say German banks are. This may well be one reason for Britain's sluggish growth rate.[90]

Once again, the comparison with financial systems of foreign competitor nations resurfaced. A fascination with how other advanced industrial economies had grown so quickly since the war reopened the old wounds, which claimed that the financial systems abroad were more effective at transferring savings into investment, and engaging with industrial borrowers. As a document given to supporters of nationalization at the 1976 conference stated, banks were not lending enough to industry, because their prices were too high, the terms of lending were too strict, and they

---

[87] Harold Wilson, Parliamentary Debates, Commons, vol. 866, cols 1165–1280 (18 December 1973).

[88] Burnham, 'The Politicisation of Monetary Policy', 414–15; Burnham, 'Depoliticising Monetary Policy', 474–6.

[89] LPA: Rd. 343, John Hughes, 'Banking and Insurance Working Party. Public Ownership and Control: The Financial Sector, why Intervene?', April 1972.

[90] LPA: Rd. 561, 'Banking and Insurance Study Group. Public Ownership in the Banking Industry', January 1973.

were routinely unwilling to finds ways of making medium-term and long-term loans. British banks were more risk averse in industrial matters, it was alleged, than their foreign cousins.[91]

UNCOMPETITIVE BANKING

The loss of control over credit allocation after 1971 brought the banking system back into the Labour left's political economy during the following decade as it sought to recapture public control. Equally important was the ongoing debate over competition in domestic banking, on which the campaigners for public ownership also placed great weight. The macro-economic concerns fed into a broader belief that the financial system generally (not simply the banks) was ill equipped to meet the needs of the nation. Yet in banking much of the emphasis was upon the value of the existing banks to depositors. As already described, a significant tension within the political economy of the Labour Party, particularly in the 1960s, was between whether industrial and commercial sectors could better serve the economy by competing or by merging. The former brought greater choice to customers, but the latter offered the realization of economies of scale and a more rationalized economy. In domestic banking this tension was evident at the end of the 1960s when the proposed merger between Barclays, Lloyds, and Martins banks was blocked by the government.[92] Anthony Crosland, as President of the Board of Trade, explained that the merger would lead to a 'less satisfactory competitive environment' in which small and medium-sized firms in particular would have fewer options for borrowing.[93] In response to this announcement, the Labour MP Alistair Macdonald—an ex-bank clerk and area treasurer for the Nation Union of Bank Employees—asked:

> Is my right hon. Friend aware that his announcement will be received with incredulous astonishment and dismay? Does he regard with equanimity the way in which the banks follow one another in opening branches simply because another bank has opened a branch in a particular area, giving the appearance of spurious competition? Does he pay no regard to the potential savings which could have been effected by this merger?[94]

---

[91] LPA: Re. 838, 'A Note on the Main Criticisms of "Banking and Finance"', November 1976.

[92] Paul Bareau, 'The Frustrated Bank Merger', *Journal of the Institute of Bankers*, 89/5 (1968), 388–94.

[93] Anthony Crosland, Parliamentary Debates, Commons, vol. 769, cols 990–4 (25 July 1968).

[94] Alistair Macdonald, Parliamentary Debates, Commons, vol. 769, cols 990–4 (25 July 1968).

The NBPI report had also supported the Macdonald view, favouring greater integration between the existing banks. But, as John Hughes noted, the monopolies commission and the government had been 'caught in the dilemma of choosing between an increasing technical efficiency...and a diminishing competition', and went on to argue that 'without the nationalisation of at least one of the main commercial banks there seems no obvious way of seeing major economies in branch banking without strengthening collusive tendencies among the banking oligopolists'.[95]

After 1971 the Labour left placed a significant degree of emphasis on the failure of the banks to engage in genuine competition. It is not that they did not want greater competition, but that they thought it impossible for such competition to take place. The 'Competition and Credit Control' policy had not engendered a great degree of faith in the first place. Roger Opie, a fellow of New College, Oxford and ex-editor of the *Banker* magazine, predicted that, despite the abolition of the cartel, there would be a continuation of 'price leadership' and that competition would continue to take place only on 'non-price' grounds.[96] The small number of banks would ensure that price competition would never truly emerge. One of the party's working party papers neatly summarized this perspective on the banking oligopoly:

> Even following the end of the clearing bank interest rate cartel in 1971, competition has hardly been cutthroat. Profits have in fact risen. In the UK, as in most other countries, banking is an oligopoly, with the usual consequences: a great reluctance to introduce real innovations; excessively high margins between borrowing and lending rates; and an archaic pricing policy which leads to different sets of customers subsidising each other in an extraordinary manner (and in particular to personal customers subsidising corporate customers on a large scale).[97]

Ian Mikardo argued his case for nationalization most comprehensively in an article for the *Bankers' Magazine* in January 1974. For Mikardo, banking was the 'most sheltered industry' in which deliberate secrecy and avoidance of public accountability was unacceptably maintained. He charged that 'they keep the world at bay by making a mystique and a mystery of their craft: they are the witch-doctors of a commercial society'. This sat squarely with left-wing concern about the power of the opaque

---

[95] LPA: Rd. 343, John Hughes, 'Banking and Insurance Working Party: Public Ownership and Control: The Financial Sector, why Intervene?', April 1972.

[96] LPA: Rd. 257, Roger Opie, 'Finance and Economic Affairs Sub-Committee: Comments on Bank and Insurance', February 1972.

[97] LPA: Rd. 561, 'Banking and Insurance Study Group: Public Ownership in the Banking Industry', January 1973.

City. More substantially, however, Mikardo argued that banking was the prime example of 'the wastefulness of a market dominated by a small number of big institutions', as it provided 'the benefits neither of rationalization at one end of the scale nor of free competition at the other'. This led to duplication of resources and 'phoney' competition, in which each high street had a branch of each of the big four banks, which each provided the same services at the same cost. The only competition came through the cinema, television, newspaper, and magazine advertising, which was 'wasteful' and 'mutually cancelling'. Inter-bank transactions were costly, where 'sensible rationalisation' would save the customer from having to pay the price. He continued:

> the banks incur all the frictional waste of resources which constitute the price of free competition but, because of concentration and cartelization in the big four, the benefits do not accrue to the customer at all. The tendency for banking concentration, and the emergence of monopoly power, had only been checked by the last Labour government. The competition introduced in 1971 September was merely a nominal abandonment of the cartel...in place of common interest rates fixed by the authorities we have common interest rate fixed by the laws of minimal—indeed, only nominal—competition.

He alleged that banks exploited their customers by giving poor value for money—doubling the profits in a single year through no effort of their own. Meanwhile, high levels of bank charges were maintained. Banks in Holland, Switzerland, and West Germany supposedly provided customers with a service that was 'more wide-ranging, more flexible and more considerate', and many people had not been given the opportunity of opening a bank account, as the banks were more concerned with existing customers.[98]

NATIONALIZATION AND ITS ALTERNATIVES

Roger Opie wrote of the banks in the *New Statesman* at the start of 1976:

> The greatest benefit for nationalizing them all would be to rationalize them all. Since the only purpose of most bank branches is to try to attract deposits by being more conveniently sited, one National Deposit Bank would need no more than a trifling fraction of the 14,000 or so branches now dotted around our city centres and prosperous suburbs...What about the loss of

---

[98] Ian Mikardo, 'Tomorrow you May Be a Civil Servant...', *Bankers' Magazine*, January 1974.

competition and variety? What variety? All banks and all branches are open at the same times, and shut at the same times. They are over-crowded at the same times, and empty but under-staffed at the same times. The only variety comes in the designs on the cheque books. And what competition? They all offer the same deposits rates, and change them on the same day.[99]

The state could more effectively provide a rationalized and efficient set of banking services to depositors. Furthermore, it was claimed that the state could provide more technologically advanced banking services to customers than the conservatively run private clearing banks, which apparently prevented their modernization to the detriment of depositors and borrowers alike. Predicting that Britain would be 'very near a cashless society' within the next fifteen or twenty years, the Labour Party Treasurer, Norman Atkinson, claimed that 'shops will be fitted with credit terminals wired to a central clearance system'. But this ideal, of 'a modern, ultra-efficient banking system', would not be made a reality without state intervention.[100]

The means by which the banking system would be brought back within public control were to be worked out specifically in the policy group set up after 1971, and in subsequent Labour Party policy groups. These were invariably overseen by the leading figure in the campaign for bank nationalization—Ian Mikardo. It was a long-standing project for Mikardo, who, in 1944, had managed to pass a Labour conference resolution calling for a much larger scale of nationalization (including of land and banking) than the leadership intended. This had provoked the personal ire of Herbert Morrison, who informed Mikardo that his motion would be responsible for losing the Labour Party the next election.[101] In leading the post-1971 policy group, Mikardo (a man once described by a House of Commons clerk as 'simply the most skilful operator in committee that any of us ever saw') campaigned forcefully for a radical expansion of public ownership of the financial sector.[102] The study group report concluded, on publication in 1973, that all clearing and overseas banks should be nationalized and brought under the auspices of a single 'British Bank' comprising a development and overseas aspects. This was to be matched by the nationalization of the top twenty-nine insurance companies into a single 'British Insurance Corporation', and the municipalization of

---

[99] Roger Opie, 'Nationalising a Bank or Two', *New Statesman*, 9 January 1976.
[100] LPA: Financial Institutions Miscellaneous 1973–76 Box 9, letter from Norman Atkinson, *lGuardian*, 9 May 1977.
[101] Dell, *A Strange and Eventful History*, 122.
[102] Quoted in Tam Dalyell, 'Mikardo, Ian (1908–1993)', *Oxford Dictionary of National Biography* (Oxford: Oxford University Press, 2004); online edn, May 2006 <http://www.oxforddnb.com/view/article/52289> (accessed 6 October 2012).

building societies under local authorities. Mikardo argued in public that the findings of the report were rooted in the interests of the consumer and the need 'to give the public a better deal', as well as the pressing need to allocate national financial resources more efficiently.[103]

An alternative approach had been developed by other members of the study group who were not keen on such far-reaching nationalization. Their alternative proposal was to inject public-sector competition in the domestic banking system, rather than take it over wholesale. This was the suggestion of Roger Opie, who argued that the banks should be brought back under the influence of the Bank of England (which in future should be under direct Treasury control) for the purposes of general credit control, but that one clearing bank should be nationalized and used as a catalyst for efficiency and price competition.[104] This line of thinking was developed into a proposal to create a 'state-owned financial conglomerate' that would meet the demands for universal financial services under the name of the British Banking Corporation (unhelpfully shortened to BBC). At its core this would comprise the existing National Savings Bank, the Trustee Savings Bank, the Giro, and at least two of the largest building societies. It would be operated through the 21,000 Post Office branches nationwide, and would also acquire capabilities in merchant banking and insurance. Nationalizing one of the clearing banks was a possibility, though not essential. If so, it would serve the purpose, as Opie had earlier suggested, of 'setting the pace' of structural changes within the banking sector as a whole.[105] This alternative, more limited, approach was ignored in the final report in favour of full-scale nationalization. It seems that this can be attributed directly to the drive of Mikardo, whose domineering approach to the group's work had alienated most of the group members (as discussed further in Chapter 3).

Less far-reaching approaches to banking reform were developed by others within the Labour movement. One significant alternative, which did not include any expansion of the public sector, or the creation of new agencies, was for reform of the Bank of England. For many this offered the best possible solution to the problem of credit direction. Lord Balogh, in rejecting the Mikardo paper in 1973, argued that the Bank of England should simply be brought under Treasury control, rather than remaining a detached entity. Writing for the *Financial Guardian* in 1976, the head

---

[103] 'Labour Unveils State Plan for Banking and Insurance', *Financial Times*, 3 August 1973.

[104] LPA: Rd. 257, Roger Opie, 'Finance and Economic Affairs Sub-Committee: Comments on Bank and Insurance', February 1972.

[105] LPA: Rd. 561, 'Banking and Insurance Study Group: Public Ownership in the Banking Industry', January 1973.

of the Cooperative Bank—Clive Woodcock—called for greater control over and public accountability of the banking sector. This could best be achieved by bringing the 'big four' and 'fringe banks' under joint Bank of England responsibility.[106] In its evidence to the Wilson committee, the Cooperative argued that the flow of funds to industry could be best achieved within the existing financial framework.[107] The evidence presented by the Union of Shop, Distributive, and Allied Workers (USDAW) in the post-1976 consultations with the party placed greater emphasis on the already existing 'enormous powers' that had been conferred on the Bank of England in the 1946 Act. These powers allowed the Treasury to issue directions as to how the banking system should operate in general, as well as being able to issue directives to individual institutions. USDAW argued that the Bank could be instructed to specify lending to certain industrial sectors.[108] The ideas did not, however, have the same visceral appeal as Mikardo's emotive campaign for wholesale public ownership of the banks.

CONCLUSION

The push for the nationalization of banking in the 1970s was the combined product of three pressures—an attempt to reassert the state's legitimate control over credit creation and allocation following the collapse of the post-war settlement in banking; the perceived impossibility of a genuinely competitive market in banking; and the need for a rationalization and modernization of the banking sector. These approaches were not only rooted in a desire to develop a banking system that might more effectively serve industrial borrowers and overcome a long-standing limit on Britain's economic development; they also sought to improve banking services for the general public as a whole. Thus the radical reformers of the banking system were interested in consumers as well as producers.

Chapters 1 and 2 have demonstrated the erosion of the material foundations on which the social democratic approach to managing credit and investment in the post-war period was built. It is important not to overstate the fixed nature of the post-war settlement, yet the basic architecture of social democratic financial policy was established in the 1940s

---

[106] Clive Woodcock, 'Co-op Bank Chief Calls for More Controls', *Financial Guardian*, 11 June 1976.

[107] FI: FI(78)98, 'Public Ownership—Note by the Secretary'.

[108] LPA: Re. 1012, 'Working Party on Banking and Insurance: USDAW statement . . .', February 1977.

and 1950s on the basis of a distinct set of institutional and organizational structures that did not remain static over the following decades. By the 1970s, as the industrial crisis challenged the fundamental assumptions of their economic strategy, social democratic thinkers and policymakers attempted to reconcile their approach with these changes. In some cases this inspired a resurgence of interwar proposals for nationalization and central direction (a proposal that gained most attention and influence), but the changes also encouraged new analysis and ideas that envisaged alternative means to revitalize the national economy. Chapter 3 assesses the reasons for the subsequent failure of these efforts to re-equip social democratic financial policy for the 1970s.

3

The Limits of Financial Reform and the Challenge to Social Democracy in the 1970s

The previous chapters have demonstrated that during the 1970s many on the left and within the Labour movement sought to reform the British financial system in an attempt to defend, reformulate, and advance the industrial political economy of post-war social democracy. This chapter considers why the campaign for financial reform was unsuccessful, and explores its ramifications for British social democracy in the period. In assessing the fate of the attempted social democratic reforms of the financial system during the 1970s, this chapter will first outline the City's political response to the threat of nationalization, before going on to describe the divisions within the Labour movement over the most effective methods of pursuing reform, as well as the resistance to reform from senior civil servants. Of principal importance, however, was the inability of the social democratic reformers to attract the support of Britain's industrialists to a coherent reform agenda. Despite superficial conflicts and frustrations between 'industry' and 'finance' at the start of the decade, and the collapse of the stock market in 1974, which starved many firms of investment capital, the left was unable to build a 'producer's alliance'. Instead, financial and industrial interests, having already formed a substantive and integrated material relationship in the post-war decades, developed a political and ideological alliance in response to the mid-decade economic crisis. This alliance was forged by the severe crisis of profitability after 1973, which saw the rate of return on investment, and the share of national income accruing to profits, decline sharply. The means to achieve the restoration of profits amounted to a simple set of proposed solutions: cut taxation on capital and personal income, eradicate inflation, and reduce government interference in the operation of economy. These proposals for government economic retrenchment as the solution to industrial decline were an outright rejection of the state-coordinated financial strategy offered by the labour movement. Furthermore, they challenged the fundamental premises of post-war social democracy—foreshadowing the 'neoliberal' agenda of the post-1979 Conservative governments.

THE CITY'S SELF-DEFENCE

Criticism of the City's negative contribution to the British economy, and the threat of state intervention, was met with a well-organized public defence from the Square Mile itself during the 1970s. This was a direct response to the highest profile aspect of the left's reform agenda—the campaign for widespread nationalization of the City, which culminated in the 1976 Labour conference motion. The increasing volume and influence of the radical reformers in the Labour Party after 1975 forced the representatives of the City institutions to discard their traditional disengagement from public debate over their role in the British economy. Ian Mikardo and the ascendant left wing of the Labour Party could not be ignored—particularly given that they were dangerously close to political power in a fractious and febrile political and economic environment. However, rather than further pursuing a voluntary reform approach (as the financial institutions had been offered by Heath and the Bank of England), the City turned its attention primarily to self-defence and a political resistance to change. The threat of nationalization encouraged the clearing banks in particular to engage in a concerted and coordinated political and public relations campaign, which sought to defend their value to the economy and resist the call for public ownership.

The clearing banks had begun seriously to consider the threat of nationalization in 1973. The Committee of London Clearing Bankers (CLCB) discussed how they might publicly respond to the calls for state ownership at the upcoming Labour Party conference, whether it would be necessary to carry out a campaign against takeover, and what the arguments for and against nationalization were. The decision was taken to establish a working party to consider these issues.[1] When it became clear that the Labour Party Home Policy committee's engagement with the issue of nationalization was giving the matter 'even greater prominence', the clearing bankers recognized the necessity of coordinating public opposition to the demands. The banks agreed to work together in providing information and resources, and accepted that they would all reject

---

[1] British Bankers' Association Papers, London Metropolitan Archives, London [henceforward BBA]: CLC/B/029/MS32276/001, 'CLCB: Informal Note of Discussions at the Meeting of the Committee', 4 April 1973.

any compromise based on the nationalization of a single bank.[2] The committee subsequently agreed to the expenditure of £25,000 on the cause.[3] The coordinated and active strategy of the banks in opposing the nationalization movement marked a break with their past unwillingness to become engaged in public debate. As an adviser to the banks, Brendon Sewill (ex-Director of the Conservative Party Research Department) explained:

> Whales are very large, kindly, and it is said, intelligent animals. They have survived through the ages because they have adopted a policy of remaining out of sight and doing no harm to anything larger than plankton. Much the same is true of the clearing banks. They have survived by remaining invisible, impartial, and strictly non-political.[4]

For Sewill this was something that the banks should not sacrifice. The 'Mr Cube' model of aggressive and populist campaigning, as pursued by Tate & Lyle in the late 1940s, would serve only to 'attract unwelcome political attention'.[5] The more effective strategy would be simply to provide the 'right wing of the Labour Party' with 'the ammunition with which it can prevail'. This campaign—'firm, influential, comprehensive, but quiet and discreet'—would attempt to persuade Labour's National Executive to 'water down' any proposals for reform, and to ensure that the Cabinet did not include any 'adverse proposals' in its legislative programme.[6] This approach would have to reject the optimistic view in the City that 'if only people understood how well [the financial system] worked they would automatically approve'. Sewill accepted that, while it was important to improve the availability of factual information to '40m. befuddled electors brainwashed with bias', something 'more positive, more orchestrated, more sophisticated in terms of political economy' was required.[7] This amounted to a concerted public relations campaign, which lobbied Members of Parliament and the newspaper-reading public through advertisements.[8]

The gathering of evidence by the Wilson Committee after 1977 provided the clearing banks with an opportunity to make a public case against

---

[2] BBA: CLC/B/029/MS32006/013, 'Bank Nationalisation', 8 January 1976.

[3] BBA: CLC/B/029/MS32006/013, 'Bank Nationalisation', 31 March 1976.

[4] BBA: CLC/B/029/MS32142/001, Brendon Sewill, 'Bank Nationalisation: An Assessment of the Situation', October 1975.

[5] Ron Noon, 'Goodbye, Mr Cube', *History Today*, 51/10 (2001), 40–1.

[6] BBA: CLC/B/029/MS32142/001, Brendon Sewill, 'Bank Nationalisation: An Assessment of the Aituation', October 1975.

[7] BBA: CLC/B/029/MS32142/001, 'Note from Brendon Sewill', 12 January 1976.

[8] BBA: CLC/B/029/MS32142/007, 'Report to the Committee from the Bank Nationalisation Working Party', 28 July 1977.

the criticisms that had intensified over the preceding decade. The CLCB took the opportunity presented to submit a lengthy (200 pages) and lavishly produced piece of evidence, which was subsequently published by Longman.[9] The core of the banks' case was to assert that their activities and practices in recent years demonstrated a clear willingness and capacity to support British industry, and that the demand for financial reform was misguided. The evidence stated:

> The clearing banks believe that the financial system in the United Kingdom is essentially sound and well equipped to meet the needs of the economy as a whole and industry and trade in particular. They do not believe there is a case for radically changing the organisation, supervision or ownership of the country's financial institutions and markets. They believe that the financial system has been effective in the particular task of meeting the demands of industry and trade for finance on reasonable terms.[10]

It was argued that the banking system had been extremely flexible in providing new opportunities for borrowers, beyond the historic and more traditional reliance on overdraft facilities for existing customers. The CLCB stated that its members had increasingly provided medium-term lending to corporate customers following the end of quantitative credit controls in 1971. Furthermore, the banks were providing instalment credit, leasing, and factoring to firms through their subsidiaries, and were active in the attempt to plug the 'Macmillan Gap' through Finance for Industry (FFI). Regarding the problem of financing small businesses, the CLCB accepted that the costs of borrowing were higher and that more stringent security requirements were required, but that every effort had been made to make access to finance easier and clearer.

The CLCB essentially told the Wilson Committee that its members had done everything within their powers to serve the needs of British businesses. However, there were limits to what could be achieved through the banks alone. Constraints upon the freedom of the banks, and structural limitations from the broader economy, were central. First, the banks were constrained by their prudential requirements—the need to protect the depositors from improvident lending. Therefore the argument that the banks held underutilized capital misunderstood the necessity of retaining prudent levels of available capital and liquidity. Secondly, the capacity of the banks to lend was determined by wider economic trends, particularly the changing overall levels of deposits and the increasing share of deposits

---

[9] Committee of London Clearing Bankers, *The London Clearing Banks: Evidence by the Committee of London Clearing Bankers to the Committee to Review the Functioning of Financial Institutions, November 1977* (London: Longman, 1978).
[10] Ibid.

managed by building societies at the expense of the banks. The clearers were thus not in a position to provide long-term loans or equity capital. Thirdly, the banks acted to serve their customers, and rejected the notion that 'force-feeding' funds to businesses would be worthwhile. Instead, the need for financing should come only from the firms themselves. This decision was the product of industrial and commercial actors, operating within the real economy, and as such was not the responsibility of the banks. Where the trade-union representatives on the committee asserted that the financial system generated a supply-side dearth of funds for investment, the banks emphasized the alternative—funds were not forthcoming because there was no demand. In a critical response to a paper written by Lord Allen and Clive Jenkins for the TUC, Sir John Prideaux (Chairman, National Westminster) and Richard Lloyd (Chief Executive, Williams and Glyn's) argued that 'what was needed above all was to get industry *wanting* to invest'.[11]

A similar defence was mounted by the pension and insurance funds. They also argued that they were doing their best to invest in Britain but that they were constrained both by the obligation to the savers whose funds they managed, and by the limited external demand for finance. The National Association of Pension Funds informed the committee that over the ten-year period 1965–75 the funds had increased their investment in company securities and property, and that there was never a shortage of available money. Unwillingness to invest was only ever determined by a 'lack of demand for capital on terms which pension funds can accept'. The funds had actively sought to develop links with other institutions in an attempt to become more responsive and involved as productive investors in the economy—particularly their involvement in schemes such as Equity Capital for Industry (ECI), Finance for Industry (FFI), and the Institutional Shareholders' Committee (ISC).[12] However, the primary objective of funds, contrary to the apparent desire to have them serve a broad social purpose, was simply to 'maximise the rate of return by investment which involves an acceptable level of risk, having regard to the nature of the liabilities'. In this pursuit of secure investment income, the institutions were bound by a legal obligation to their trustees, which prevented the pursuit of any other objective. Furthermore, much of the criticism laid against apparently 'unproductive' investment practices was misplaced. It was argued that property investment helped companies by preventing them from having to tie up their capital in long-term assets

---

[11] FI: 1/5, 'Minutes of 5th Meeting', 14 June 1977; 1/10, 'FI(77)39 Comments by Sir John Prideaux and Mr Lloyd on the TUC evidence', 9 June 1977.
[12] ECI and FFI are described in more detail later in this chapter.

(thus making money available for operating capital), and provided a direct economic stimulus to the economy through the building industry. Overseas investment, though only a small percentage of funds invested, improved the nation's reserves and, where profitable, reduced the cost to companies of financing their pensions.[13]

The written evidence of the Insurance Company Associations (the British Insurance Association, the Life Offices Association, the Associated Scottish Life Officers, and the Industrial Life Offices Association) emphasized to the committee that the UK capital market was highly competitive and efficient. Insurance company funds played a significant role in this market, with a fivefold increase in the flow of funds into investment holdings over the previous fifteen years. The association warned, however, that any attempt to direct investment that might result in returns below market rates would 'penalise policyholders and discourage much-needed long-term saving'. In addition there was a 'danger that the centralization of decision-making power would, as a result of political pressure, be used to sustain declining industries and thus impede rather than accelerate the procession of industrial regeneration'.[14] Meanwhile, the Stock Exchange told the committee that the idea of establishing a tripartite (government, TUC, and employers) organization that would direct a proportion of funds from the savings institutions was against the 'best interests of investors', as it would not be responsible to the policyholders and potential pensioners whose funds would be managed. Furthermore, it was reiterated that 'the problem affecting the flows of funds into industry and trade is not a lack of funds but rather of demand'.[15]

LABOUR DIVISIONS

The banking and financial institutions mounted a coherent self-defence that argued that Britain's low rates of investment were due to a lack of demand, not supply, and that their immediate responsibility to savers took precedence above all else. The organization and clarity of the City's self-defence undoubtedly helped to resist the pressure for radical changes to the financial system, yet the weakness of their political opponents made

[13] FI: 1/12, 'FI(WE)102 Memorandum by the National Association of Pension Funds', 19 July 1977.
[14] 'Written Evidence by the Insurance Company Associations', in *Committee to Review the Functioning of Financial Institutions: Evidence on the Financing of Industry and Trade*, iii (1978).
[15] Stock Exchange, *Evidence to the Committee to Review the Functioning of Financial Institutions: The Role and Functioning of the Stock Exchange* (London, 1977).

this task relatively easy. The nationalization agenda pursued by Mikardo and his supporters deeply divided the Labour movement. As described in the previous chapters, there were a number of proposals for how to reform the financial sector to meet the demands of the whole British economy. It was, however, wholesale nationalization that became adopted as Labour policy in the party's committees during 1973, and subsequently at the 1976 conference vote. This radicalism can probably be attributed to the force of Mikardo himself, whose domineering approach to the 1973 Banking and Insurance Study Group had alienated most of the group members. Eleven of the sixteen other committee members expressed reservations about the group's report—primarily over the section on banking.[16] In a joint note to the committee, the economists Nicholas Kaldor and Robert Neild—both strong proponents of changing the financial system in some form—expressed reservations. They stated:

> Irrespective of the merits of the case for nationalizing the financial institu-
> tions of the country at the present stage we do feel however a certain
> hesitation in supporting such far reaching and comprehensive proposals for
> inclusion in the election manifesto...These proposals are bound to arouse
> the most virulent hostility of the capitalist press and radio; and the com-
> parative ease with which wholly unreasonable fears can be aroused in this
> rather obscure field by an unscrupulous and dishonest campaign makes one
> hesitate whether the benefits to be gained are sufficient to justify the political
> risks which the advocacy involves. The ordinary voter's ideas about money
> are crude in the extreme, and as the experience of 1931 has shown, masses of
> people can be persuaded that the socialist government would be out to 'grab'
> everybody's savings. The scope for arousing such fears and suspicions could
> be greatly reduced by a more 'Fabian' approach that confined the immediate
> reform to a selective extension of the public sector in the City rather than a
> comprehensive nationalisation.[17]

This view was supported by Lord Thomas Balogh in his refusal to support the proposals on the basis that they represented 'a violent break for which neither the party nor the country is prepared'.[18] Even if the members of the committee had all agreed, senior Labour figures outside the study group were in complete opposition. Jim Callaghan (at that time head of the Home Policy Committee) was described by the *Financial Times* as 'willing to go to the stake' against the 1973 committee paper being

---

[16] 'Labour Unveils State Plan for Banking and Insurance', *Financial Times*, 3 August 1973.
[17] LPA: LP/RD/9/3, Nicholas Kaldor and Robert Nield, 'Banking and Insurance Study Group Report: A Note of Reservation', 7 July 1973.
[18] LPA: LP/RD/9/3, Lord Balogh, 'Remarks on the Banking and Insurance Study Group Report', n.d.

published.[19] William Rodgers, a former Treasury minister, condemned the paper and appealed for a 'mood of sanity'. He argued that the party should focus its energies on 'a number of simple social issues related to housing, employment and education, the quality of life and inequality', rather than foolishly pursuing a set of ideas so wide-ranging that it exposed 'as many flanks to the enemy as a polygon has sides'.[20] Radical proposals for the direction of pension fund investment were also resisted by the party leadership. Where the Labour Party's parliamentary left was keen to pursue a general policy of institutional direction and control—admittedly in a far less considered way than John Hughes—the Labour government was not convinced. In December 1975, speaking notes prepared for a Treasury minister's response to a backbench motion for directing institutional funds asserted that the 'prime responsibility' of the institutions was to 'those who have invested their savings in them', and that investment was not being restricted by a lack of external funds.[21] Speaking in the debate, the minister Denzil Davies accepted that there had 'clearly been a massive failure of investment . . . to enable us to compete in the markets of the world with our industrial competitors', yet he was unwilling to commit to the proposals put forward.[22] The insurance industry and the Conservative opposition appealed to the government not to proceed with such proposals. Harold Wilson personally assured those concerned with the prospect that the funds might be 'directed' that such ideas were not, and would not become, government policy.[23] It was not until he had left office that Wilson became personally concerned with the power and influence of pension and insurance funds, leading eventually to his support for intervention.[24] It is clear that within the post-1974 Labour government itself enthusiasm for harnessing the power of the institutions was muted.

When the 1976 Banking and Finance motion was proposed to the party conference, the increasingly radical Tony Benn, at that time Secretary of State for Energy, described the proposals as 'a long term solution to

---

[19] 'Labour Party not to Publish Banking-Insurance Paper', *Financial Times*, 28 June 1973.
[20] 'Labour Unveils State Plan for Banking and Insurance', *Financial Times*, 3 August 1973.
[21] TNA: T 386/348, K. J. Jordan, 'Private Member's Motion: 12 December', 11 December 1975.
[22] Denzil Davies, Parliamentary Debates, Commons, vol. 902, cols 840–911 (12 December 1975).
[23] TNA: T 386/348, letter from Kenneth Clarke to Barbara Castle, 24 April 1974; letter from Harold Wilson to E. F. Bigland (Chairman of the British Insurance Association), 8 October 1975.
[24] 'Wilson Warns of Pension Fund Power', *Guardian*, 24 January 1981.

unemployment and to low growth in this country'.[25] Yet, despite their overwhelming popularity with the conference delegates, a MORI poll commissioned by the CLCB demonstrated that only 14 per cent of the public agreed with the plans—and that most Labour voters were opposed to large-scale nationalization of finance. The Conservative *Daily Telegraph* savaged the 'vicious proposals':

> Our savings are to be removed from the care of prudent men to whom we have entrusted them and squandered on lame ducks by a pack of politicians who, on the evidence of the policy document, cannot even write proper English, whose boasted 'experience of industry' is in fact disastrous or nil, and whose record in picking industrial winners could be bettered by a child drunkard with a pin.[26]

The proponents of City nationalization, despite their public dominance in the debate over financial reform (obscuring the more nuanced aspects of the left's analysis and policy ideas) and strong support from party activists, faced the reality of hostile public opinion, negative press reaction, and a campaign of resistance on behalf of financial interests. In the light of this, Callaghan, as Prime Minister in 1976, continued to refuse to accept the policy on the basis that it would be 'an electoral albatross'.[27] When the conference vote referred the issue to the trade unions for consultation, it discovered another block on public ownership—the white-collar unions. 94 per cent of all members of the Insurance Staff Association were recorded in December as being against the proposals for nationalization. In February Leif Mills, representing the National Union of Bank Employees (NUBE), expressed his members' concerns that possible nationalization would lead to a direction of funds into 'unprofitable' firms—a policy of which his members were firmly opposed. The Union of Shop, Distributive, and Allied Workers (USDAW), while supporting the nationalization of insurance (as it had done for many years previously), argued strongly against the expensive proposals on the grounds that it was not clear that there was a lack of funds for industry. Both the Association of Professional, Executive, Clerical and Computer Staff (APEX) and the Association of Scientific, Technical, and Managerial Staffs (ASTMS)— both of which were affiliated to the Labour Party—rejected the proposals.

---

[25] 'Labour Plan for Banking Takeover', *Financial Times*, 8 September 1976.
[26] Quoted in Kynaston, *City of London*, iv. 539.
[27] LPA: LP/RD/9/21, 'Statement Made by James Callaghan at a Meeting of the NEC in Blackpool', 24 September 1976; LP/RD/48/4, Norman Stagg (Deputy General Secretary of Post Office Workers), 'Union of Post Office Workers: The Development of the Giro Service, the National Savings Bank, and the Work of the Paymaster General's Department into a Common State Banking Service', 21 April 1977.

The National Union of Insurance Workers stated that the NEC document embodied 'the worst of all worlds' because the proposals would 'provide a huge bonus to the remaining private companies and leave the public sector to compete with both hands tied behind its back. They would demoralise staff and provide crushing ammunition for the opponents of nationalisation.'[28] By 1978, with the publication of the working party's interim report into the Banking and Finance proposals, Labour had abandoned any plans for mass nationalization of City institutions in the face of such trade-union opposition.[29]

Given its unpopularity with the electorate, and the divisions and conflicts it engendered within the Labour Party itself, it is not surprising that the nationalization policy went no further than the party conference and figures within the parliamentary left wing. Despite its popularity with the grass-roots members, it was never likely to become a policy pursued by the party's governing leadership. This is probably the reason why such limited historiographical coverage has been afforded to this aspect of Labour's economic policymaking during the 1970s.[30] Yet it is clear that approaches to reforming the financial system went beyond the rather simplistic nationalization agenda. Why were these alternative ideas never implemented?

TREASURY RESISTANCE

One reason for this can be attributed to the orthodoxy and conservatism of Treasury civil servants. In the midst of the mid-decade economic and financial crisis, and the left's push for nationalization, Harold Lever, the Chancellor of the Duchy of Lancaster and the government's expert on financial matters, sought to develop new approaches to the financial system that might assist the ailing industrial economy. Lever was unconvinced by the basic proposition that there was any shortage of funds available for equity investment and preferred instead to try to generate a

[28] 'Ballot Rejects Labour's Finance Sector Plan', *Financial Times*, 21 December 1976; Christian Tyler, 'ASTMS Conference Rejects Bank Nationalisation Plan', *Financial Times*, 23 May 1977; LPA: Re. 1011, Leif Mills (General Secretary NUBE), 'Nationalisation of Banking and Finance: NUBE's Attitude', February 1977; Re. 1012, 'Working Party on Banking and Insurance: USDAW Statement on Banking and Finance', February 1977; Re. 1013, 'USDAW Statement on Insurance', February 1977; Re. 1034, 'The Banking and Finance Sector: A Statement by APEX', March 1977.

[29] Rupert Cornwell, 'Labour Buries Bank Nationalisation Plan', *Financial Times*, 6 September 1978.

[30] Wickham-Jones, *Economic Strategy and the Labour Party*, 64–6; Callaghan, 'Rise and Fall', 116–18.

mechanism by which cheaper medium- and long-term loans could be provided to industry.[31] In a letter to the Leeds North East constituency Labour Party, which had recently condemned his refusal to countenance nationalizing banking, insurance, and pharmaceuticals, he informed his critics that 'there is no need to coerce funds into manufacturing industry, because funds can be obtained voluntarily for sound and profitable projects'.[32] Harold Lever negotiated the extension of FFI that took place at the start of 1975. Designed by the Governor of the Bank of England, FFI had been formed from a merger between Finance Corporation for Industry and Industrial and Commercial Finance Corporation to demonstrate that the clearing banks were willing to do more to lend to industry.[33] The purpose of the expansion was to provide a way for the banks to transfer short-term savings into long-term investment in industry through loans at lower rates than previously available.[34] It was intended that the fund was to be built up to provide £1,000 million of loans to industry. The fundamental purpose of FFI was not to canalize institutional savings into productive investment, but instead was an attempt to meet the specific crisis in the financing of medium and large firms in 1974–5.[35] It was in no way conceived of, or implemented, as a means to 'save' or prop up struggling industry—it simply provided loans at lower cost to low-risk companies according to a set of commercial criteria. This was distinct from the notion that the financial institutions could oversee the reconstruction and expansion of the British economy according to social needs.[36] Indeed, six months after the establishment of the new lending facility, the *Guardian* described it as 'more of a City bank developed by the Bank of England to provide the City with an important industrial conscience'.[37] Clive Jenkins, leader of the white-collar ASTMS, wrote to *The Times* at the end of November 1974 to query the value of FFI. He argued that the lack of information about its activities, and its fundamentally conservative nature in which simple 'old customer relationships' were preserved, ensured that the body had 'no relevance to national social objectives' and that 'the vital worker relationship is not even on the agenda'. For Jenkins, like many others seeking more significant reforms,

---

[31] TNA: T 386/37, 'Lever Doubts on Equity Plan', *Guardian*, 5 November 1975.

[32] LPA: Re. 745, 'Home Policy Committee: Nationalisation of Banking, Insurance, and Pharmaceutical Industries', August 1976.

[33] Capie, *The Bank of England*, 804; FCI and ICFC were founded by the Bank of England in the 1940s (see Introduction).

[34] TNA: T 233/3014, Harold Lever, 'Finance for Industry', 27 January 1975.

[35] TNA: T 233/3014, letter from Denis Healey to Barbara Castle, 24 February 1975.

[36] Roy Levine, 'The £1bn. Investment Programme', *Financial Times*, 11 March 1975.

[37] TNA: T 233/3014, 'In Search of a Role', *Guardian*, 9 July 1975.

the FFI did not meet the demands for an institution that could coherently oversee the effective (worker-friendly) investment of national resources.[38] In 1976 the Bank of England would also attempt to create a new institution in the form of Equity Capital for Industry (ECI), which was intended to give struggling firms access to investment at the height of the mid-decade crisis. However, City conservatism prevented it from taking on anything other than a minor role.[39]

More significantly, Lever proposed the idea of establishing a British Enterprise Bank (BEB) at the start of 1975. This investment bank could act as a subsidiary of the NEB but would operate as an independent body with the purpose of mobilizing private funds for lending to industry at either fixed or variable rates of interest. As with FFI, the bank would provide loans, rather than equity investment, to firms in which the NEB was investing, as well as those in which it was not. The latter lending would be determined by whether the loan would both be profitable and 'serve a useful economic or social purpose'. It would aim to attract, and lend, an estimated £200 million–£300 million over the first two years of its existence. The bank would raise its funds directly from the general public, but perhaps also from institutional investors. The attraction would be that it provided a means by which investors could channel funds into public enterprise, assured that the risk of doing so was offset by a government guarantee. Furthermore, a minimum return would be assured with the prospect of additional returns linked to profitability. Patriotism or community-consciousness could be used to appeal to small savers, with the bank making a clear connection between saving with the bank and investing in British public industry.

In a note written by Walter Ulrich, a senior civil servant in the Cabinet Office, it was acknowledged that success could be achieved so long as 'its direct link with public enterprise could fire the imagination of the investment public'.[40] However, Ulrich observed in a revised note that pension funds and other institutions with overseas investors would not be drawn to the scheme, as the 'public enterprise flavour' would suggest that government interference could inhibit returns.[41] Ulrich's report was ultimately negative in its appraisal of the enterprise bank idea, as he believed it would merely direct funds into industry in a slightly different, and not altogether

[38] Letter from Clive Jenkins, 'Proposed Lending Capacity of Finance for Industry', *The Times*, 29 November 1974.

[39] Kynaston, *The City of London*, iv. 537–9.

[40] TNA: T 224/3324, W. O. Ulrich, 'The Proposed "British Enterprise Bank"', 31 January 1975.

[41] TNA: T 224/3324, W. O. Ulrich, 'The Proposed "British Enterprise Bank"', 13 February 1975.

useful, way.[42] This lack of enthusiasm frustrated Tony Benn, who found Ulrich's appraisal 'disappointing in the restricted range of possibilities examined and hence the conclusions about an NEB Bank's ability to attract funds'. Furthermore, he disagreed with the notion that the 'public enterprise flavour' would deter the institutions and other savers.[43] Subsequently Benn, as the Secretary of State for Industry, wrote a short paper arguing that the Industry bill be amended to establish a British Enterprise Bank with substantial borrowing powers.[44] However, Harold Lever, accepting the orthodoxy and ambivalence of Ulrich's report, recommended that the policy not be pursued. Instead, he offered an alternative of establishing a trust fund that could attract small savers to invest directly in British industry. Established by the government, the trust fund would offer shareholdings to members of the public and other bodies such as trade unions, and would invest in equities on their behalf. Although this might not tap into new sources of unutilized funds, the trust would 'give our people, as they invest their savings, a sense of identifying with their country's future by directly linking that investment with the prosperity of the particular firms that provide them and their fellow workers with employment and the hopes of prosperity'.[45] Neither Benn's scheme, nor Lever's, appealed to the Under-Secretary to the Treasury Gordon Downey. Writing to John Page at the Bank of England, Downey expressed that the minimum guaranteed return implicit in a state unit trust implied a potential 'objectionable' subsidy. Downey argued that Benn's proposal was confused—it would be constrained in attracting funds as it was associated with the NEB, and should not engage in equity investment in companies in which the the NEB was already investing.[46] The response of the Permanent Secretary to the Treasury, Douglas Wass, to the Benn proposal was succinctly recorded as: 'This must be resisted. It goes miles beyond the White Paper [Cmd 5710, The Regeneration of British Industry] and there is no proven need for it.'[47]

A particular objection from Treasury officials to the enterprise bank was that it would amount to a straightforward increase of public-sector

---

[42] TNA: T 224/3324, W. S. Ryrie, 'Proposed British Enterprise Bank', 26 February 1975.

[43] TNA: T 224/3324, Alison Macfarlane (Private Secretary to the Secretary of State for Industry), 'British Enterprise Bank', 16 April 1975.

[44] TNA: T 224/3324, R. E. Dearing, 'British Enterprise Bank', 7 May 1975.

[45] TNA: T 224/3324, memorandum by the Chancellor of the Duchy of Lancaster, 'The Proposal for a "British Enterprise Bank"', 7 May 1975.

[46] TNA: T 224/3324, letter from G. S. Downey to J. B. Page, 'British Enterprise Bank', 8 May 1975.

[47] TNA: T 224/3324, M. T. Folger, 'British Enterprise Bank', 6 May 1975.

borrowing of £1,000 million at a time in which expenditure was being cut.[48] Bank of England officials were in agreement that neither plan was worthwhile owing to the implicit increase in public expenditure. A state unit trust, the Bank argued, would struggle to attract investors, who would undoubtedly worry that public policy influences would restrict the freedom of the trust's managers to pursue investors seeking the best returns.[49] Deputy Secretary Leo Pliatsky asserted to the Chancellor that 'Mr Benn's proposal . . . must be decisively rejected. There can be no compromise on this.' He said that the Lever plan could be explored further, but only on the grounds that it might serve as a useful tactic to offset Benn's more radical proposals.[50] The subsequent report for the Cabinet Office concluded that an investment trust would have to become a state unit trust with the investor's capital at risk and would probably duplicate the provisions already existing in the market.[51] Lever's response to the report was to recommend that the state trust—an idea that he continued to favour as a means of attracting small savers into industrial investment—be 'deferred until times are more propitious for introducing such a scheme' (that is, when the economic and financial crisis had passed).[52] Of course, this demonstrates the fundamentally limited nature of Lever's original proposal, which was not concerned with radically raising the rate of industrial investment, or challenging the fundamental architecture of the nation's financial system. As Downey subsequently acknowledged, the meagre £50 million that was to be raised was 'trivial and much of it would in any case be switched saving'.[53]

In the push for financial system reform, the Labour movement was divided in methods and goals. The nuanced ideas of the activist thinkers on the left, such as Hughes, struggled to find a subtle or realistic political expression until the Wilson Committee (which, ultimately, published its proposals too late). The unwavering commitment to wholesale nationalization by senior figures on the left wing of the Labour Party was politically insensitive and unable to secure the support of the Labour leadership or the financial sector trade unions. That said, it is clear that even moderate ideas for reform, led by Lever, were constrained by the Treasury conservatism.

---

[48] TNA: T 224/3324, J. S. Beastall to Alison Macfarlane, 'British Enterprise Bank', 8 May 1975.

[49] TNA: T 224/3324, letter from T. Coleby to L. Pliatsky, 12 May 1975.

[50] TNA: T 224/3324, L. Pliatsky, 'British Enterprise Bank', 14 May 1975.

[51] TNA: T 224/3324, Cabinet Office, 'Proposal for a State Trust: Note by Officials', 14 July 1975.

[52] TNA: T 224/3324, memorandum by the Chancellor of the Duchy of Lancaster, 'The Proposal of a State Trust', 25 July 1975.

[53] TNA: T 224/3324, G. S. Downey, 'State Trust', 30 July 1975.

THE RELATIONSHIP BETWEEN FINANCE
AND INDUSTRY

The failure of the Labour movement to achieve financial system reform must be placed in a broader context that takes account of the relationship between finance and industry in post-war Britain. At the beginning of the decade the notion that the City and its financial institutions were uninterested in domestic industry seems to have been a widely accepted fact that appears to have been supported by many industrialists. It is important to remember that when John Davies queried the City's capacity to support modern industry in 1970 he was speaking as an ex-Director General of the CBI.[54] The *Financial Times* editorial published in the wake of the minister's speech supported his main contentions, stating that Davies had 'undoubtedly put his finger on a genuine problem'. The editorial acknowledged the historical roots of the disconnection between the British banks and industry, as compared with the close financial and personal integration that was commonplace on the Continent. Furthermore, the rise of institutional investment funds had not led to more effective support for firms. Instead they tended to 'vote with their feet' by divesting themselves of shares on the basis of bad news, rather than seeking to regenerate the firms in which they had invested. Where institutional shareholders did take an active role, they often did so with a damaging degree of ignorance.[55] In the summer of 1973 the financial journalist Hamish McRae noted the apparent divisions between the City and industry. McRae described the cultural gulf between the two entities, quoting unfavourably a 'senior man from one of our clearing banks' as saying that 'he had no interest in industry and the thing he disliked most was having to go and look at factories'. McRae claimed that industrialists tended to view the City as a 'den of thieves'.[56] A 1972 seminar, sponsored by the Manchester Business School, on the relationship between finance and industry had concluded that the Square Mile was 'completely out of touch' with industry. This was confirmed by an Inter-Bank Research Organization report that noted: 'the City is not generally well-regarded by industry, by educated and professional people, or even by the populace at large. Even in the City itself, some people say privately that some of our financial

---

[54] 'Davies, Rt Hon. John (Emerson Harding)', *Who Was Who*; online edn (Oxford: Oxford University Press, 2012) <http://www.ukwhoswho.com/view/article/oupww/whowaswho/U153750> (accessed 28 April 2013).
[55] Editorial, 'He who Pays the Piper', *Financial Times*, 6 November 1970.
[56] Hamish McRae, 'How the City Is Failing Industry', *Financial Times*, 7 August 1973.

institutions are sluggish and complacent...'[57] McRae drew further attention to the fact that, despite having the most developed market for trading existing shares in Europe (in the form of the London Stock Exchange), relative to GNP it raised half the amount of 'new funds' of stock markets on the Continent. McCrae quoted the view of a member of the EEC commission that the City was 'a great place for bookies, but it didn't breed very good horses'.[58] The revisionist Labour journal *Socialist Commentary* even quoted a 'well-heeled construction industrialist and property developer' in the autumn of 1974, who argued that 'Wedgwood Benn will be the saviour of British capitalism' because Labour's plans for industry were 'a far better source of investment capital than Arab Eurodollars, Jim Slater's millions...and the increasingly undependable supplies of the City, a snooty club geared not to development enterprise, but to shareholders' profits'.[59] Yet this incipient coalition of labour and industry centred on a critique of the nation's financial sector never materialized as a political force in the latter half of the decade.

How far this divide between industry and the City actually existed is uncertain—indeed the evidence presented here is somewhat superficial and impressionistic. Despite the 1974 stock market collapse, which starved industry of equity investment, any divide between the two 'fractions' of British capitalism that did exist did not widen with the decade's economic crisis.[60] Where in the early 1970s the reformist left had found some common ground with frustrated industrialists, by the time the Wilson Committee had been established the representatives of British industry expressed almost unequivocal support for financial orthodoxy. Large firms stated that they had a perfectly good relationship with financial institutions. Unilever described its relationship with the suppliers of finance as 'uniformly good', and the institutions as more keen to lend than for them to borrow.[61] Courtaulds Ltd, the largest textiles company in the world, also experienced no problems with a lack of access to funds.[62] The manufacturing holding company Tube Investments stated that 'the City has been willing and able to provide adequate funds for industry in recent years on a reasonably competitive basis'.[63] A survey conducted by the Engineering Employers' Federation described an 'extremely close

[57] Inter-Bank Research Organisation (Cabinet Office), *The Future of London as an International Financial Centre: A Report* (London: HMSO, 1973).

[58] Hamish McRae, 'How the City Is Failing Industry', *Financial Times*, 7 August 1973.

[59] Catalpa, 'In & Out of Parliament', *Socialist Commentary*, September 1974.

[60] Nicholls, 'Fractions of Capital'; Anderson, 'Origins of the Present Crisis'.

[61] FI: 1/5, 'FI(WE)52, Written Evidence: Memorandum by Unilever', 31 May 1977.

[62] FI: 1/29, 'Written Evidence: Memorandum by Courtaulds Limited', 3 August 1977.

[63] FI: 1/7, 'Written Evidence: Submission by Tube Investments', 13 June 1977.

relationship with arrangers of finance' in the form of merchant banks, stockbrokers, clearing and foreign banks. As such, there was 'no shortage of long-term funds to finance investment or short-term funds to cover current asset needs'.[64] R. H. Grierson, a director at General Electric (GEC), told the committee in a personal submission of evidence: 'I have never come across evidence to support the charge that the traditional source of finance in this country, whether investors or lending, have "failed" UK industry.' Grierson went to great lengths to dispel the apparent myths that characterized the debate over the City's apparently poor relationship with industry. He dismissed the notion that finance tended to take a 'short-term, greedy view of lending and investment' compared with the 'patient, long-term, public-spirited view' of finance abroad as 'complete fantasy'. The belief that British industry should seek expansion by becoming more 'highly geared' with borrowed money was 'hair-raising' in its recklessness. The logic that, because German industry is at once more heavily indebted and is more efficient and that therefore British industry should increase its debt–equity ratio, was dismissed as foolish. Furthermore, the idea that there was a weaker *rapport* between banks and industry in Britain than abroad was 'the most entrenched myth of all. Lack of representation of bankers on the boards of their customers isn't beneficial to the industrialist anyway—bankers tend to cling to them mainly for prestige reason and to avoid important accounts moving to competitors.' The notion that foreign banks were better organized to solve the problems of their customers was also denounced as a myth—many industrialists abroad were jealous of the 'less partisan lending habits of UK banks'. He continued: 'And as for "guidance" from bankers, critics should rest assured that this quaint notion of omniscient bankers prodding myopic industrialists into making desirable investments is as unheard of in Tokyo and Paris as in London. Banking is not a moral rearmament crusade among industrialists.'[65] The exoneration of the financial institutions was cemented by the evidence presented by the CBI. Having consulted with 'a wide range of CBI member companies, and in particular the views of our Small Firms Council', the organization concluded that 'it has not been a shortage of external finance that has restricted industrial investment but rather a lack of confidence that industry will be able to earn a sufficient return'.[66]

---

[64] FI: 1/5, 'Written Evidence: Submission by Engineering Employers' Federation', 25 May 1977.

[65] FI: 1/7, 'Written Evidence: Submission by R. H. Grierson', 20 June 1977.

[66] FI: 1/10, 'Industry and the City: The CBI's Evidence to the Wilson Committee', 1977.

A report from the accountancy firm Coopers and Lybrand of a survey of 'medium-sized firms' (consisting of forty-eight firms with annual turnover of between £5 million and £150 million) noted that, although their interviews were intended to place much of their focus on discussing the problems of 'external fund raising', the businesses spoken to had expressed a 'general lack of comment or criticism—indeed a remarkable disinterest—on this topic'. Indeed, Coopers and Lybrand heard of 'no instance of specific investment proposals ... rejected for lack of finance or term or conditions imposed by lenders'.[67]

That is not to say that there were not some expressions of frustration regarding the difficulty of obtaining funds, or the cost of borrowing. This was especially true among smaller businesses, which were slightly more ambivalent towards finance. For example, the Machine Tool Trades Association, summarizing evidence given by its membership of primarily small companies, noted that long-term finance was too expensive in view of the large profits made by financial institutions, and that the financial institutions should give more help to small companies.[68] The Association of Independent Businesses expressed concern that small firms were at a disadvantage compared to their foreign counterparts in the financial services available to them, as the banking system in Britain was far less integrated with domestic business than abroad. The capital required to start or expand a business in Britain had to be drawn from the entrepreneur himself, with only a small reliance on external funds, whereas 'in some European countries' it was possible for the entrepreneur to obtain financial support, which meant that only 20 to 30 per cent of assets would have to be self-financed. Furthermore, the banking system in Britain was deemed to be too risk averse, requiring extensive security, personal guarantees, or imposing charges. The evidence stated:

> We cannot entirely blame the banks for their attitude; they are protecting their depositors. They believe that banks should not borrow short-term and lend long-term ... This obsession with security has meant that British small firms are at a severe disadvantage compared with their European counterparts. It seems that the British banking system has been too conservative in its approach.

The association argued that banks could relax their 'rigid rules' on security and the ratio of long- and short-term lending. The comparison was made

---

[67] FI: 1/17, 'Report by Coopers and Lybrand on Survey of Medium-Sized Firms', 11 January 1978.
[68] FI: 1/4, 'Written Evidence: Memorandum of the Machine Tool Trades Association', 4 May 1977.

with the building societies, which managed to achieve this maturity transformation in a prudent manner and with low margins.[69] Outside the banking system the necessity of establishing an over-the-counter market in unlisted securities was also pressed.[70]

The difference in views on this matter, between medium-sized and large industrial concerns, seems to reflect the long-standing argument, first articulated in the findings of the 1931 Macmillan Committee, that the British capital markets failed to provide adequate support for smaller firms.[71] However, it is also likely that it was a function of the fact that the relationship between large firms and financial institutions had grown steadily more integrated in the previous decades. There is significant evidence to demonstrate that the financial and industrial 'fractions of capital' in Britain had become far closer since the Second World War. The 'merger mania' of the 1960s—which witnessed the formation of larger firms with the encouragement of the state—was overseen by the merchant banking community of the City. The forging of large-scale enterprises through the intermediation of financial institutions served to develop a genuine form of 'finance capital' (an integration of finance and industry) previously absent in Britain.[72] The growth of occupational pension funds, owned and managed by non-financial firms, also undermined the dichotomy between industry and finance. In addition to these material changes, there was an emerging political relationship between industrialists and financiers taking place through the CBI. In 1968 Sir Stephen Brown, the president of the CBI, invited the chairmen of the major City organizations to dinner to discuss the forging of greater ties between industry, banking, and commerce.[73] This was followed in 1969 by formal invitations from the CBI to numerous financial institutions to become members of its organization. In a letter sent to the heads of various banks, the CBI stressed the 'indivisibility of the business operation—from the provision of capital through production and distribution', and that 'interests common to the City and to manufacturers seem to us to be increasing both in significance and in number'.[74] In 1973 E. J. N. Warburton (Vice Chairman of Lloyds)

[69] TUC: MSS.2920/462.2/1, the Association of Independent Businesses, 'Memorandum to the Committee to Review the Function of Financial Institutions', June 1977.

[70] FI: 1/10, 'Written Evidence: Memorandum by the Association of Independent Businesses', 23 June 1977.

[71] Cmd 3897, *The Report of the Committee on Finance and Industry* (London: HMSO, 1931), para. 404.

[72] Wilson, *British Business History*, 181–93.

[73] Dennis Topping, 'Closer City-Industry Links Sought by CBI Chief', *Financial Times*, 26 March 1968.

[74] CBI: MSS.200/C/3/P3/?1-59, letter from CBI to D. A. Sterling (Chairman, Natwest), 13 January 1969.

and D. S. G. Adam (a general manager at Barclays) were elected to the CBI Grand Council.[75] The CBI's chief economic advisor in the 1970s, Donald Macdougall, also recalls in his memoirs his own successful efforts to overcome the perceived division between industry and services prevalent within the organization.[76] As the 1970s progressed, the relationship between finance and industry became politically much stronger, with a motion at the 1978 CBI conference explicitly rejecting the notion that there was a divide between the two fractions of British capital.[77] Smaller firms, unlisted on the London Stock Exchange, had not been exposed to this process and were therefore more alienated from financial institutions than larger firms.

THE PROFITS CRISIS

The economic and political relationship between industrialists and the financial sector had become much closer in the post-war decades, thus making the former less receptive to proposals for substantial financial sector reform. However, this increased integration was made concrete—in polit-ical terms—by the economic experience of the 1970s. From the middle of the 1960s both the share of national income accruing to profits, and the rates of pre-tax and post-tax profitability, were in decline in Britain (see Figs. 3.1–3.3). This was demonstrated throughout the 1970s in the work of the economist Andrew Glyn (alongside co-authors Bob Sutcliffe and John Harrison).[78] Working within a Marxist/Kaleckian framework, Glyn argued that the crisis in British capitalism was a crisis of profitability, and for the capitalist economy to survive it was necessary for the profits to be restored.[79] The evidence of this declining rate and share of profits is substantial.

---

[75] BBA: CLC/B/029/MS32006/012, Minutes of the Committee of London Clearing Bankers, 1 May 1973.

[76] Donald MacDougall, *Don and Mandarin: Memoirs of an Economist* (London: John Murray, 1987), 235–7.

[77] Wyn Grant, *Business and Politics in Britain* (1st edn, London: Macmillan, 1987), 75–9.

[78] Andrew Glyn and Bob Sutcliffe, 'The Critical Condition of British Capital', *New Left Review*, 66 (1971), 3–33; Andrew Glyn and Bob Sutcliffe, *British Workers and the Profit Squeeze* (Harmondsworth: Penguin, 1972), 3–33; Andrew Glyn and John Harrison, *The British Economic Disaster* (London: Pluto, 1980).

[79] Glyn's analysis did not replicate the orthodox Marxist theory of the long-run tendency of the profit rate to fall. Rather it emphasized—influenced by Michael Kalecki—the specific context in which full employment and welfare state protections under the post-war social democratic settlement had served to increase wages and erode profits. For a concise summary of Glyn's argument, see Stuart White, 'The Economics of Andrew Glyn', *Renewal*, 6/3–4 (2008), 134–8.

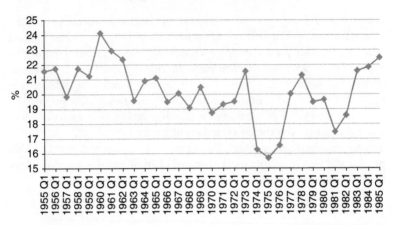

Fig. 3.1. Gross operating surplus of corporations, % of GDP, 1955–85
Source: Office for National Statistics.

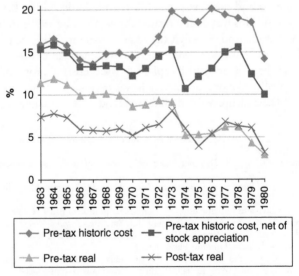

Fig. 3.2. Rates of return on trading assets, 1963–80
Source: *Bank of England Quarterly Bulletin*, 21/2 (1981), 228–31.

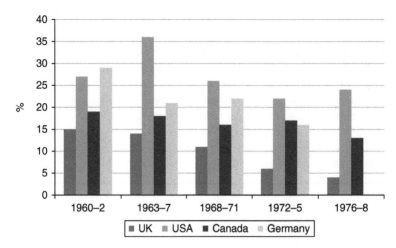

Fig. 3.3. International profitability of manufacturing: net pre-tax rates of return, annual average, 1960–78

Source: Cmd 7937. Committee to Review the Functioning of Financial Institutions: Report (London: HMSO, 1980), table 36.

Between 1973 and 1975—with the onset of severe inflation—profitability declined sharply. This declining rate of profit has been employed subsequently as an explanation of the 'neoliberal' economic policies implemented in the 1980s—portraying them simply as a political strategy to reassert the share of national income accruing to profits.[80]

The crisis of profitability dominated business discourse at the time of the 1974 stock market collapse. This event was framed by two general elections in which Labour formed a minority government in February and a small majority in October, and by two Budgets delivered by the Chancellor Dennis Healey in March and November. The first Budget coincided with the onset of industry's liquidity crisis. The imposition of taxes on capital and profits significantly undermined the capacity of firms to reinvest, because they reduced company profits at a time in which rapid inflation was eroding their value. In the *Investors Chronicle* the journalist Alan Stanbrook gave the example of

> a well-known British company [which in 1972] made net profits of £92m after tax distributed gross dividends of £67m to its shareholders and ploughed over £24m back. In that same year it provided £132m depreciation on plant and equipment whose average age was 6½ years. During those 6½ years, however, general prices ... increased by just over 45 per cent.[81]

[80] Duménil and Lévy, *Capital Resurgent*, 21–8.
[81] Alan Stanbrook, 'Taking the Illusion out of Company Profits', *Investors Chronicle*, 17 May 1974.

The *Investors Chronicle* condemned 'Mr Healey's Robin Hood Budget' in the light of its 'confiscatory' tax policies and its seemingly deliberate attack on profits. The Chancellor justified the policies of increasing the national insurance contributions of companies and increasing corporation tax on the grounds that 'companies have in general been doing better in the last year or two, and profits have reached a very high level'—yet this was a money illusion.[82] For the *Investors Chronicle* Healey carried a 'direct Government attack on profits further than ever before'. Many alleged that this was a deliberate strategy, orchestrated by Benn at the Department of Industry, 'actively [to] arrang[e] the condition' by which the liquidity of companies was squeezed so significantly that it would force them to approach the government as the lender of last resort and in doing so allow the state to take progressive ownership of the economy.[83] Writing in September, the journalist Michael Brody correctly recognized that such a claim was a groundless conspiracy theory that obscured the 'violent personality and policy clashes between socialist fundamentalists and the social democratic centrists within the Labour cabinet'—however, it exemplified the paranoia and fear surrounding the possible collapse of the free capitalist economy all together.[84] In the four days after the Budget the Financial Times Ordinary Share Index fell by 8.8 per cent.[85] In its quarterly industrial survey taken during the first months of the July, the CBI highlighted reductions in industrial production, a reduced willingness to invest in the near future, and a decline of 'business optimism'.[86]

An anonymously authored article in the *Investors Chronicle* in May 1974 by a partner in a firm of financial advisors claimed that 'the movement to the left in the policies of the two principal political parties over the last few years' had been so great that it was 'now no more than commonsense to question whether dividends and rents [would] ever again be allowed to rise in a totally unfettered fashion'.[87] Indeed, it was the Heath government that had first introduced dividend controls. Norman Freeman of the ICI pension fund argued that fund managers were faced with two problems. First, the need to maintain the real value of pension

---

[82] Denis Healey, Parliamentary Debates, Commons, vol. 871, cols 277–329 (26 March 1974).

[83] 'Mr Healey's Robin Hood Budget', *Investors Chronicle*, 29 March 1974.

[84] Michael Brody, 'Hand to Mouth Finance Cannot Save British Industry', *Investors Chronicle*, 30 September 1974.

[85] Nigel Bolitho, 'Companies Weight the Cost of the Budget', *Investors Chronicle*, 2 April 1974.

[86] Michael Brody, 'Investment Plans Curtailed as the Gloom Deepens', *Investors Chronicle*, 3 August 1974.

[87] 'Fund Manager's Lament', *Investors Chronicle*, 10 May 1974.

savings and investment in the face of inflation; and, secondly, the constant attack by governments on the freedom of investment. Dividend restraint was 'the most overt and obvious' example of this. This was conjoined with the 'attack of profits' that had begun under phase II of the Heath government's counter-inflation policy in 1973. On top of this, the inevitable move into direct property investment by companies drew public criticism of 'property speculation' (excoriated by the Labour left), which forced governments of both colours to impose taxes and freeze rents. The outcome was to place institutional investors in a difficult position, politically constrained and unable to find investment yields sufficient to keep pace with inflation.[88] A later editorial in the same journal claimed: 'As it is the present controls negate the capitalist system because shareholders are not allowed to receive the rewards of success while still being liable for the results of failure.' The editorial argued that it was necessary for City bodies to work with the pension and insurance funds to inform the public of the damaging effects of their investments engendered by the controls.[89] Many other financial figures called for a political campaigning effort to assert the importance and necessity of revitalizing private profit so that the free economy might continue to function. Freeman asserted:

> It is essential that industrialists are not defeatist at this point; they must not be apologetic. They must rather make plain their belief in profits and in capitalism and why, and do their best to make clear that everything has to be paid for, in a socialist society as much as in a capitalist one.[90]

The outcry was substantial and significantly influenced Healey's November Budget. Recognizing the lack of working capital available to firms as a result of inflation, and that 'present tax rules, impos[ed] burdens which industry was never meant to carry', Healey acknowledged the government's 'duty to see that firms which are alert and vigorous can be profitable as well ... but that such firms can be profitable only if the system of price control and taxation within which they operate makes this possible'.[91] In response to pressure from the CBI, Healey offered tax relief on stock appreciation and reduced price controls.[92] Of course this was not a statement of nascent 'neoliberal' intent, but was perfectly in

---

[88] Norman Freeman, 'Political Decisions Are Hitting Pensions—and Industrial Investment', *Investors Chronicle*, 28 June 1974.

[89] 'Time to Campaign', *Investors Chronicle*, 7 June 1974.

[90] Norman Freeman, 'Political Decisions Are Hitting Pensions—and Industrial Investment', *Investors Chronicle*, 28 June 1974.

[91] Denis Healey, Parliamentary Debates, Commons, vol. 881, cols 432–549 (13 November 1974).

[92] Plender, *That's the Way the Money Goes*, 51–2; MacDougall, *Don and Mandarin*, 213.

keeping with the model of investment that had characterized the political economy of post-war social democracy. However, for the remainder of his period in office the commitment to a wealth tax was not fulfilled, and taxes on capital constituted a diminishing proportion of the Treasury's total tax intake.[93] Reflecting on these measures in 1982, the financial journalist John Plender observed that Healey 'arguably fought a better rearguard action for the rich and for investors...than any other holder of the Chancellor's office since the war.'[94]

Regardless of Healey's readiness to change course in 1974, and his public commitment to restoring the profitability of British firms, the crisis cemented the issue at the heart of economic discourse in the second half of the decade. Both financial and industrial interests coalesced around the need to increase the rate of profit for the purpose of securing economic dynamism through investment. As a result, when the Wilson Committee came to take evidence on how best to approach financial reform, industrial representatives were not interested in structural changes designed to advance the state's role in the administration of a social democratic economy. The problem was defined, by representatives of finance and industry alike, as one of poor profitability limiting the demand for investible funds. The stockbroking firm Cazenove & Co. argued that the new issue market could be built only upon a general share market in which investors could actually make a profit on their investments.[95] Stockbrokers Parsons & Co. pressed that companies would seek to expand only if there was a prospect of an attractive rate of return on any investment.[96] The Unit Trust Association stated that the primary means of encouraging personal savings to flow into British industry and commerce was 'by the restoration of conditions favourable to a material increase in the profitability of British companies'.[97] In a paper for the National Economic Development Council's 'Committee on Finance for Investment', I. J. Fraser (Chairman of the City Capital Markets Committee) argued: 'It cannot be overemphasised that the prime motive for investing for all company engagements is to make profits in the medium or long term for the shareholders...'[98] In a public speech in 1975, Sir Eric Faulkner, the chairman of Lloyds bank, made the

[93] Plender, *That's the Way the Money Goes*, 210–11 n. 7; Howard Glennerster, 'Why Was a Wealth Tax for the UK Abandoned? Lessons for the Policy Process and Tackling Wealth Inequality', *Journal of Social Policy*, 41/2 (2012), 233–49.

[94] Plender, *That's the Way the Money Goes*, 51–2.

[95] FI: 1/4, 'Memorandum by Cazenove & Co.', 28 March 1977.

[96] FI: 1/4, 'Memorandum by Parsons & Co., Stockbrokers', 1977.

[97] FI: 1/16, 'Memorandum by the Unit Trust Association', 10 June 1977.

[98] TUC: MSS.2920/462.21/1, I. J. Fraser (Chairman, Capital Markets Committee), 'Committee on Finance for Industry: Capital for Manufacturing Industry—Development of Supply and Demand over the Next Period', 16 March 1976.

case that blaming the City for lack of investment was deeply misguided when the true problem facing the British economy was the erosion of profit. He argued that falling profitability reduced the retained profits, which were the main source of new funds for capital investment. 'It cannot be said too often or too loud,' he argued; 'it must be driven home to all political parties, to employees and the trade unions, to the media, and to the general public' that investors need confidence in the viability of industry—'and that means its profitability'.[99] Sir John Prideaux stated to his fellow committee members that 'for investment to rise there needed to be a sustained rise in the share of national income going to profits'.[100]

It could be claimed that this was simply a justification on the part of the financial institutions for their conservatism and unwillingness to take a greater responsibility for overseeing the regeneration of the economy. Yet it found loud echoes of support from industry, which argued that the general economic climate was the primary cause of underinvestment. The product of this lack of profitable opportunities could be associated with, and blamed primarily upon, the state. The evidence of the British Chambers of Commerce stated baldly that 'the key to solving the problem of investment is profitability'.[101] The Engineering Employers' Federation supported this, claiming:

> It can only be said that recent Governments have failed to create an environment in which industry can hope to operate at reasonable profitability . . . The financial problems of the engineering industry have in no way been caused by the financial institutions; they are entirely the responsibility of the Governments which appear to have no comprehension of how industry works.[102]

The CBI stressed that industrialists would invest only if there was the prospect of a profit, and that the only means to enhance investment would be through a marked improvement in earnings.[103]

CHALLENGING THE SOCIAL DEMOCRATIC ECONOMIC MODEL

The financial and business community was most animated by the impact of taxation in hampering the operation of the capitalist economy. The

---

[99] 'The City is "Supporter and Organiser of Markets"', *Financial Times*, 7 November 1975.

[100] FI: 1/5, 'Minutes', 14 June 1977.

[101] FI: 1/16, 'At Whose Expense? First submission from the ABCC to the Committee of Enquiry into the Role and Functioning of the Financial Institutions', August 1977.

[102] FI: 1/5, 'Submission by the Engineering Employers' Federation', 25 May 1977.

[103] FI: 1/10, 'Industry and the City: The CBI's Evidence to the Wilson Committee', 1977.

Association of Independent Businesses, representing smaller firms, argued that it was vital for the government to reduce high rates of income tax to levels similar to those in France and Germany, and to place a much greater tax burden on indirect rather than personal taxes. Capital gains and transfer taxes needed reform, and corporation tax reduced (because small firms could not afford the financial advice available to larger firms in finding corporation tax loopholes.) The organization argued that 'the decline of vitality of the independent business sector has been caused by a political climate which has been unsympathetic towards it. This climate has allowed the development of the tax system which tends to stifle enterprise which is particularly onerous for small and medium-sized firms.'[104] The issue of high taxation, particularly taxation of wealth, was especially important, owing to the nature of the funding methods of small businesses. Because of the reliance of small business on retained earnings as the primary source of investment funds, taxes on capital and dividends were viewed as an expropriation of the motors of expansion and growth. The concern to create new institutional structures, or simply to change the behaviour of the financial institutions, was peripheral to the far more pressing need to reconstruct the framework within which an industrial capitalist economy could function effectively. This perspective was most explicitly expressed in a 'Joint Statement on Taxation' presented to the committee by the Association of British Chambers of Commerce, the Association of Independent Businesses, the Institute of Directors, the National Farmers' Union, and the Unquoted Companies Group. In their presentation they stated that the UK had the highest rates of both income and capital taxes 'in the Western world'. The result of the present level of taxes on capital were such that 'most, if not all, successful and substantial privately owned and thus unquoted companies will, within a generation, need to be sold up. Taxes are now penal upon the owners, who are usually also the managers, of efficient and successful enterprises.' The primary concern was with capital gains tax, capital transfer tax, and the Labour government's proposal of a wealth tax.[105] The CBI's Smaller Firms Council argued that small firms were being 'taxed out of existence' in a political climate hostile to their existence, and pressed for a comprehensive review of the tax system. Among the many proposals put forward, the group campaigned for the planned wealth tax to be abandoned, the top

---

[104] TUC: MSS.2920/462.2/1, the Association of Independent Businesses, 'Memorandum to the Committee to Review the Function of Financial Institutions', June 1977.

[105] FI: 1/10, 'Joint Statement on Taxation by the Association of British Chambers of Commerce, the Association of Independent Businesses, the Institute of Directors, the National Farmers' Union, and the Unquoted Companies' Group', October 1976.

rate of income tax reduced to 60 per cent, and the investment income surcharge abolished.[106] In addition, the Coopers and Lybrand survey of medium-sized firms found that 'several family owned companies saw no incentive to borrow to finance significant expansion of the business; if the profit was successful the profits were likely to be largely absorbed, eventually, by taxes on capital and income . . .'.[107]

The small and medium-size industries were not alone in their rejection of onerous taxation as a root cause of squeezed profits. Sir Arnold Weinstock, the managing director of GEC, expressed that it was in fact remarkable that such a high level of industrial investment continued to take place in Britain in the face of 'political and economic conditions adverse to free enterprise, and under taxation laws based on the premise that highly skilled and (formerly) highly paid industrial managers are (in the Chancellor's words) pips that must be made to squeak'.[108] The CBI called for a 'reduction in the mounting burden of taxation on capital' to encourage saving and investment, and a decrease in income tax in order to 'restore incentives and spur expansion'.[109]

In the representations of the City firms to the committee there was an unambiguous demand for taxation reduction. Cazenove demanded that the return of the private investor be heralded by allowing profits to rise through investment income tax reduction and the decontrolling of dividends. The Stock Exchange's official evidence stated that the advocacy of increased taxes on individuals, and on the purchase and sale of equity shares, plus the limiting of dividends, adversely affected profits and removed individual incentives.[110] The result was to undermine the confidence necessary to spur industrial expansion. In the body's official representation to the Chancellor in 1977 regarding the reform of taxation, it argued for changes in the next Finance bill 'to help industry and commerce and savers who provide capital to them'. This meant the reduction of the top rate of income tax from 83 per cent to 60 per cent, an abolition of the investment income surcharge, and the reduction of stamp duty on purchases of equities to levels commensurate with the EEC, and, 'if abolition is out of the question', concessions on capital gains tax.

[106] FI: 1/10, CBI Press Release, 'Small Firms Taxed out of Existence: Ease Burden before they Disappear, Says CBI', 4 October 1977.
[107] FI: 1/17, 'Report by Coopers and Lybrand on Survey of Medium-Sized Firms', 11 January 1978.
[108] FI: 1/7, 'Memorandum by Sir Arnold Weinstock', 23 June 1977.
[109] FI: 1/10, 'Industry and the City: The CBI's Evidence to the Wilson Committee', 1977.
[110] FI: 1/12, 'Memorandum by the Stock Exchange', 28 July 1977; TUC: MSS.2920/463/2, 'Stock Exchange Commentary Leaflet No. 1: An End to Dividend Control', n.d.

Although the imperatives were different for small and large businesses, a consensus political position developed among the various shades of industrial capital, and finance itself, against current levels of taxation. This push against the apparent excesses of the social democratic state by business appears as a forerunner of the Thatcherite revolution after 1979—though, as already noted, it is important to acknowledge the impact and influence of these campaigns on the post-1974 Labour governments.

The issue of taxes was complemented by a more wide-ranging critique of the government's economic policies. The issue of inflation was particularly pertinent. The Stock Exchange placed 'a sharp reduction in the rate of inflation' at the top of its list of priorities for future policies.[111] Eric Faulkner told his audience in 1975, as part of his comprehensive condemnation of the British economic climate:

> It is the government's failure to control inflation which has so dangerously eroded your profitability and reduced the retained profits from which most new capital investment traditionally comes...Inflation is not a plague inflicted by God. Inflation is, as it has always been, man-made. The creation of man's materialism and self-indulgence, it can be controlled only by man's self-discipline...To get this recognised by the British people requires courageous leadership.[112]

As with taxation, it was not simply the City's representatives that regarded inflation, or uncertainty about the rate of inflation, as the block on profits and investment. The capacity to plan, and to earn a decent return on investment, was consistently undermined by inflationary pressures. Furthermore, the effect of inflation was deemed to be at the root of high loan costs, rather than the fault of the institutions.[113] As Courtaulds noted, the effect of high rates of inflation was to increase the working capital requirements of firms—in Courtauld's case by £152 million in the two previous years, and by an estimated £45 million in the coming year. This meant that new investment had to be reduced to meet these necessities.[114] Inflation, when combined with capital gains tax, still had the effect of acting as a tax on existing capital rather than gains—despite Healey's tax relief.[115] Arnold Weinstock argued that inflation brought 'confusion and

---

[111] Stock Exchange, *Evidence to the Committee to Review the Functioning of Financial Institutions: the role and functioning of the Stock Exchange* (London, 1977).

[112] 'The City is "Supporter and Organiser of Markets"', *Financial Times*, 7 November 1975.

[113] FI: 1/5, 'FI(WE)52, Written Evidence: Memorandum by Unilever', 31 May 1977.

[114] FI: 1/29, 'Written Evidence: Memorandum by Courtaulds Limited', 3 August 1977.

[115] TUC: MSS.2920/462.2/1, The Association of Independent Businesses, 'Memorandum to the Committee to Review the Function of Financial Institutions', June 1977.

unpredictability into the economy', leading businesses to become 'chary of investing since they cannot tell whether any contemplated investment will earn a reasonable return'. For Weinstock, as with Faulkner, the fault of this inflation could be simply attributed to the pursuit by the government of 'popular but often mutually irreconcilable objectives, such as a full employment, increasing levels of (wasteful?) public expenditure and guaranteed improvement in living standards'.[116]

More broadly, financiers and industrialists were agreed that the general economic climate in which they were required to seek profits was consistently undermined by a practice of economic policymaking that lacked consistency and created uncertain expectations. For example, the Insurance Company Associations claimed in their evidence that the volatility in investment markets was a 'reflection of greater uncertainty and of more extreme changes in government fiscal policy' in addition to unstable exchange, interest, and inflation rates.[117] For the Stock Exchange what was necessary was to enact 'fewer changes in fiscal and economic legislation and less interference with industry and trade'.[118] It was further argued that the excessive borrowing of the government, which had increased significantly in the middle of the decade, was not merely the cause of inflation, but also served to reduce the capacity for industry to access funds at affordable interest rates. Investment in industry would continue to be limited so long as the state claimed an increasing share of investable funds to finance its expanding deficit.[119] Furthermore, it was argued that bringing public expenditure on 'non-productive services into a better relationship with total national resources would create confidence in the future and increase the demand by industry and trade for funds'.[120]

Finally, the CBI and the City also found common ground in opposing exchange controls. As is described in the next chapter, the City asserted that the ongoing existence of exchange controls in the 1970s limited its capacity to earn income from abroad—to the detriment of the nation. Meanwhile, in 1967 the CBI defended the value of overseas investment,

---

[116] FI: 1/7, 'Memorandum by Sir Arnold Weinstock', 23 June 1977.

[117] FI: 1/12, FI(WE)64, 'Memorandum by the Insurance Company Associations', 8 November 1977.

[118] Stock Exchange, *Evidence to the Committee to Review the Functioning of Financial Institutions: the role and functioning of the Stock Exchange*, (London, 1977).

[119] FI: 1/4, 'Memorandum by Cazenove & Co.', 28 March 1977; 1/14, 'Evidence by the Accepting Houses Committee', 27 July 1977; 'Written Evidence by the Insurance Company Associations', 'Written Evidence by the Stock Exchange', (1978); TUC: MSS.2920/462.21/1, Fraser (Chairman, Capital Markets Committee), 'Capital for manufacturing industry', 16 March 1976; MJO: Gordon Pepper, '"Crowding Out": Myth or Fact?', 3 February 1977.

[120] 'Written Evidence by the Stock Exchange', (1978).

which required the removal of controls on capital export. The CBI argued that, 'if the benefits of international specialisation are to be realised, capital must be given more, not less, freedom to move. International investment stimulates prosperity and expansion of trade.'[121] The increasingly multi-national organization of industrial firms brought them into a political alignment with the City over exchange controls. The City's historic role in the export of capital, which was so often associated with the starving of the domestic industrial base, was now supported by industrial firms whose operations crossed national boundaries and thus required the free movement of capital.[122]

CONCLUSION

The left's attempt to reshape the financial system in the 1970s failed in the face of industry's indifference to change. Despite the superficial prevalence of disgruntled voices within industry at the beginning of the decade, the chance to achieve financial reform faded with the onset of the mid-decade economic crisis. The subsequent crisis of profitability, in which both the rate of return on investment and the share of national income accruing to profits declined rapidly, forged a political coalition between the financial and industrial 'fractions of capital' that sought to restore profits in order to revive the effective functioning of the economy. The means to achieve this, it was asserted, was for the state to reduce its involvement in the free operation of the economy. The opportunity to advance the social demo-cratic settlement in Britain during the 1970s, through an expansion of the public role into the operation of the financial system—already a divided and weakened cause—was thwarted by a concerted challenge to the social democratic attempt to improve national economic performance through state intervention. This episode supports Adam Pzreworski's assertion that social democratic economic control is constrained by the need to maintain private profits, and for capitalists to allocate these profits effectively in order to increase productivity. According to Pzreworski, the 'efficacy of social democrats . . . depends upon the profitability of the private sector and the willingness of capitalists to cooperate. This is the structural barrier which cannot be broken: the limit of any policy is that investment

---

[121] CBI: MSS.200/C/3/INT/2/2, CBI, 'Overseas Investment: Why and How?', (1967)
[122] John M. Stopford, 'The Origins of British-Based Multinational Manufacturing Enterprises', *Business History Review*, 48: 3, (1974), 303–5; Neil Rollings, 'Multinational Enterprise and Government Controls on Outward Foreign Direct Investment in the United States and the United Kingdom in the 1960s', *Enterprise and Society*, 12: 2 (2011), 398–434.

and thus profits must be protected in the long run.'[123] Where Michał Kalecki had argued that social democracy contained the seeds of its own destruction in the asymmetrical power relations brought about by full employment, this chapter suggests that it was the shock of inflation and economic uncertainty that unified Britain's business class, and that provoked its anti-social democratic counter-revolution.[124]

This chapter has argued that the attempt to reform the financial system during the crisis decade of the 1970s was prevented by political conflicts within the Labour movement, but that these were rooted in a more fundamental crisis of the material conditions in which the post-war social democratic settlement was built. Attempts to reformulate social democratic economic strategy in the 1970s were subject to strong resistance from across the British business class—both industrial and financial. The following chapter puts these constraints on social democracy in the context of a political and cultural struggle over the future of the national economy—a debate in which the City of London was central.

---

[123] Adam Przeworski, *Capitalism and Social Democracy*, (Cambridge: Cambridge University Press, 1985), 42–3.

[124] Michał Kalecki, 'Political Aspects of Full Employment', *Political Quarterly*, 14: 4 (1943), 322–30.

4

The City of London and the Politics of 'Invisibles'

So far this book has focused on the City of London's position at the heart of the domestic financial system. The responsibility of the City's institutions and mechanisms for allocating credit and investment to the real economy ensured that its role was exposed to the demands of a social democratic economic strategy based on the desired development of the industrial economy. But what about the City of London's international activities? Today the City of London stands as a pre-eminent international financial centre providing a host of financial and commercial services to an integrated global economy. In September 2008 London was responsible for 20 per cent of global cross-border lending, and held bank assets worth £7.5 trillion. In 2007 London accounted for over 30 per cent of world foreign-exchange business, as well as acting as the centre for trading in gold and silver. In the same year the City could claim a 46 per cent share of global foreign equity trading, and a 70 per cent of international bond trading. The London International Financial Futures Exchange (LIFFE), established in 1982, was responsible for 47 per cent of all the world's cross-border derivatives turnover with 1,224 million futures and option contracts traded there in 2007. In the same year, 80 per cent of European hedge fund assets, worth $2,250 billion, were managed in London. London simultaneously provides the world's leading international insurance market, as well as hosting a major centre for international arbitration, and a management consultancy sector worth almost £3 billion. In 2007 financial and professional services accounted for 11 per cent of UK GDP, and the trade surplus in financial services equalled £35.6 billion.[1]

How did the City of London achieve its position as a pre-eminent international financial centre; and why has the international City become so significant a part of the British national economy? It is possible to argue that the outcome was inevitable. London's status as an international

---

[1] Leila Simona Talani, *Globalization, Hegemony and the Future of the City of London* (London: Palgrave Macmillan, 2012), 172–7.

financial and commercial hub was established at the start of the nineteenth century as the product of the nation's increasingly dominant position as a major trading and colonial power. In the eighteenth century, as the Industrial Revolution had taken off at home, the City's activities grew to meet the requirements of expanding overseas trade. This expansion had little to do with domestic industrial development, but was dependent on the growing demand, in Britain and across Europe, for consumer goods produced in the new world. The capacity of the City to meet these conditions was rooted in preindustrial institutions and practices, such as its commodity and marine insurance markets, as well as its specialized banking system.[2] The City's international significance was boosted by the increasing dominance of London-based merchant banks on the inter-national loan market—particularly loans to foreign governments—from around the time of the Napoleonic Wars.[3] The importance of the City in the world economy was assured by its centrality to the multilateral trading networks wthat flourished during the nineteenth century. Banking and insurance were attendant to the demands of international commercial interactions, and the City's success owed a great deal to its geographical location on the Thames—though the financing of third-country trade, in which goods and merchandise did not physically move through London itself, grew increasingly significant from the middle of the century. The height of the City's international pre-eminence as a financial and com-mercial centre coincided with the pinnacle of the British Empire in the four or so decades prior to the First World War. This was in part the product of imperial dominance, but largely due to the depth of global trading integration, which characterized the period. Mass migrations of people, capital, and goods saw the first age of globalization reach its peak. The principles of free trade, a non-interventionist state, and the commit-ment to the gold standard underpinned London's centrality to this trading and commercial structure. In this environment, foreign banks were drawn to London on a large scale.[4] It is often argued that this internationalist history explains the City's late-twentieth-century resurgence. The matur-ity of the City's financial and commercial institutional architecture ensured that, with the revival of the liberal international trading envir-onment in the latter decades of the twentieth century (following its disruption and break-up between 1914 and 1945), London was perfectly

---

[2] Cassis, *Capitals of Capital*, 15–19.   [3] Ibid. 22–4.
[4] Mae Baker and Michael Collins, 'London as an International Banking Center, 1950–1980', in Youssef Cassis and Eric Bussière (eds), *London and Paris as International Financial Centres in the Twentieth Century* (Oxford: Oxford University Press, 2005), 247–8.

placed to revive its historic role. This was helped by the fact that London speaks English, the language of the hegemonic economic and financial power (the United States), and that it is conveniently situated midway between New York and Tokyo, with easy access to European financial centres.

An alternative explanation is explicitly *political*. From this perspective, the City's resurgence is attributed directly to the policies of Margaret Thatcher's post-1979 Conservative governments—the abolition of exchange controls in 1979, large reductions in taxation on incomes and capital, and major deregulatory reforms of the City in the middle of the decade (the 'Big Bang'). The focus on Thatcher constitutes an article of faith for many contributors to contemporary public discourse on the City. On the political right the government's policies of deregulation are widely celebrated as averting national economic disaster and overcoming social democratic 'decline'; on the left they are deemed responsible for legitimating financial sector greed and excessive wealth accumulation at the expense of domestic industrial development and economic stability.[5] The Conservative policies were undoubtedly vital to the City's late-twentieth-century expansion, yet to focus solely on them is short-sighted. This perspective assumes that the Thatcher government operated in a vacuum and was simply able to impose its predetermined ideological will on an infinitely malleable world. As described in this chapter, it is quite evident that the City's role as an international financial centre was already expanding and progressing long before Thatcher's arrival in Downing Street. It is more fruitful to evaluate the conditions that shaped the eventual policy choices made by her government.

The most substantive explanation of the City's trajectory over recent decades has focused on the origins and development of the Euromarkets in London from the 1950s onwards. This process saw the City transform itself from being the centre of an international banking and payments system based on sterling as an international trading and reserve currency, to an international banking centre based largely on the US dollar. Operated by foreign and domestic banks in London, the Eurodollar market was one in which non-sterling denominated currencies could be deposited and lent outside the exchange controls imposed on sterling. Most of the deposits were US dollars, arising from the combined effects of a US domestic policy that imposed a cap on saving interest rates; the US balance

---

[5] e.g. Patrick Minford, 'City's 'Big Bang' Helped Boost UK's Economy', *Daily Telegraph*, 13 April 2013; Heather Stewart and Simon Goodley, 'Big Bang's Shockwaves Left us with Today's Big Bust', *Guardian*, 9 October 2011. For a recent historical evaluation of 'Big Bang', see Bellringer and Michie, 'Big Bang in the City of London'.

of payments deficits of the 1950s, which increased external dollar hold-ings; the multinationalization of American firms that needed a means of transferring capital between their domestic and international sites; the unwillingness of Soviet bloc countries to hold their dollar deposits in banks on the US mainland (owing to the danger of their being frozen in the event of a diplomatic/military crisis); and the general post-war return to convertibility of European currencies.[6] These deposits were managed separately from the banks' sterling liabilities, and so conceptually existed 'offshore' and outside the exchange control restrictions that had been in place since the war and codified in the 1947 Exchange Control Act. The Eurodollar market grew rapidly in the 1960s, and evolved an additional international capital market known as the Eurobond market (taken together these are referred to simply as the Euromarkets). The success of these non-sterling markets divorced the City from its reliance on sterling as a trading and reserve currency, which enabled London to succeed as an entrepôt financial centre. The rise of the Euromarkets in London is viewed as the key explanatory reason for the City's ability to reassert its inter-national role in the post-war decades. This can be seen as a financial and economic process by which the market, responding rationally and effi-ciently to impediments on its free functioning, simply innovated a way around the restrictions of government barriers to the liberal international monetary order. London was able to oversee this process because of its inherited skills and institutions—including an informal regulatory structure.[7]

Alternatively, Eric Helleiner has suggested that the process was in fact encouraged and promoted by the British state itself. Rather than being seen as something that existed despite the strictures of social democratic states, the Eurodollar market was largely the product of deliberate efforts by Britain and the United States—with the former seeking to revive London as an international financial centre. Helleiner attributes this to a 'kind of hegemonic "lag"', and cites the fact that the Bank of England chose not to regulate the market to any significant degree and actively

---

[6] On the Euromarkets, see Baker and Collins, 'London as an International Banking Centre'; Geoffrey Bell, *The Eurodollar Market and the International Financial System* (London: Macmillan, 1973); Kathleen Burk (ed.), 'Witness Seminar on the Origins and Early Development of the Eurobond Market', *Contemporary European History*, 1/1 (1992), 65–87; E. W. Clendenning, *The Eurodollar Market* (Oxford: Oxford University Press, 1970); Paul Einzig, *The Euro-Dollar System* (London: Macmillan, 1964); Catherine Schenk, 'The Origins of the Eurodollar Market in London, 1955–63', *Explorations in Economic History*, 2 (1996), 1–19.

[7] Gary Burn, 'The State, the City, and the Euromarkets', *Review of International Political Economy*, 6/2 (1999), 226–7.

encouraged its growth.[8] The most in-depth historical analysis of the evolution of the Euromarkets has been produced by Gary Burn. Burn corrects Helleiner's simplistic conflation of the Bank of England and the British state. As is well understood, the Bank was as much an agent of the financial interests of the City as it was of the state. The Bank oversaw, encouraged, and legitimized the development of 'offshore' markets, yet did not do this with the explicit consent of successive governments. This escapes the narrow, technocratic, and market-centric explanation, yet Burn does not fall into Helleiner's state-centric position. Therefore, for Burn, the market dynamic operated through the unique institutional structure that governed the City, and permitted its expansion without any serious hindrance. This contrasts with the experience of financial centres in other nations. According to Burn, the process should be viewed instead as a deliberate effort to re-establish the pre-1931 freedoms afforded to the 'financial aristocracy', and to escape the constraints of the state.[9]

The historical accounts of how the City came to revive its international role through the Euromarkets have successfully challenged the *post hoc ergo propter hoc* reasoning that has embedded itself in many contemporary assumptions. They explain the process, and the mechanisms, through which revival occurred in a concrete historical setting. Importantly, Burn has shown that this process was not simply a naturally occurring phenomenon, but was the product of changing economic conditions and regulatory regimes that were filtered through the prism of a deliberate *political* project on behalf of the City's supporters working through the Bank of England. Yet there is a problem with Burn's account. His argument assumes that the process by which the City revived its international role occurred obscured from public view—conducted in the deliberate regulatory vacuum constructed by the Bank of England. This suggests that the rise of the international financial City was relatively frictionless, and that it did not impinge upon the wider public sphere. But where did the process of reinternationalization fit in contemporary public and political discourse? Was the resurgence of the City really absent? Given the nature of the social democratic model of economic management and its goals, encouraging and permitting the City to restore its pre-1931 liberal certainties should have been problematic. This chapter

---

[8] Eric Helleiner, 'Explaining the Globalization of Financial Markets: Bringing States back in', *Review of International Political Economy*, 2/2 (1995), 320; Eric Helleiner, *States and the Reemergence of Global Finance: From Bretton Woods to the 1990s* (Ithaca, NY: Cornell University Press, 1994).

[9] Gary Burn, *The Re-Emergence of Global Finance* (Basingstoke: Palgrave Macmillan, 2006); Burn, 'The State, the City, and the Euromarkets'.

argues that the resurgence of the City's international role was accompanied by a distinct political and public relations campaign that sought to persuade the state (of elected governments and civil servants) of the necessity and value of permitting the City to develop and expand its international activities. This campaign sought to legitimize the City's role according to the contemporary pressures of social democratic economic policy, and the constraints in which it was required to operate, in Britain. It attempted to argue the case for the City in terms of national economic benefit, and not simply the preferences of the City itself. It was not explicitly tied to the Euromarket phenomenon, though it was inevitably embedded in City's ongoing material reglobalization. It presented an argument for the City that did not conform to the assumption that its success was tied to the widespread use of sterling as a trading and reserve currency. Furthermore, it was embedded in a historical reconceptualization of the national economy that challenged the assumption that Britain was fundamentally *industrial* in nature by presenting evidence of its historic *commercial* and *financial* supremacy and importance.

THE CITY AND STERLING

The outbreak of the First World War destroyed the foundations upon which the City of London was permitted to operate as an international financial centre. The free movement of goods and capital was restricted and the gold standard was suspended. The interwar period was spent trying to revive these conditions, yet the financial crisis of 1931, in the context of new democratic pressures in Britain and Europe, pushed Britain back off the gold standard and saw trade barriers erected across the world. The merchant banks, traditionally focused on foreign trade and investment, were forced to operate within a much more restrictive environment of capital controls. The effect of the Second World War on the international City was to see these controls extended further, while the nation's foreign investments were sold to finance the war. The various markets operating in the City—capital and commodity—were heavily restricted. Victory in Europe left the City, and the British economy, severely damaged, but the attempt to revive London as a financial centre got underway almost immediately after hostilities had ceased. The British delegation to the Anglo-American talks over a loan to assist in the nation's post-war economic recovery were determined to restore the City to its former position as an international banking centre, with sterling as a key international currency. This was done with the support of the Attlee

Labour government.[10] Sterling and the international City were intimately entwined. Since its pre-1914 zenith, the role of sterling as an international reserve and trading currency was key to the City's global role. It provided a common, trusted, and stable currency upon which international transactions could take place, and ensured that such transactions took place in London. The 1931 crisis forced sterling off the gold standard, and in its wake emerged an informal group of nations that pegged their currencies to sterling (the 'sterling bloc'). This bloc was cemented by the war, and then formalized in the designation of 'scheduled territories' in 1947. The members of the bloc, as well as pegging their currency to sterling, maintained common exchange controls with the UK and maintained their national reserves in sterling. Within the sterling area, direct investment was permitted without formal request, and the sterling area nations were given privileged access to the London capital markets.[11] Following the aborted attempt to achieve full convertibility of sterling in 1947 (a condition of the post-war American loan), and the 30 per cent devaluation of the pound in 1949, the widely held presumption remained that the international role of the City depended directly on the strength of sterling. Without its international role—achievable only by committing to the maintenance of a high, fixed exchange rate—it was believed that the City would wither.[12] As Kynaston has noted, the strength of sterling and the sterling area was 'equated, automatically and unquestionably, with the strength of the City'.[13] The problem was that the pound was particularly exposed to volatility as a result of its wartime accumulation of debts ('sterling balances'). At the end of the war these amounted to five times the level of the UK foreign-exchange reserves, which meant that they could not be immediately liquidated. This mismatch of foreign liabilities to reserves was not resolved and remained a threat to sterling, as, in the event that confidence was lost, the balances could be run down and threaten the currency's value.[14]

From the mid-1950s the value of Britain's commitment to retaining sterling's international role, and to the sterling area, was increasingly questioned. The economist A. C. L. Day, writing in 1954 on the future of sterling, queried the 'wisdom of directing our efforts to maintaining and developing sterling's position as an international currency'.[15] In doing so

[10] Ingham, *Capitalism Divided?*, 203.
[11] Catherine Schenk, *Britain and the Sterling Area: From Devaluation to Convertibility in the 1950s* (London: Routledge, 1994), 8–12.
[12] Catherine Schenk, *The Decline of Sterling: Managing the Retreat of an International Currency, 1945–1992* (Cambridge: Cambridge University Press, 2010), 207.
[13] Kynaston, *The City of London*, iv. 4.
[14] Schenk, *Britain and the Sterling Area*, 11.
[15] A. C. L. Day, *The Future of Sterling* (Oxford: Clarendon Press, 1954), 1–2.

he challenged the retention of London as the 'chief pivot of the world payments', arguing that the strains imposed by such a commitment were larger than Britain could endure.[16] This argument against the maintenance of sterling was developed further by Andrew Shonfield, the economic editor of the *Observer*, in his 1958 book entitled *British Economic Policy since the War*. Shonfield argued, in the light of the apparently poor performance of the British economy in the preceding decade, and the tendency for growth to come in fits and starts according to inconsistent government policy, that the weakness of the economy could be attributed to the combined effects of excessive foreign investment, inflated overseas government expenditure, and the adherence to maintaining sterling's role. The sterling area, and the official desire for the pound to be widely employed as a trading currency, imposed a heavy burden on the British balance of payments. The effect was to prevent the steady growth of domestic investment vital for improving the nation's productive capacities and ability to export goods that might strengthen the weak balance of payments position. Shonfield's view reflected the norms of domestic economic policy set immediately after the war. He argued:

> the more extensively sterling is used in international trade and payments, the more Britain is exposed to speculative flurries... Each time they are countered by crisis measures of restriction, bearing inevitably on the investment programme as the biggest and easiest target immediately in sight, and the result is that British industrial development is held up again for another couple of years or so. In retrospect, the enormous effort made by the British authorities since the war to encourage the ever wider use of sterling in international trade payments appears an extraordinarily hazardous venture.[17]

The balance of payments was the perennial problem facing the post-war British economy. It was the central indicator of economic performance and it was the key goal of successive governments from the end of the war until the mid-1970s to overcome its almost constant deficit. As described in the Introduction to this book, Tomlinson has demonstrated that the post-1945 Labour government asserted the absolute necessity of increasing the nation's manufactured exports in order to finance its imports. This approach was shaped by practical constraints (most notably the wartime loss of foreign income), as well as by Labour's inherent bias towards industrial production—part moral and cultural; part a function of the need to ensure full employment; and part a function of the party's need to

---

[16] Ibid. 6.
[17] Andrew Shonfield, *British Economic Policy since the War* (Harmondsworth: Penguin Books, 1958), 151.

appease its industrial electoral base. The Attlee government's approach to solving the balance of payments problem, through the expansion and modernization of manufacturing industry, subsequently formed a central component of the post-war governing consensus.[18] From the late 1950s, as worries about national economic decline grew in response to the impressive catch-up performance of continental competitor nations, the belief in the need to expand and modernize industry became even more pronounced. The Conservative Party's move towards indicative planning in the early 1960s, and its more thoroughgoing application by the post-1964 Wilson governments, exemplified this.

WILLIAM M. CLARKE AND THE CITY'S INVISIBLE EARNINGS

The seemingly existential threat posed to the City of London by the growing scepticism about maintaining sterling's international status at the end of the 1950s provoked the journalist William Clarke to mount a defence of the City. Born in Lancashire in 1922, Clarke was a grammar-school boy who had interrupted his undergraduate degree in History at the University of Manchester to become an RAF flying instructor in Canada during the war. On return to university he switched to study economics and subsequently became a financial journalist at the *Manchester Guardian*. In 1955, after two years at *The Times*, he became its City editor.[19] It was during his time in this role that Clarke published his first book entitled *The City's Invisible Earnings: How London's Skill Serves the World and Brings Profit to Britain*.[20] Essentially a short pamphlet, rather than a full-length book, it was the third publication of the Institute of Economic Affairs (IEA)—an organization established in 1955 with the express purpose of championing liberal economics and free market principles, and which was later to be feted for its role in the ideological overthrow of the post-war social democratic 'consensus' via its influence on Margaret Thatcher's Conservative governments.[21]

The sterling crisis in the summer of 1957 had inspired Clarke to write the pamphlet. Despite the nation running a balance of payments surplus,

---

[18] Tomlinson, 'Balanced Accounts?'.

[19] 'Obituary: William Clarke', *Daily Telegraph*, 26 May 2011; Robert Pringle, 'William Clarke Obituary', *Guardian*, 1 June 2011; David Kynaston, 'Chronicler of London Finance who Made Invisibles Real', *Financial Times*, 6 May 2011.

[20] William M. Clarke, *The City's Invisible Earnings: How London's Financial Skill Serves the World and Brings Profit to Britain* (London: Institute of Economic Affairs, 1958).

[21] Cockett, *Thinking the Unthinkable*, 122–200; Jackson, 'The Think-Tank Archipelago'.

sterling was exposed to speculative pressure that had forced the Bank of England to deplete its dollar holdings in defence of the parity. Bank rate was raised from 5 to 7 per cent—the highest it had been since 1921—and planned increases in public-sector investment were curbed.[22] In the wake of this, the City of London had, in Clarke's words, come in for a 'good deal of critical discussion' in which its role 'as the centre of this unique payments system, underwent a searching examination'.[23] As already noted, it had led many to question whether it was 'worth all the trouble of acting as the sterling area's banker and as the centre of an international payments system' if crises could occur regardless of economic fundamentals. Indeed, in the preface to *The City's Invisible Earnings*, the financial journalist and regular IEA contributor Harold Wincott identified that the events of September 1957 had generated the notion that the City was 'a liability, not an asset' because 'the good that honest toilers, working with their hands, have done [to generate a surplus in the balance of payments] can be undone by the machinations of speculators'.[24] More fundamentally, the change in Britain's post-war position from a creditor to a debtor nation suggested that, 'valuable though the City's institutions have been in the past, their current earnings are insufficient recompense for the risks inherent in trying to continue to act as the world's financial centre on inadequate reserves'.[25] Shonfield and Day argued that it would be better to escape this arrangement, curtail Britain's overseas commitments, and accept that the nation could no longer afford such an international status. The natural corollary of this was that the City of London would have to accept its diminished role as an unexceptional domestic financial centre, forced to disengage from international business as its trading networks were dismantled and its currency devalued. Clarke did not agree, and set out in the book to demonstrate the value of the City to the national economy. In this he simply attempted to calculate (or recalculate in response to recent estimates of a House of Commons answer given in February 1957) how much foreign exchange the various components of the City generated in their international activities—their 'invisible earnings'.[26] In this context 'the City', for Clarke, was defined as the institutions, organizations, and markets engaged in banking, insurance, commodities, shipping and air charter, and foreign investment.[27]

---

[22] Capie, *The Bank of England*, 91–5.   [23] Clarke, *City's Invisible Earnings*, 15.
[24] Harold Wincott, 'Preface', in ibid. 9.   [25] Ibid.
[26] Clarke, *City's Invisible Earnings*, 92; Parliamentary Debates, Commons, 5th ser., vol. 564, cols 77 (5 February 1957).
[27] As discussed in the Introduction to this book, the term 'the City' is subject to context-dependent shifts in meaning. In this chapter, 'the City' will be used as William Clarke understood it—an international financial centre providing a range of financial and

In the balance of payments net invisibles are classified as income generated by services provided to non-residents, minus payments to non-residents for services, plus income generated overseas.[28] When Clarke published his first book, the concept of 'invisible earnings' was not new. According to W. A. P. Manser, the term originally came into use during the debates over the balance of payments in the latter decades of the nineteenth century, and it had been adopted by the Board of Trade as an official term in the 1930s.[29] At the height of the City's international role in the nineteenth century, Britain had consistently produced a large 'invisible' surplus, which kept the balance of payments in overall surplus—bridging the deficit in its visible balance. This invisible income was primarily generated by the commercial and financial services that the City provided to global trading networks, and to a lesser extent from interest and receipts earned through capital export. This norm had been eroded in the interwar period, and then subsequently devastated by the Second World War. The collapse of the reconstructed gold standard, the break-up of international trading networks, the loss of foreign assets during the war, and the destruction of much of the City's physical infrastructure during the Blitz were responsible for this. In the immediate aftermath of the war, as the government's policy for national economic revival became focused on increasing domestic industrial production in order to increase exports and thus to solve the massive balance of payments deficit, invisible income largely disappeared from public discourse.[30] Even before the war, the notion of invisibles had not embedded itself in public understanding of the economy, largely because of the lack of statistics available on the subject. Before 1946 these had not been published officially at all.[31] Clarke's book on the City was notable not for its discovery of anything uniquely new, but for its attempt to popularize the concept of private invisible income and its production in the City. Clarke acknowledged that the post-war City was not entirely the same as that which had preceded the Second World War. The export of capital to the rest of the world, which had been so significant a part of the City's historic banking operations, had all but evaporated following the years of government control and declining surplus funds for investment. What capital the nation did export was increasingly undertaken outside the

commercial services to the world economy. We must recognize, however, that Clarke's definition was a rhetorical device that sought to emphasize the City's international activities.

[28] A. E. Holmans, 'Invisible Earnings', in D. J. Robertson and L. C. Hunter (eds.), *The British Balance of Payments* (Edinburgh: London: Oliver and Boyd, 1966), 42.

[29] W. A. P. Manser, *Britain in Balance* (Harmondsworth: Penguin, 1973), 15.

[30] Tomlinson, 'Balanced Accounts?', 867.   [31] Manser, *Britain in Balance*, 50.

traditional City channels through the internal transfer of funds from domestic firms to their overseas operations.[32] Most importantly, the nation had been transformed from net creditor to net debtor.[33] Yet, despite these fundamental changes, Clarke observed that the City still had the capacity to play an international role. He wrote that,

> in spite of the decline of one of the City's main functions—the raising of long-term overseas capital—it is remarkable how well it has maintained its lead as a centre of foreign trade financing. The machinery for both *settling* and *financing* international payments is still intact. In spite of all the difficulties of the past decade, sterling continues to be used to settle 40 per cent of the world's visible trade and an even greater share of its invisible transactions. This is the basis on which the City's institutions are still functioning.[34]

Clarke's primary argument throughout the short text was that the City still had the capacity to be a success even within the new climate. The world's largest international insurance market, a host of commodity markets progressively freed from wartime restrictions in the 1940s and 1950s, the bullion market, shipping, and the chartering of planes in the City all brought income to Britain. As such they should be championed, and further decontrolled, for the sake of the nation because, 'in spite of great progress in the past five or six years, the City of London [was] still far from working to capacity'.[35] Clarke acknowledged that the success of these activities did not directly rely on sterling's international role, which raised the question of why these activities could not be encouraged, while international banking was left to wither? This was the suggestion put forward by Shonfield, who argued that much of the City's strength, particularly in insurance, would not be adversely affected by rolling back the use of sterling. He had estimated in 1958 that perhaps £40 million worth of earnings would be lost by 'putting some armour on the pound sterling and withdrawing the country from a number of activities, which render its economic life intolerably exposed to international pressures'—but that £125 million of foreign-exchange earnings generated by the City would remain intact.[36] Clarke thought this inadvisable, because the City operated as a whole system in which each component relied on the banking and discount market institutions at its heart.[37] You could not abandon some activities and assume that others would remain unaffected. Furthermore, many of the ancillary activities still relied upon the stability and ease of

---

[32] Clarke, *City's Invisible Earnings*, 23–4, 85.   [33] Ibid. 23.   [34] Ibid. 24.
[35] Ibid. 98.   [36] Shonfield, *British Economic Policy*, 158–9.
[37] Clarke, *City's Invisible Earnings*, 97.

international settlement that sterling provided.[38] This aspect of Clarke's argument was not well developed, and did not go much beyond asserting the importance of sterling and international banking with limited evidence.

Clarke's argument set out the simple case for why the City was valuable to the nation—it earned income abroad, totalling an estimated £150 million per annum, which contributed to the balance of payments.[39] Deregulation and permitting the operation of the City's institutions and mechanisms—as had occurred progressively under the Conservatives since 1951—was vital to continued success in this area, as was maintaining sterling as an international currency. However, despite the mercantilist bent of Clarke's primary argument, he remained idealistically committed to the City's central importance to the world economy. In the concluding section of the book he stated:

> the true measure of the City's value is not just this invisible income... London is still providing the mechanism for a large share of the world's finance and commerce. Surprising as it may seem in a decade in which the pound has remained officially inconvertible, no other financial centre has even attempted to take over the mantle from London. Whilst this is not an altruistic role, the City does play an invaluable part in creating a truly international society in which commercial co-operation and economic inter-dependence loom larger than national rivalries. In addition to the fees and commissions from their services, these institutions are also providing the basis on which the United Kingdom can develop an expanding multilateral trade with the rest of the world. It is basically on these grounds rather than the size of its invisible earnings, large as they are, that the City of London fulfils itself.[40]

In 1965 Clarke expanded his core argument into a more substantive and detailed analysis of the City's activities and their earning power. Once again published by the IEA, though also reprinted by Penguin as part of its Pelican series in 1967, *The City in the World Economy* was essentially a longer, more-detailed, version of *The City's Invisible Earnings*. The top line argument of the book was that the City earned an estimated annual £185 million in foreign exchange, representing an almost 25 per cent increase on his last measure.[41] In this extended work, Clarke engaged more explicitly with the fundamental questions:

> Can London maintain its position as an international financial centre, when Britain is no longer the top industrial nation and no longer commands vast economic resources? More important, should it?[42]

---

[38] Ibid. 101.   [39] Ibid. 93–5.   [40] Ibid. 103.
[41] William Clarke, *The City and the World Economy* (Harmondsworth: Penguin, 1967; first published London: Institute of Economic Affairs, 1965).
[42] Ibid. 10–11.

And:

> whether the City of London, still regarded by many as the world's leading financial centre, can play as useful and profitable an overseas role in the future as it has over the past 150 years, without undermining economic expansion at home? Is the City simply another anachronism left over from Britain's age of power or can it still serve a useful purpose? And even if it can, is the effort worthwhile?[43]

This second book was written in the shadow of increasingly commonplace sterling crises, which had taken place following the return to full convertibility in 1958. These had exposed the City to ever greater criticism, which made the urgency of defending its ongoing existence even more substantial. This was pertinent because the City itself, according to Clarke, was 'not the most articulate of places', with 'a natural tendency...to dwell overmuch on its illustrious past'. Clarke understood the need to justify its ongoing role according to the contemporary requirements of economic management.[44] As he had acknowledged in 1958, the debate over the City primarily centred on its reliance upon the status of sterling as a trading and reserve currency. In his previous publication, he simply asserted the necessity of sterling in underpinning the various activities of the City—whether immediately relevant or not. Yet, in the years of subsequent crisis Clarke was forced into a more substantive assessment. Acknowledging Shonfield et al.'s critique of the damaging impact of the pound's status, Clarke repudiated the assumptions (both pro- and anti-City) that the maintenance of a strong pound within a strong international monetary system was vital for the success of the City. For Clarke, this was an inaccurate faith that a return to pre-1914 currency arrangements would bring success on a similar level—an argument that mistook 'the shadow for the substance'.[45] Though he rejected the notion that all the nation's economic difficulties of 'stop-go' growth could be attributed to the check on expansion engendered by the sterling commitment, Clarke favoured the managed creation of some form of new reserve currency. What was important, in this analysis, was that the City's strength did not emerge from its currency alone but that it was the skills and institutions of the City that were the root of its success. He stated:

> There is little doubt that the links between the international role of the pound and the City's activities have been over-emphasized in the past... Most discussions on this topic seems to begin from the wrong end. It is not so much that the City's earnings depend on the holding of pounds in London, though they do, but rather that the City's services lead to the

---

[43] Ibid. 15.   [44] Ibid. 10–11.   [45] Ibid. 184.

holding of pounds . . . It is the City's usefulness both to Britain and to the world that attracts pounds to London, not the prestige surrounding a reserve currency.[46]

He told the Royal Institute of International Affairs in 1966 that the key conclusion to be taken from his argument was that the various sectors of the City did not rely on whether sterling was an international reserve currency, but whether it was a freely convertible currency. Shipping, commodity, and insurance markets did not depend on the *prestige* of sterling; they merely required 'currency freedom' to flourish.[47] That is not to say that stability of sterling was not helpful to many of the institutions in the City. In a letter to the *Financial Times* in 1972, following the emergence of the Eurodollar market (of which Clarke was a keen observer—he is said to have coined the 'Eurodollar' term), he made his position clear:

> [The City] has, in effect, been moving towards a Eurocurrency standard. In these circumstances the City would, in my view, lose little from a running down of Britain's reserve currency role, provided that currency convertibility were maintained and provided that the negotiations were handled with a knowledge of existing City activities. But the City would gain immeasurably from any moves designed to bring greater stability to the pound itself . . .[48]

The purpose of Clarke's two publications on the contribution of the City to the British economy was to challenge the 'declinist' narrative, which saw its continued existence as a drain and limitation upon the British economy.[49] The City gave Britain a significant role on the international economic stage by providing 'the basis on which the United Kingdom [could] develop an expanding multilateral trade with the rest of the world'.[50] Yet it also earned a significant degree of invisible income, which positively contributed to the nation's perennially weak balance of payments. The logic of this perspective was that greater liberalization of the City—allowing it to engage with the rapidly growing international economy—was for the benefit of the nation as a whole. This brought the interests of the City directly in line with the interests of the country—a far more legitimate argument for freeing the City than the desire to return to the nineteenth-century glory days of economic liberalism. Indeed, Clarke argued that 'both the country and the City . . . should be pulling in the

---

[46] Ibid. 244–5.

[47] BOE: 7A1/1, William M. Clarke, 'How Far Does the City Depend on Sterling: Study Group', *Royal Institute of International Affairs*, 21 November 1966.

[48] William Clarke, 'Letter: The City's Movement towards a Eurocurrency Standard', *Financial Times*, 10 November 1972; David Kynaston, 'Chronicler of London who Made Invisibles Real', *Financial Times*, 6 May 2011.

[49] Tomlinson, 'Thrice Denied'.   [50] Clarke, *City's Invisible Earnings*, 102–3.

same direction. Government policies on exchange control towards trade and currency problems generally should be pursued because they benefit the country, not the City.'[51] Significantly, Clarke made the case for a City that was reliant not on sterling, but on freedom to operate. This accepted the growing critique of the role of sterling, but sought to ensure that the institutions of the City were not lost as the international role of the pound was demoted. Clarke argued a new case for the City, which responded to the constraints of domestic economic priorities, which, after a brief lull during the years of Tory government, became increasingly significant as criticisms of 1950s political economy grew.

What exactly is the relevance of William Clarke, and his arguments, to our understanding of the economic politics of post-war Britain? In this we are faced with what Roger Middleton has described as 'the generic problem facing all contemporary historians of thought and policy . . . what is the influence of any one individual and/or work?'[52] Of course, as a senior reporter for *The Times*, Clarke's views would have carried more weight than most (at the time of writing his second book he had become the paper's financial and industrial affairs correspondent).[53] The fact that his second work was republished so soon after its original print run, and this time in a popular paperback format available for general consumption, also ensured that he played an important role in the public debate over the British economy in this period. It stands as a significant contribution to the contemporary debate, which has, in historical accounts of the period, been dominated by Shonfield and other 'declinists'. Yet more significant is the fact that Clarke, rather than operating simply as a writer and journalist, translated his arguments into a distinct public relations and political campaign on behalf of the City, which gained a great deal of influence over public affairs in the subsequent two decades.

THE COMMITTEE ON INVISIBLE EXPORTS

In 1964 the Secretary of State for Industry and Trade and President of the Board of Trade, Edward Heath, established the British National Export Council (BNEC). Its purpose was

> to initiate, guide and inspire export efforts in all markets; to advise upon the formation of bodies to foster British exports in particular areas of the world;

---

[51] Clarke, *The City and the World Economy*, 245.

[52] Roger Middleton, 'Brittan on Britain: "The Economic Contradictions of Democracy" Redux', *Historical Journal*, 54/4 (2011), 1141.

[53] 'Obituary: William Clarke', *Daily Telegraph*, 26 May 2011.

to provide a means of co-ordination between such bodies and of the country's export effort generally; and to provide the necessary finance and services for this purpose.[54]

The BNEC was part of the expansion of the state's role in encouraging trade and economic growth—an example of the shift to a more interventionist, indicative planning approach to economic policymaking engendered by widespread concerns that domestic industry was failing to keep pace with its continental counterparts. William Clarke's attempts to popularize the concept of invisible earnings in the late 1950s and early 1960s paid off when in 1966, a year after the publication of his second book for the IEA, he was appointed by the BNEC as the director of a study into Britain's invisible earnings. This investigation was to be undertaken by a committee consisting of fourteen of the most senior businessmen operating in the City, including—for example—the chairman of the British Export Houses Association and the chairman of Lloyd's insurance brokers (see Box 4.1). The committee, which was entitled the Committee on Invisible Exports (COIE), operated under the chairmanship of Sir Thomas Bland (deputy chairman of Barclays bank), with Cyril Kleinwort (chairman of Kleinwort Benson) as his deputy.[55] Its purpose was to examine the 'invisible element within the balance of payments and to consider ways in which invisible exports could be promoted and stimulated'.[56] Where Clarke had previously focused on the earnings of the City alone, this study was nominally set up to examine all invisible earnings from businesses and industries operating in all sectors and regions of the British economy. Therefore, the committee, despite remaining fundamentally rooted in the City (in terms of its membership at least), was required to look beyond the Square Mile in its attempts to calculate the size of the nation's invisible income. This led the committee to approach industries and organizations that supported the balance of payments without the physical export of goods, such as the Royal Institute of British Architects and the Casino Association. The committee even approached The Beatles, whose song and image rights would have been significant invisible earners, for information on their income. The band was not forthcoming, which suggests that they were not particularly interested in the nation's balance of payments worries (during 1967 the band recorded and released two albums (*Sgt Pepper's Lonely Hearts Club Band* and *Magical Mystery Tour*), discovered Eastern spiritualism, and lost their manager to a drug

---

[54] Parliamentary Debates, Commons, 5th ser., vol. 699, cols 32–9 (20 July 1964).

[55] '"Invisible" Exports Body Formed', *Financial Times*, 26 May 1966, 8.

[56] Financial Advisory Panel on Exports (British National Export Council), *Britain's Invisible Earnings: Report of the Committee on Invisible Exports* (London, 1967), 9.

Box 4.1. **Members of the Committee on Invisible Exports**

Appointed June 1966

Sir Thomas Bland, TD, DL (Chairman)
  Chairman, Financial Advisory Panel on Exports
  Deputy Chairman, Barclays Bank Ltd
C. H. Kleinwort, Esq. (Deputy Chairman)
  Deputy Chairman, Financial Advisory Panel on Exports
  Chairman, Kleinwort Benson Ltd
Alex Abel Smith, Esq., TD
  Director, Kleinwort Benson Ltd
D. W. Beharrell, Esq.
  Chairman, British Export Houses Association
F. B. Bolton, Esq., MC
  President, Chamber of Shipping of the UK
Sir George Bolton, KCMG
  Chairman, Bank of England and South America Ltd
Sir Charles Denman, Bt MC
  Chairman, Tennant Guaranty Ltd
The Right Hon. The Viscount Harcourt, KCMG, OBE
  Managing Director, Morgan Grenfell & Co. Ltd
E. J. W. Hellmuth, Esq.
  Director and Deputy Chief General Manager (International), Midland
Bank Ltd
The Right Hon. Lord Kilmarnock, MBE
  Chairman, The Baltic Exchange
R. E. Liddiard, Esq.
  Chairman, British Federation of Commodity Associations
F. E. P. Sandilands, Esq. CBE
  Chairman, British Insurance Association
R.W. Sturge, Esq.
  Chairman, Lloyd's
P. H. Swan, Esq. DSO, DFC
  Member of the Council of the London Stock Exchange
R. L. Wills, Esq., CBE, MC
  President, Association of British Chambers of Commerce

---

overdose).[57] While the committee remained dominated by senior City figures with an undoubted interest in promoting their own successful contribution to the national economy via the income they generated, the committee obtained the status of a semi-official body through its

---

[57] BOE: 7A1/2, 'Minutes', 23 May 1967; Robert Head, 'Spotlight on the Exporters who Sell you Things you Can't See: The Invisible Men', *Daily Mirror*, 19 October 1967.

association with the BNEC. Furthermore, it operated with direct ties to other official bodies of the state. The investigation was assisted throughout, in its statistical analysis at least, by the Treasury, the Board of Trade, the Central Statistical Office, and the nationalized Bank of England. Inevitably, this gave the committee a great deal of legitimacy and influence.

'A COMMERCIAL AND FINANCIAL NATION'

After an investigation of over a year, the COIE published its findings in October 1967. With the assistance of a newly formed consultancy firm called the Economists Advisory Group (EAG), led by Professors E. Victor Morgan and John H. Dunning, the committee found that all previous estimates of UK invisible earnings had been significantly underestimated.[58] The committee reported that in 1966 private invisible receipts totalled £2,823 million (compared with £5,100 million for 'visible' exports and re-exports). Thomas Bland, in his preface to the report, reiterated the value of these sizeable earnings in contributing to 'our' (Britain's) standard of living through their contribution to the balance of payments.[59] The report asserted that the contemporary importance of invisible income was not a new phenomenon. In fact, the committee's historical analysis showed that, whereas Britain had achieved a visible trade surplus in only 7 out of the previous 175 years, it had maintained a continuous surplus on invisibles.[60] This historical account permitted the committee to promote a redefinition of the British economy that challenged the industrial tendency of contemporary discourse (embodied in the Labour government's National Plan), stating that 'Britain is and has been for well over a century and a half as much a commercial and financial nation as a manufacturing nation'.[61] At a time in which recurrent balance of payments crises continued to disrupt the stability of the post-war British economy, causing endless consternation to the Labour government, the success of invisible earnings seemingly offered the solution to this intractable problem. The report demonstrated that Britain had historically buoyant, yet much-neglected, export sectors on which future stability and prosperity could be based. British economic success, it could be concluded, should be sought in permitting invisibles to grow. Particularly

---

[58] Financial Advisory Panel on Exports, *Britain's Invisible Earnings*, 7–8; Morgan, alongside other EAG members Sir Alan Peacock, Dennis Lees, and Jack Wiseman, were all members of the advisory council of the Institute of Economic Affairs—Alan Peacock, 'A Career as an Economic Advisor', 10 May 2011 <http://www.iea.org.uk/blog/a-career-as-an-economic-adviser> (accessed: 22 March 2012).

[59] Financial Advisory Panel on Exports, *Britain's Invisible Earnings*, introduction.

[60] Ibid. 15–19.   [61] Ibid. 19.

important was the fact that, at a time in which the economy was widely perceived to be in decline owing to its relatively slow record of economic growth in comparison with competitor European nations, Britain was the second best performing country in the world when it came to invisibles. With world invisible trade showing major expansion in recent years, the Britain trailed only the US in gross invisible receipts and its net invisible surplus. Third-placed Italy earned under half the amount of invisible income of Britain.[62]

This new historical narrative, in which the invisible earnings contribution spearheaded by the City acted as the saviour of the British economy, was a powerful rhetorical tool to reconceptualize the way in which the British economy could be 'thought about'. During a decade in which industrial growth in output and employment was the key aim of economic policy, the committee's conclusions challenged the prevailing orthodoxy, which viewed Britain as an industrial nation. This perspective was developed further by the economist W. A. P. Manser. Writing in 1971, he set out to explain more explicitly, and with less political sensitivity, than the invisibles committee (but on the basis of its findings), 'the simple fact that the deficit on trade in goods is not new. We have had it all through our history. Through prosperity and privation, through peace and war, victory and defeat, century after century, this country has run a continuous visible deficit.'[63] In *Britain in Balance*, published by the IEA, Manser argued that Britain's historic economic success should be traced back not to the Industrial Revolution of the eighteenth century, but to the expansion of seaborne trade in the sixteenth century. International trade brought merchanting, which brought insurance, which expanded the need for credit and banking, and encouraged the expansion of overseas investment. Since the mid-nineteenth century, food, raw materials, and semi-processed goods had all been vital imports necessary for industrial expansion, generating a deficit that was financed by the private invisible surplus. Invisibles were the 'essence of our economy'.[64] The committee was highly successful in publicizing this historical reassessment. The ex-Chancellor of the Exchequer Reginald Maudling claimed that 'this will come as a shock to those who, like myself, always thought that in the last century it was the exports of British textiles and British machinery and British coal that built up the overseas investments from which we now draw so much of our invisible income'.[65] Even the Duke of Edinburgh (or his official speechwriter at least) was persuaded, as he stated that 'these invisible earnings seem to be particularly suited to the British character'.[66] What is particularly of note

[62] Ibid. 25–33.   [63] Manser, *Britain in* Balance, 4.
[64] Ibid. 33–9.   [65] Quoted in ibid. 50.
[66] Quoted in Julian Critchley, 'British Achievements: The City and its Expertise Succeed in a Changed Role', *Financial Times*, 17 November 1969, 11.

is the way in which the City and invisibles were made synonymous in the committee's report. As a 'group of commercial and financial institutions' engaged in insurance, merchanting, brokerage, and banking, the City was responsible for an estimated £205 million–£225 million of a total national private invisible net income of £609 million.[67] Though this was clearly a very substantial contribution, the report—which was produced by the City's elite representatives—placed most of its emphasis on the importance of the City. 'The City' and 'invisibles' were deliberately conflated. This was continued by Manser, who claimed that the effect of the report was to generate a 'fancy that!' reaction outside Whitehall—'if it had not been for those chaps in the City, where would we be?'[68]

On the basis of these findings, the committee made a large number of recommendations. The most basic was for the Central Statistical Office and Bank of England to undertake regular enquiries into the size of British private invisible earnings and for the establishment of a permanent organization tasked with 'keeping a watch on the whole field of invisibles'.[69] Another proposal was for invisible exporters to be made eligible for the Queen's Award to Industry—thus attempting to equate service provision with the general notion of industry, and therefore to break down the division that gave priority to manufacturing over services.[70] Most importantly, the report argued that the most promising means of increasing invisible earnings would be to establish favourable levels of taxation and to remove 'other obstacles' that hampered growth in invisible sectors. This notably focused on ways in which the effects of the Selective Employment Tax (SET—discussed later in this chapter) could be mitigated, and the extension of the 'Export Rebate Scheme' for invisible income earners.[71] The report stressed that the recent increases in invisible earnings over the previous fifteen years could be attributed to the removal of restrictions rather than the 'provision of positive incentives'.[72] The committee therefore pressed for a 're-examination' of exchange controls and for a removal of those that provided 'no particular defence to the balance-of-payments and the pound'. It is important to note that this did not amount to a campaign for the complete abolition of controls—largely because of a conscious effort on behalf of the committee to 'avoid dogmatic recommendations' and to refrain from making demands with overtly 'political overtones.'[73] But the principle was clear—invisible earnings were to the benefit of all

[67] Financial Advisory Panel on Exports, *Britain's Invisible Earnings*, 187–93.
[68] Manser, *Britain in Balance*, 50.
[69] Financial Advisory Panel on Exports, *Britain's Invisible Earnings*, 266.
[70] Ibid. 246.   [71] Ibid. 241–6.   [72] Ibid. 237.
[73] Ibid. 66; BOE: 7A1/4, 'Minutes', 12 July 1967.

through their contribution to the balance of payments, and thus allowing invisible exporters the freedom to operate with fewer controls and reduced tax disincentives was imperative.

On publication in October 1967, the report received wide coverage in the broadsheet press—presumably helped by Clarke's journalistic background. William Keegan wrote a full-page article for the *Financial Times* that provided a detailed summary of the report's findings; as did Peter Jay in *The Times*.[74] The former essentially regurgitated an abbreviated version of the report. Yet the report also captured the imagination of business and City editors in the popular press, likely to have been attracted by the mysterious notion of 'invisibles.' Commentators in the right-wing dailies recognized the value of the report in countering left-wing 'suspicion and hostility' towards the City.[75] For Patrick Sergeant, the City editor of the *Daily Mail*, the report successfully 'exploded' the historical critique originated by Karl Marx and William Morris in the nineteenth century that 'services' were a vice compared with the virtues of physical production.[76] Harold Wincott, Clarke's earlier collaborator and an established defender of economic freedoms in the City, used the report to claim that the Labour Party in government did not understand invisible exports, because it was a party that remained wedded to the notion that 'unless you go home with dirty hands and an aching back you're not really a worker'.[77] This view was supported by Manser, who argued that the post-war Attlee government had deliberately chosen not to encourage the growth of invisibles. Manser wrote that

> Labour party members really did not like our apparent dependence on invisible exports, particularly in the form they were imagined to take. If they were the product of financiers' paper-pushing in the City, the profits of men 'making money out of money', then socialists would rather do without them. Lloyd's, the Stock Exchange, merchant banks, discount houses, and the like, had high places in the roll of Socialist demonology. Much better to base the country's international solvency on the healthy product of sinewy labour in the mines or factories. In the old aphorism: 'If it doesn't hurt when you drop it on your foot, it isn't an export.' Little in this has changed in Labour Party mythology ever since . . . [78]

[74] William Keegan, 'Major Survey of Britain's Invisible Earnings', *Financial Times*, 19 October 1967; Peter Jay, 'Surpluses on Neglected Invisibles Are Crucial', *The Times*, 19 October 1967.

[75] BOE: 7A1/5, Patrick Ellis, 'Praise for Invisible Earners', *Daily Express*, 19 October 1967.

[76] Patrick Sergeant, 'Help the Invisible Men', *Daily Mail*, 19 October 1967.

[77] Harold Wincott, 'The Old Man of the Sea on Britain's Shoulders', *Financial Times*, 24 October 1967.

[78] Manser, *Britain in Balance*, 63.

Furthermore, in keeping with the notion of a consensus amongst the parties, Manser argued that 'such was the force of the early post-war statement of policy and the apparent economic logic of the need for exports, that you will hear views little different in Conservative Central Office'.[79] For right-wing journalists, the image of Britain's economy as being service based, specializing in trade and commerce, was deeply attractive. However, it was not only the right-wing press that was drawn to the report's findings, as the Labour-supporting *Daily Mirror* also praised the 'invisible men' identified by the committee as 'the unsung heroes in our economic war'.[80]

Despite providing administrative and statistical support in the preparation of the report, the response of officials at the Treasury, and in some quarters at the Bank of England, was generally more muted. Kit McMahon, an advisor to the Governors of the Bank at the time, expressed concern that the report had a 'slight air of whitewashing' owing to the fact that the committee's make-up was so 'exclusively "City"'.[81] An unidentified Bank official concurred with McMahon, believing that a 'little more *self*-criticism would have been a good thing' for the City figures who produced the report.[82] Meanwhile, the Treasury appears to have felt somewhat aggrieved by the fact that the committee sought willingly to give the impression that they had 'discovered' the invisible account. This suggested that, in their constant battle to strengthen the balance of payments by boosting physical exports, governments had embarrassingly missed the obvious solution.[83] In a letter to the Governors of the Bank of England, Derrick Layton, an advisor to the Bank's Economic Intelligence Department, retorted that discovering the invisible account was

> in a sense … precisely what they have done. Hitherto Government has put excessive emphasis on visible trade and has taken the private invisible surplus for granted. The Government and the informed public will not be able to ignore the importance and value of invisible exports after the publication of this Report.[84]

[79] Ibid. 64.
[80] BOE: 7A1/5, Robert Head, 'Spotlight on the Exporters who Sell Things you Can't See: The Invisible Men', *Daily Mirror*, 19 October 1967.
[81] BOE: 7A1/5, McMahon to the Governors, 'The Atlas Report', 19 September 1967.
[82] Ibid.
[83] BOE: 7A1/5, Layton to the Governors, 'The Atlas Committee's Report on Invisibles', 6 October 1967; Layton to the Governors, 'The Atlas Committee's Report on Invisibles',16 October 1967.
[84] BOE: 7A1/5, Layton to the Governors, 'The Atlas Committee's Report on Invisibles', 6 October 1967; Layton to the Governors, 'The Atlas Committee's Report on Invisibles', 16 October 1967; Capie, *Bank of England*, 720.

As already noted, the concept of invisibles was not new, but the report publicized and politicized them in a way that had been missing in contemporary discourse. Indeed, as Peter Jay said in his coverage of the report, this 'vital element... [had] been strangely neglected by academic students and government alike'.[85] More substantially, the Treasury expressed consternation at the fact that the report had explicitly compared the surplus of private invisible income with the larger deficit of invisibles generated by government overseas expenditure. The committee's approach challenged the government's traditional method of publishing the nation's invisible balance, which grouped the large government overseas deficit with private receipts (in 1966 the official statistics had recorded an invisible surplus of £92 million, but it would have been far larger if not for the drain of £457 million government expenditure abroad).[86] The logic of this was simple—if the state rolled back its foreign military and diplomatic commitments, the private invisible account would keep the balance of payments in permanent surplus. Layton reported to the Governors that the hostile reaction from the Treasury was due to a misinterpreted belief that the report was a 'deliberate attack on the government'. Layton thought this an unfair assessment of the committee's desire to demonstrate the positive contribution of private invisibles, though he acknowledged that this emerged only 'as a result of disentangling the Government and private elements in the invisibles account'. This conflict remained hidden from public view, as the Bank, in agreement with Harold Copeman at the Treasury, ensured that it did not become a 'public wrangle about the respective merits of Government and private invisibles'.[87] Yet, as Peter Jay put it in his analysis of the report, 'there is a theme running through the report, even if it is never fully explicit in the carefully objective prose. It is crudely and exaggeratedly put, that the City keeps the nation afloat in spite of the extravagance and folly of governments.'[88] In this area the report subtly, though not explicitly, aligned itself with Shonfield's 'overstretch' argument.[89] The less politically hamstrung Manser identified

---

[85] Peter Jay, 'Surpluses on Neglected Invisibles Are Crucial', *The Times*, 19 October 1967.

[86] William Keegan, 'Major Survey of Britain's Invisible Earnings', *Financial Times*, 19 October 1967.

[87] BOE: 7A1/5, Layton to the Governors, 'The Atlas Committee's Report on Invisibles', 6 October 1967; Layton to the Governors, 'The Atlas Committee's Report on Invisibles', 16 October 1967.

[88] Peter Jay, 'Surpluses on Neglected Invisibles Are Crucial', *The Times*, 19 October 1967.

[89] BOE: 7A1/5, Layton to the Governors, 'The Atlas Committee's Report on Invisibles', 6 October 1967; Layton to the Governors, 'The Atlas Committee's Report on Invisibles', 16 October 1967; Shonfield, *British Economic Policy*, 104.

government overseas expenditure as 'the real problem', and stated baldly that 'Britain does not run a commercial deficit; she runs a political and military deficit . . . If there were not Government spending, there would be no deficit, and no balance of payments problem.'[90]

The committee, conscious of its position, never made such an assertion—though it did not have to. In the light of the Bank's support, the Treasury grudgingly accepted that the government should welcome the report in public on the basis of its 'excellent statistical analysis'.[91] Meanwhile the report's significant impact on political and economic discourse was demonstrated by the fact that it sold out its entire first print run, and had to go to a second printing in February 1968.[92] Its first major effect was to enforce a change in the way invisibles were recorded in the official statistics (the annual 'Pink Book'), by splitting private and government invisible income. No longer was the private invisible surplus 'mopped up by the entries for Government spending'.[93] The importance of this change should not be underestimated. As Adam Tooze has argued, it is only through 'the gathering of statistics' that 'the abstract conception of the "national economy" is turned into objective reality'.[94] Thus the extraction and presentation of private invisibles in the official statistics changed the way in which the British economy was conceptualized and 'imagined'.

A PERMANENT COMMITTEE

Almost immediately after the successful publication of the report in October 1967, the decision was taken by the committee members to establish a permanent body that retained the same name and sought to work towards implementing the recommendations made.[95] Though Thomas Bland was unable to continue as chairman and was succeeded by his deputy, Cyril Kleinwort, William Clarke retained his role as Director.[96] The agenda of the committee was outlined at its second meeting in early 1968. The COIE sought 'to promote recognition of

---

[90] Manser, *Britain in Balance*, 24.
[91] BOE: 7A1/5, D. F. Hubback to Sir Denis Rickett, 'Britain's Invisible Earnings: Report of the Committee on Invisible Exports', 17 October 1967.
[92] 'New Printing of invisibles Report', *Financial Times*, 29 February 1968.
[93] Manser, *Britain in Balance*, 51, 54.
[94] Adam Tooze, 'Imagining National Economies: National and International Economic Statistics, 1900–1950', in Geoffrey Cubitt (ed.), *Imagining Nations* (Manchester: Manchester University Press, 1998), 214.
[95] BOE: 7A1/5, 'Financial Panel on Exports', 8 November 1967.
[96] 'Committee on Invisible Exports Formed', *Financial Times*, 10 February 1968, 14.

invisibles to U.K. balance-of-payments...to co-ordinate efforts to promote individual invisible services...[and] to help in promotion of "City" as a financial centre'.[97] This statement of purpose exemplifies the unique strategy of the committee. It was committed to invisibles in general (which were produced by a variety of economic activities performed across the country), but specifically sought to place the City of London at the centre of attention. In this the committee successfully conflated the concept of invisibles with the City in the public imagination, but also created a pressure group coalition of service exporters in which the City's institutions were presented as part of a broader constituency. Thomas Bland's introduction to the original report captured this most clearly:

> What has enabled this country to pay its way has been its 'invisible' earnings. The performance of a British play on Broadway, the shipping of foreign goods in a British vessel, the insurance of a foreign factory, the raising of capital in London by a foreign borrower, the purchase of British industrial 'know how' by a foreign firm, the interest on investments overseas...[98]

The focus was on City activities, with an appealing nod to the more eye-catching sources of non-City earning in an attempt to prevent the report from being deemed 'too City'.[99] The coverage given to the original report by the *Daily Mirror* demonstrates the successful nature of this strategy:

> Who are the Invisible Men? There is the banker sitting in his oak-panelled parlour earning fees and commissions for overseas customers. There is the waiter at the Savoy serving breakfast to Frank Sinatra...A croupier at Crockford's rakes in cash from a French gambler. Stockbrokers, insurance men, ship-owners, grain merchants, airline pilots...the list of Britain's invisible earners is almost endless.[100]

Yet the populist appeal to readers of the *Mirror* did not continue to inform the activities of the permanent committee and its public relations strategy. The COIE operated according to a distinct strategy that combined its semi-official nature with a narrow goal of seeking to influence elite attitudes to invisible exports.

As we have seen, the original committee had been established by the BNEC and had formal relations with the Bank of England and the Treasury. This relationship continued with the establishment of the permanent

---

[97] BOE: 6A375/1, 'Second /meeting of COIE–CIE 68.4 Promotion and Public Relations Policy', 17 July 1968.
[98] Financial Advisory Panel on Exports, *Britain's Invisible Earnings*, introduction.
[99] BOE: 7A1/5, McMahon to the Governors, 'The Atlas Report', 19 September 1967.
[100] BOE: 7A1/5, Robert Head, 'Spotlight on the Exporters who Sell Things you Can't See: The Invisible Men', *Daily Mirror*, 19 October 1967.

committee. The Governor of the Bank of England, Sir Leslie O'Brien, invited individual members to serve on the COIE and appointed the chairman, while the Bank provided office space and a secretariat (consisting of a secretary and '2½' staff) until permanent offices were found in the mid-1970s.[101] Furthermore, a representative from both the Bank and the Treasury sat on the committee. This was inevitably an outgrowth of its continuing relationship with the BNEC, yet it also served a particular purpose. In the first year of the permanent COIE, tensions arose between Kleinwort and the 'official' members. The Chairman was keen for the Treasury and Bank representatives to leave the committee so that it could become a more activist and vocal pressure group, free from the constraints of having to be tentative and moderate to satisfy the cautious Treasury officials.[102] Furthermore, Kleinwort's outspoken tendency had served to irritate Frank Figgures (committee member and third secretary to the Treasury), who did not feel comfortable with some of the recent public statements Kleinwort had made without first consulting the committee as a whole.[103] This fundamental fault line in the committee was recognized by O'Brien. The Governor felt strongly that the private–public alliance was vital to the success of the invisibles campaign, and sought to bridge the divide between Kleinwort and the Treasury. He advised Kleinwort that pleas on behalf of invisible exporters were much more likely to be heard in Whitehall if a joint committee was maintained.[104] He repeated this conviction at the Lord Mayor's Dinner later that year, in which he asserted:

> there are some I know who would like to turn this Committee into a militant pressure group speaking loudly whenever possible on behalf of City interests. I believe the method so far chosen, under which representatives of the various Government authorities concerned are full members of the Committee, is a better one. Admittedly it offers less scope for uncompromising public utterances, but it does provide continuing opportunity for the careful examination of problems in an atmosphere of co-operation, which should in the long run lead to more tangible results.[105]

Yet O'Brien's practical support for cooperative and moderate activism was also rooted in a desire to resist contemporary demands, emanating from

---

[101] BOE: 7A70/5, Clarke to Governor's Private Secretary, 'Committee on Invisible Exports', 2 June 1978.

[102] BOE: 6A375/1, Governor's Note, 'P.I.B. and City Enquiry: City Neddy', 25 June 1968.

[103] BOE: 6A375/1, Figgures to Parsons, 6 November 1968.

[104] BOE: 6A375/1, Governor's Note . . . , 25 June 1968.

[105] BOE: 6A375/2, 'Governor's Speech at the Lord Mayor's Dinner', 17 October 1968.

the TUC, for the establishment of a 'City Neddy' (mirroring the corporatist NEDC, which had set up in 1962 to coordinate industrial development) that might seek to direct investment and bank lending for the purposes of national planning.[106] O'Brien felt that, as part of a strategy to offset the establishment of such a body, the COIE could be presented as already fulfilling a similar role. However, if the official members were to drop out and the COIE were to become a 'shrill pressure group', the task of resisting a 'City Neddy' might become much more difficult.[107] O'Brien successfully managed to hold the COIE together—though for Frank Figgures the discomfort proved too great, and he was replaced by another Treasury representative.[108]

O'Brien's role tells us something unique about the role of the Bank of England as the interface between the City and the British state that has previously been overlooked—not least in the recent official history of the central bank.[109] There is a well-established argument that the Bank operated in a way that sought to champion the City's preferences (particularly with relation to economic policy and sterling), and more recently in Gary Burn's work its role in championing the City as an international financial centre.[110] The former stresses the explicit exercise of influence over government economic policy on behalf of the City's interests, while the latter emphasizes the way in which the Bank created regulatory space that was insulated from the impositions of the democratic state. However, in this instance, we see how the Bank also acted as a distinctive political actor in the campaign to legitimate the City's international role. This was not explicit, nor was it hidden, but it was a subtle exercise of power and influence that colours our understanding of the Bank's unique position in the political economy of post-war Britain.

The formal connections with the Bank and Treasury formed part of the committee's broader public relations strategy. Sir Robert Bellinger (Lord Mayor of London 1966/7) had been a particularly proactive mayor who sought to use his tenure to popularize the contribution of the City to Britain through its invisible earnings.[111] He most notably assisted in the creation and publicity of a film entitled *The Hidden Strength* to achieve this end.[112] Also, as we have seen, the popular press was particularly

---

[106] TNA: T 326/938, Trades Union Congress, 'EDC for Banking, Insurance and Finance', 6 August 1968.
[107] BOE: 6A375/1, Governor's Note..., 25 June 1968.
[108] BOE: 6A375/1, Figgures to Parsons, 28 November 1968.
[109] Capie, *Bank of England*.
[110] Burn, *The Re-Emergence of Global Finance*, 99–134.
[111] BOE: 7A1/1, 'Minutes', 14 September 1966.
[112] Sir John Benn, '"Invisibles" Need More Publicity', *The Times*, 17 April 1967.

responsive to the committee's original report. Yet the COIE's public relations strategy was deliberately less populist, and was directed towards a highly specific notion of the 'public'. The committee was not concerned with the general public, but instead sought to focus its attention on those identified as opinion-formers—namely, press, politicians, and civil servants in Whitehall. In 1970 the Sub-Committee on 'Promotion and PR identified 2,000 such influential individuals and sent copies of an 'Invisibles Information Card' to each.[113] In 1968 and 1969 *The Times* (as *the* paper of the 'opinion-forming' classes) published lengthy supplements on 'Invisible Exports' written by William Clarke and a number of other committee members. These supplements were interspersed with numerous advertisements by City firms that employed their contribution to invisible earnings as both a public relations campaign and a personal selling point (for example, Lloyds bank used its advertising space in both supplements to highlight the extent of invisible earnings by *all* banks (Fig. 4.1).[114]

Reflecting on the committee's operations in 1976, Clarke acknowledged that they had 'deliberately not attempted to influence the broad mass of the public, partly for reasons of expense, partly because we have been concerned primarily with policy makers'.[115] Another aspect of the COIE's attempt to influence the opinion-forming classes was through its continued association with the EAG. Throughout the 1970s, the committee employed the group to investigate and publish studies on various issues relating to invisible earnings. For example, in 1969 the EAG undertook economic investigations into the factors that influenced international company decisions to base themselves in Britain, and into the effect of the selective employment tax on invisible earnings.[116] By being able to appeal to the findings of academic economists, working under the auspices of the EAG, the committee was provided with a basis of scholarly evidence upon which to support its campaign to promote invisibles. Undoubtedly the committee was aware that the apparent expertise of these reports was particularly useful when attempting to persuade civil servants of the merits of their proposals.

---

[113] BOE: 7A70/3, 'Sub-Committee on Promotion and PR', 3 March 1970.
[114] 'Invisible Exports: A Special Report', *The Times*, 19 March 1968; 'Invisible Exports: A Special Report', *The Times*, 21 March 1969.
[115] BOE: 7A4/1, Clarke, 'COIE: Past and Future: Some First Thoughts', 31 March 1976.
[116] BOE: 6A 375/3, 'The International Company and Britain's Invisible Earnings', *EAG*, April 1969; BOE: 6A 401/1, Prof. A. T. Peacock, 'Second Memorandum on the Selective Employment Tax and Invisible Earnings', *EAG*, January 1969.

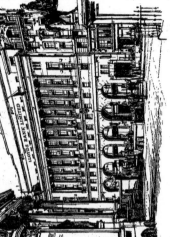

Fig. 4.1. Advertisements referring to invisible exports

Source: The Times, 19 March 1968. Reproduced with permission of Legal and General, and the Lloyds Banking Group Archives.

Finally, the committee also had an international public relations role. This became especially important in the second half of the 1970s. In a letter to the Governor, William Clarke explained that, having 'broken the back of publicity at home', the committee was now devoting 'increasing attention *abroad*' by holding conferences that sought to promote the City. Conferences were held in cities across the globe, from Jakarta to Rio, Tokyo to Trinidad.[117] The committee was even fortunate enough to have the Labour Chancellor of the Exchequer, Denis Healey, accompany their mission to Tehran in 1975.[118]

'PLUCKING THE GOOSE WHICH LAYS THE GOLDEN EGG'

What was the purpose of the promotional activities of the committee? The original committee's report in 1967 had sought to redefine the nature of the British economy to place greater emphasis on the contemporary and historic success of services, and to demonstrate how invisible earners (primarily in the City) kept the balance of payments in surplus. This allowed Clarke and his co-members to challenge the notion of the City as a sectional interest group, and to demonstrate that its interests were aligned with the national interest. It was on this basis, which had been popularized in the most influential quarters of Britain, that the committee could then launch a campaign for greater freedom of the service economy—most notably a liberalization of financial and commercial services in the City. This campaign focused itself around two key aspects: an attack on exchange controls and a demand for the alleviation of taxation on invisible earners.

The effects of different types, and various rates, of taxation on economies, industries, and individuals are highly contentious and difficult to assess. Yet it is undeniable that, to whatever degree, taxes do impose costs on firms and individuals. Forgoing any ideological desires to increase the incidence of taxation, individuals and firms prefer to reduce their exposure to taxation. However, arguments for reductions or removal of taxation on the grounds of pure self-interest are difficult to justify. The concept of invisible earnings and their beneficial contribution to the British economy allowed the members of the COIE to campaign legitimately for reductions

---

[117] BOE: 7A70/5, Clarke to the Governor's Private Secretary, 'Committee on Invisible Exports', 2 June 1978.
[118] 'Mr Healey Taking Part in Iran Conference', *The Times*, 11 April 1975.

in the incidence of taxation on the service industries that they represented. Rather than being a self-interested campaign to reduce exposure to taxation, the committee argued that reducing the taxation of financial services would increase invisible earnings and thus benefit the nation as a whole. In the decade following the founding of the committee, it campaigned to reduce or remove various taxes that were identified as impediments to the invisibles sector.

The 1967 report had proposed a number of taxation changes, yet the most prominent proposal put forward (and one that had garnered most press support and attention) had been for an alteration to the Selective Employment Tax (SET). Having been introduced in 1966 by the Labour Chancellor Jim Callaghan, SET imposed a lump sum tax for each person employed in 'service trades' and construction. At its highest level in 1969 this tax amounted to 10 per cent of wages in the service trades. The principal originator of this tax had been Callaghan's special economic advisor, Professor Nicholas Kaldor, who had designed the tax as a means of redressing the balance between taxes on manufacturing and services (the latter having previously been less taxed) and to encourage labour efficiency in the service sector in order to increase the availability of labour 'for the expansion of the manufacturing industry'.[119] SET exemplified the 'productionist' bias of social democratic economic policy with its explicit emphasis on the centrality of manufacturing to improving national economic performance. The COIE identified the tax as a major impediment to invisible trade. The 1967 report appealed to the government to 'consider ways of mitigating' the effects of the SET because 'a major tax which on balance imposes a burden on a sector that has a persistent payments surplus over the years and which provides a deliberate premium to a sector that invariably produces a payments deficit is in need of some adjustment'.[120] Seeking to remain moderate in its approach, the committee proposed four possible ways to reduce the effect of the tax on invisible exporters: to extend SET exemption to 'insurance, banking and finance, professional services . . . hotel and catering services (as part of the tourist trade); employ the employment exemption on a narrower front; abolish the tax; or place a flat-rate poll-tax on all employers'.[121] These solutions

---

[119] Nicholas Kaldor, 'The Economics of the Selective Employment Tax', in *Reports on Taxation I: Papers Relating to the United Kingdom* (London: Duckworth, 1980), 200–29; Richard Whiting, 'Ideology and Reform in Labour's Tax Strategy, 1964–1970', *Historical Journal*, 41/4 (1998), 1135–7; Martin J. Daunton, *Just Taxes: The Politics of Taxation in Britain, 1914–1979* (Cambridge: Cambridge University Press, 2002), 293.
[120] Financial Advisory Panel on Exports, *Britain's Invisible Earnings*, 243.
[121] Ibid. 243–4.

would all have undermined the fundamental macroeconomic purpose of the tax—a purpose that, of course, the committee did not accept as necessary.

The committee's critique, moderated in its proposals by its semi-official position, happened to coincide with a strident attack on the tax by the Conservative Party in opposition. Ian McLeod (then shadow Chancellor of the Exchequer) promised to repeal the tax when the party was returned to power, while Selwyn Lloyd (Chancellor of the Exchequer, 1960–2) acted as Chairman of the Committee for the Repeal of the Selective Employment Tax.[122] In the face of such criticism, the Labour government established an inquiry into the effects of SET, led by the Cambridge economist W. B. Reddaway, which received a substantial submission of evidence gathered and presented by the COIE.[123] SET was eventually abolished by the Conservative government in 1973. It is difficult to measure the impact of the COIE, given that the Conservatives were already opposed to the tax in opposition. However, the conflict over the necessity of the tax highlighted the tensions between the manufacturing priorities of the economic strategy that dominated the 1960s, and the alternative, international service-based vision for prosperity popularized by the COIE.

Over the following decade the COIE conducted a campaign against all forms of taxation that were deemed to act as a disincentive to invisible earnings. A COIE document from July 1974 expressed frustration that 'invisible earnings have trebled since 1967. City invisible earnings have doubled since 1967: they have trebled since 1965. But invisible exporters still get little encouragement in taxation matters.'[124] Further to this annoyance, the committee regularly asserted the need to establish rates of business taxation that would not deter foreign businesses, investors, and service professionals from establishing their business in Britian—or, more specifically, in London. The COIE argued that the incidence of high taxation served to 'undermine the City's competitive position'.[125] Estate duty, corporation tax, and the 'anachronism' of stamp duty (which applied to the purchase of securities) were significant barriers that prevented London from fulfilling its potential of becoming *the* major financial centre. In a world in which other financial centres (such as Zurich)

---

[122] Kaldor, 'The Economics of the Selective Employment Tax', 207; BOE: 6A401/1, letter from Selwyn Lloyd to Cyril Kleinwort, 12 September 1968.

[123] Kaldor, 'The Economics of the Selective Employment Tax', 206–7; BOE: 6A401/1, letters from Kleinwort to various institutions requesting members for a sub-committee to produce evidence for the Reddaway Committee, July 1968.

[124] BOE: 6A401/4, 'Invisible Earnings and Taxation Constraints', July 1974.

[125] Ibid.

could competitively absorb business, the COIE argued that it was vital to reduce the burden of taxation on the City.[126]

The COIE (its policies shaped by a dedicated subcommittee on taxation) also campaigned for a number of tax reliefs and incentives related to the taxation of foreign income. The committee called for tax relief on income earned abroad to offset the local taxes on, for example, income dividends that were payable to foreign governments.[127] Arguments for tax reliefs of this sort were based solely on their beneficial impact on invisible earnings, and were often backed by EAG research.[128] The committee regularly appealed directly to the Chancellor on specific tax issues. For example, following an appeal from the COIE not to impose UK tax on the worldwide income of non-UK domiciled persons resident in the UK, Denis Healey conceded to Cyril Kleinwort that 'it has never been our intention to drive foreigners out of the business and cultural life of this country' and agreed to withdraw clause 18 from the 1974 Finance bill. Instead, only 75 per cent of earnings relating to UK employment would be taxed if an individual was resident for 'nine out of the ten preceding years'.[129] This episode exemplified the elite, semi-official operation of the committee.

The COIE's campaign against the purportedly stultifying effects of taxation on the City's ability to earn invisible income culminated in its evidence given to the Wilson Committee. The COIE's evidence drew on its established narrative of the City's historic role as the pre-eminent global financial centre and its invaluable contribution of invisible income to the balance of payments.[130] This success, it was reiterated, was based on the City's long-standing 'capacity for adaption'—a capacity that had to be retained by 'maintaining conditions (including both working conditions and post-tax income) that will make the City attractive to men and women of foresight and initiative'.[131] For the COIE, this meant that it was imperative that there were reductions in the 'high marginal tax rates

---

[126] Ibid.; Michael Blanden, 'UK Tax Policies Hit Invisibles', *Financial Times*, 11 July 1974, 4; BOE: 6A401/4, Richard Powell to Denis Healey, 6 June 1974.

[127] 'Tax Incentives Urged by Invisibles Committee', *Financial Times*, 8 January 1970, 20.

[128] BOE: 6A375/3, 'The International Company and Britain's Invisible Earnings', *EAG*, April 1969; BOE: 6A375/4, 'Report of Working Party on "The Role of International Companies..."', 23 December 1970; BOE: 6A375/4, letter from Kleinwort to the Chancellor, 27 January 1971.

[129] BOE: 6A401/5, Healey to Kleinwort, 19 July 1974.

[130] 'Written Evidence by the Committee on Invisible Exports', in *Committee to Review the Functioning of Financial Institutions: Second Stage Evidence*, ii (London: HMSO, 1979), 113–14.

[131] Ibid. 120.

on personal incomes' and an abolition of 'discrimination against "unearned" income'. The committee argued that post-tax earnings of management in Britain were 'way below' their equivalent in the United States and most European countries, and as a result it was becoming 'increasingly difficult to attract and retain key personnel'. This was especially pertinent, given that the professionals employed in the City tended to be extensive global travellers and were therefore keenly aware of the different tax treatments 'accorded to their foreign counterparts'.[132]

The COIE's campaign to reduce various forms of taxation was rooted in the concept of the City's invisible earnings as vital to the health of the national economy. It was not solely in the interest of financial service firms to reduce their exposure to taxation, but it was in the national interest to do so too. This campaign fed into a new dynamic in which the internationalization of financial services demanded that competitive tax regimes were promoted as vitally necessary if international business was to be retained. The logic of the committee's position on tax matters was questionable. If the City was already a national success story, why were reductions in taxation necessary? The original key argument made by Clarke was that the City's skills and institutions were unavailable in other places—so the likelihood that customers would go elsewhere is uncertain. Taxation had not deterred international financial and commercial transactions from taking place in London. Yet in this regard the committee did not simply exist to provide an explanation of the value of the City—it was a pressure group designed to further the interests of its members.

The demand for tax reductions by the committee was combined with a concomitant campaign for the liberalization of the City through the removal of exchange control restrictions that limited the capacity of firms to transfer capital overseas. The 1967 report had replicated William Clarke's early arguments, set out in his IEA publications on the City, that the successful growth of Britain's post-war invisible earnings in financial and commercial activities could be attributed to progressive liberalizations of the City. The logical follow-on, according to Clarke and the committee, was that further liberalizations would serve only to do more to assist its expansion. For the committee, the continuing existence of various forms of exchange controls that restricted the global role of the City in the 1960s and 1970s were a serious impediment to the earning of invisible income. The primary control that dominated the committee's frustrations was the '25 per cent arrangement'—more commonly known as the '25 per surrender'. This measure, which had been introduced to bolster

---

[132] Ibid. 127–8.

the balance of payments during the 1965 sterling crisis, demanded that 25 per cent of all proceeds derived from premium currency investments had to be made available to the authorities for the purpose of managing the official reserves.[133] The committee argued against this control on the basis that it posed a significant barrier to British investors from earning income from foreign portfolio investment.[134] Cyril Kleinwort regularly wrote to Chancellors of both parties to plead for a reduction or abolition of the requirement in order to give greater support to 'a most important source of invisible exports'.[135] He told Anthony Barber in January 1972: 'When so much is done to support exports, both financially and with foreign exchange in other directions, it is indeed disappointing to see invisible exports penalised in this way. An example, if you will excuse the metaphor, of plucking the goose which lays the golden egg.'[136] The committee sought to demonstrate the extent to which controls, despite their intended purpose of maintaining a healthy balance of payments, actually undermined its long-term prospects. Relaxing exchange controls, rather than tightening them, was the solution to Britain's balance of payments instability—a point asserted in an EAG report that had been commissioned in 1970 and argued for a loosening of the rules on direct overseas investment.[137] Once again the COIE attempted to challenge the prevailing orthodoxy, which saw the City as a threat to the national economy that had to be restrained. Instead, if the City was given free rein to invest globally, the benefits accrued via an improved balance of payments would reduce, rather than increase, instability.

The impact of demands for exchange control relaxations was generally limited for most of the period following the committee's first publication. The dominant notion of the British economy as fundamentally weak and vulnerable to an almost perpetual balance of payments deficit continued to underpin official commitment to exchange controls designed to uphold the value of sterling. Kynaston has noted the limited impact of Clarke's committee on this issue.[138] In December 1978, only a year before their complete abolition, Denis Healey clarified the purpose of controls to the

---

[133] Ibid. 73.

[134] BOE: 6A401/4, 'Invisible Earnings and Taxation Constraints', July 1974;.

[135] BOE: 6A375/1, Kleinwort to the Chancellor, '25% Surrender of Premium $', 7 June 1968.

[136] BOE: 6A375/4, Kleinwort to the Chancellor, '25% Surrender Regulation', 21 January 1972.

[137] BOE: 6A375/4, 'Report of Working Party on "The Role of International Companies . . ."', 23 December 1970; BOE: 6A375/4, William Keegan, 'Overseas Income Rules may be Hitting UK Invisibles', *Financial Times*, 6 May 1970, 19.

[138] David Kynaston, 'The Long Life and Slow Death of Exchange Controls', *Journal of International Financial Markets*, 2/2 (2000), 38.

Chairman of the British Insurance Brokers' Association (BIBA). He told Francis Perkins that 'overseas direct investments must be made without cost to the reserves' and that a relaxation on exchange controls, despite the contribution of invisible earnings made by BIBA members, was not appropriate at that time.[139] However, a change in the external balance as a result of oil discoveries in the North Sea served to change the terms of debate. A year earlier, in December 1977, the COIE had established a working party on exchange controls founded on the basis that 'relaxation of controls was now a very live topic in the light of North Sea oil revenue, an improved balance-of-payments and the present strength of sterling'.[140] The working party's first priority was to campaign for the removal of the 25 per cent rule—primarily for the benefit of the Stock Exchange and Association of Investment Trusts.[141] Fortunately for the working party, the rule was actually abolished six days later, though a whole array of controls remained in place—notably restrictions on the financing of third-country trade.[142]

Against the favourable conditions created by the improvement in the balance of payments generated by North Sea oil, the committee's representations to the Wilson Committee argued for the 'progressive dismantling' of exchange controls. The proposals, formulated by the working party, deliberately did not demand the 'total abolition' of controls on the basis that it would be an unrealistic outcome. However, it was felt by the working party members that, given the change in the external position, the 'onus' was on the authorities to 'justify controls rather than that there should merely be a continuing acquiescence'.[143] In their Wilson Committee submission, the COIE estimated that the cost to the current account caused by barriers to financial mobility was £600 million of annual invisible earnings.[144] To solve this, it was proposed that restrictions on the use of sterling in financing third-party trade and British exports should be abolished, restrictions on the reinvestment of overseas profits and purchase of foreign currencies relaxed, greater freedoms afforded for the holding of foreign currencies, and the the investment currency pool phased out.[145]

[139] BOE: 7A5/1, letter from Healey to Francis Perkins, 21 December 1978.
[140] BOE: 7A5/1, 'Exchange Control Working Party Committee', 14 December 1977.
[141] Ibid.
[142] BOE: 7A5/1, 'Exchange Control Act 1947, Supplement No. 34: The 25% Requirement', 22 December 1977; BOE: 7A5/1, 'Exchange Control Working Party Committee', 26 January 1978.
[143] BOE: 7A5/1, 'Exchange Control Working Party Committee', 12 April 1977.
[144] 'Editorial: Invisible Barriers', *Financial Times*, 16 February 1979, 24.
[145] 'Written Evidence by the Committee on Invisible Exports', in *Committee to Review the Functioning of Financial Institutions: Second Stage Evidence*, ii. 132.

In the wake of the total abolition of exchange controls by Sir Geoffrey Howe on 24 October 1979, an anonymous clearing banker told the *Financial Times*, reeling from the shocking announcement, that 'I am sure we have planned for this... but I've yet to find the man who did it'.[146] The members of the Committee on Invisible Exports were probably as shocked as the clearing banker, though they had spent the previous decade pushing for the removal of exchange controls. The activism of the committee had contributed over the course of the previous decade to a reframing of the City's contribution to the British economy—challenging the notion that it was a liability that needed to be tightly controlled in order to prevent a return to the havoc of the interwar period. Instead, freedom from controls for the City's invisible earners was a vital precondition for long-term stability in the earning of invisible income. The importance placed on abolishing the controls runs counter to some of our expectations in the light of the Eurodollar-centric explanation of the City's resurgence. This market had developed because it was not exposed to these controls. We might expect, then, that exchange controls would not have been a concern for those seeking the success of the City. However, we must remember that the committee operated on behalf of a whole host of City interest groups not engaged in the specialized Euromarkets.

CONCLUSION

The impact of the invisibles campaign was significant in changing elite perceptions of the British economy, and more specifically the importance of the City to the national economy. There are numerous examples of how the invisibles idea infiltrated public understanding of the economy. When Harold Lever, a senior Labour minister in the Wilson and Callaghan governments, was condemned by the North-East Leeds constituency Labour Party for not supporting proposals to nationalize the banking system, he informed them in a letter that the success of 'our banks' makes an important contribution to 'our balance of payments' in the form of invisible overseas earnings.[147] As he told the House of Commons in May 1976:

---

[146] Quoted in Kynaston, 'The Long Life and Slow Death of Exchange Controls', 37.
[147] LPA: Re. 745, 'Home Policy Committee: Nationalisation of Banking, Insurance and Pharmaceutical Industries', August 1976.

The Government have no intention of nationalising any company in the banking industry... Our branch banking system is unrivalled throughout the world, and our banks adjusted to Britain's changing position in the world with remarkable advantage to our country... They continue to make a major contribution to our invisible earnings.[148]

When in 1975 Harold Wilson was made a freeman of the City of London, he assured his audience at the Guildhall of his 'very deep regard for the long traditions of the City, and for the expertise which has made—and is still making... in increasing measure—so vital a contribution to our invisible exports'.[149] The recognition of the importance of invisibles on behalf of the Labour governments was developed further by the incoming Thatcher government. Speaking to an audience of overseas bankers at Plaisterers' Hall in 1978, Thatcher stated a case in support of the City that closely resembled that which the COIE had been making for the previous decade. She announced:

> In 1976... this country bought goods to the tune of over £3.5 billion more than it sold overseas... But in the same year our private sector invisible earnings— partly the shipping, banking, insurance and other services provided for the world community by the City of London—brought in £4.5 billion. This was not the achievement of politicians. The services provided by the City of London attract no subsidies, no hidden subventions, from Government. On the contrary, I fear that the politicians mostly contribute to the City of London's performance by the barriers they place in the way of its improvement, including a crippling burden of taxation on those who work long hours and take the risks to produce these results and increasingly indefensible restraints on productive outward investment. If the industries which have fallen under the direct control of government in this country began to match the performance of the City of London, we should have the strongest currency in the world.[150]

Once in office as Prime Minster she continued her support by personally ensuring, at the request of the COIE, that the Department of Trade's monthly press notice made clear that the invisible balance projections were composed of a government deficit and a City-led private surplus (as in the Central Statistical Office's 'Pink Book').[151]

---

[148] Parliamentary Debates, Commons, 5th ser., vol. 911, cols 1453–684 (19 May 1976).

[149] Harold Wilson Papers, Bodleian Library: 'Prime Minister's Speech at the Guildhall', 12 December 1975.

[150] Margaret Thatcher Foundation [MTF]: Margaret Thatcher, 'Speech to Overseas Bankers', 7 February 1978.

[151] TNA: PREM 19/36, Sir Francis Sandilands CBE et al. to Prime Minister, 3 October 1979; TNA: PREM 19/36, Prime Minister to Sir Francis Sandilands CBE, 15 October 1979.

From the end of the 1960s the committee had successfully promoted the concept of invisibles, and, by association, the value of the City to the British economy. It reconceptualized the British economy in the eyes of its Whitehall administrators. Though the attachment to industry as the source of national economic well-being remains prevalent today (especially following the financial crisis of 2008), the period saw the balance in priorities between manufacturing and service activities redressed in 'public' conceptions of what the British economy actually was. During the 1980s, financial deregulation and policies designed to encourage internationalization, in addition to the significant reductions in taxation on incomes and capital, permitted the City to fulfil its potential as a major international financial centre. Meanwhile, in the political and economic discourse of subsequent decades, industry was rhetorically demoted as the source of national wealth and prosperity. The extent to which the politicization, and popularization, of 'invisibles' played a causal role in this transition is difficult to judge without further historical research.[152] However, the findings here give us a clear idea of the context in which the post-1979 Conservative governments took power.

Regarding the question of what *caused* the City of London's resurgence as an international financial centre in the final third of the twentieth century, the findings set out in this chapter are uncertain. In particular, the evidence presented on the COIE does not directly challenge or undermine the materialist accounts of the City's resurgence through the Euromarkets. Furthermore, we must place this in the context of a broader shift in the character of the British economy from manufacturing (especially in primary sectors) to services that took place over the twentieth century. Yet the chapter reminds us that economism can obscure the political–economic contest in which such material changes take place. In this case, the findings suggest that the City's internationalization via the burgeoning global capital markets was embedded in a broader reconceptualization of the British economy achieved in part by the COIE. This super-structural phenomenon did not simply reflect these material changes within the financial sector, but did generate favourable conditions, which allowed those changes to take place. From this perspective,

---

[152] The Committee on Invisible Exports was renamed the 'British Invisible Exports Council' in the 1980s. The name changed to 'British Invisibles' in 1990, then 'International Financial Services London' in 2001, and is now called 'TheCityUK': '30 Years of the LOTIS Committee', *TheCityUK.com* <http://www.thecityuk.com/media/latest-news-from-thecityuk/30-years-of-the-lotis-committee/> (accessed 16 April 2014); David Litterick, 'British Invisibles Given a Makeover', *Daily Telegraph*, 5 February 2001.

the growth of the Euromarkets and the activities of the COIE were two independent processes that impacted upon, but were not dependent upon, each other.

This chapter has considered how the relationship between the City of London and the British economy was 'thought about' and conceptualized in the period of increasing internationalization in the 1960s and 1970s. This was a period in which the City transformed itself from a banking centre based on sterling to one based on foreign currencies deposits outside the controls of the state. The chapter has demonstrated that in the late 1950s, as the 'declinist' critique of post-war British political economy was popularized, an alternative anti-'declinist' interpretation was developed. In many ways this perspective accepted the premises of the Shonfield critique—particularly that government expenditure overseas was excessive, and that the commitment to sterling was not necessarily vital to the City's international role. The argument of Clarke and his committee that Britain's strength lay in its provision of international invisible services reconceptualized, historically as well as contemporaneously, the nature of the British economy. It challenged the manufacturing and 'productionist' bias of post-war domestic economic policy, and argued instead that Britain was a specialist service and commercial economy. The campaign conflated 'invisibles' with the City in a deliberate attempt to build a cross-services political alliance, yet the primary focus of the pressure group was to pursue liberalization and deregulation of the City—to restore its pre-1931 freedoms. The committee did not discover 'invisibles'; it merely politicized them. It employed them as a tool through which to argue for economic policy changes to suit the interests of the commercial and financial firms it represented. The campaign was a political effort by representatives of the City to extricate the international financial centre from the demands of domestic social democratic policies. However, this was rooted in a deeper cultural contest over the nature of the British economy that can be traced back as far as the eighteenth century. In this sense, we can see that the social democratic project was resisted by interest groups, but was also hampered by underlying tensions prevalent in modern British history—between industry and services; production and trade; the domestic and the international.

5

The City of London and the Evolution of British Monetarism

The capacity of the City of London's financial interests to dictate and determine the economic policies of the state is a well-established notion that has influenced contemporary and historical analyses of Britain's political economy since the nineteenth century. This idea has been popularized by many critical analysts of Britain's economic development, including Hobson, Anderson, Ingham, and Cain and Hopkins.[1] Since the end of the First World War, in the age of twentieth-century mass democracy, the City's financial interests are seen to have maintained their power and influence, despite democratic tendencies towards economic interventionism on behalf of the state. The most immediate example of this in the interwar period was the decision to return to the gold standard at the pre-war parity in 1925, and the subsequent events of 1931, in which the bankers of the Square Mile were alleged to have manipulated a crisis to impose their desire for a balanced budget (achieved by cutting unemployment benefit) on the Labour government.[2]

Despite the setback caused by the physical destruction and new constraints imposed during the Second World War, it was routinely alleged by critics that the City was able to rebuild its control and influence over economic policy in the social democratic age. This influence was expressed in the commitment to maintaining sterling's role as an international trading and reserve currency, despite the costs imposed on the domestic economy by the policies required to uphold this position, as well as an apparent failure to wrest control of monetary policy away from the conservative Bank of England.[3] The experience of the post-1964 Labour governments seemingly supports this view. Harold Wilson's governments attempted to pursue an economic strategy of state coordinated growth, on the basis that the means to achieve 'steady industrial expansion and a strong currency' could be achieved only through 'purposive economic

---

[1] See Introduction.   [2] Williamson, 'A "Bankers" Ramp?', 770–1.
[3] Tomlinson, 'Labour Party and the City', 174–92.

planning' and a commitment to economic expansion.[4] Yet, immediately following the general election victory in October, the new government was faced with a current account deficit of £800 million (twice what had been forecast). This led to a bout of speculation that a devaluation to improve the payments position was imminent. Throughout the following years, such speculation against the pound was endemic, and the government was forced to defend the exchange rate by gradually dismantling its modernization agenda through wage freezes and cuts to public expenditure on investment. By 1966 the National Plan had been largely abandoned.[5] The decision to devalue to a new parity of $2.40 eventually came in November 1967, although by that point the possible advantages of such a manoeuvre had been lost. For many contemporary critics on the left, it was clear that the blame lay at the door of 'the City'.

Both contemporaries and, until recently, historians have judged Wilson's resistance to devaluation harshly. For left-wing critics, the willingness to prioritize sterling over the promises of domestic economic reform represented not only Wilson's stubborn reluctance to allow Labour to be dubbed 'the party of devaluation' (as had occurred in 1949), but a surrender to the power of international financiers and the orthodoxy of the City.[6] Historians have subsequently revised this view and have challenged the notion that the Labour government simply acquiesced to the demands of the City and its typical deflationary agenda in pursuit of a high and stable sterling exchange rate. They have highlighted the complexities of the drama, and the strong resistance put up by Wilson to the pressures of the international foreign exchange markets. Furthermore, Tomlinson has demonstrated that Wilson and Callaghan saw Labour as having a responsibility to defend the institutions of the international economy in which stable fixed exchange rates were embedded in the Bretton Woods

---

[4] Cmd. 2764, *The National Plan*, (London: H.M.S.O., 1965), 395.

[5] Scott Newton, 'The Two Sterling Crises of 1964 and the Decision not to Devalue', *Economic History Review*, 62/1 (2009), 73–4.

[6] Catherine Schenk, *The Decline of Sterling: Managing the Retreat of an International Currency, 1945–1992* (Cambridge: Cambridge University Press, 2010), 155–7; Tim Bale, 'Dynamics of a Non-Decision: The "Failure" to Devalue the Pound, 1964–7', *Twentieth Century British History*, 10/2 (1999), 192–217; Newton, 'The Two Sterling Crises', 73–5; Scott Newton, 'The Sterling Devaluation of 1967, the International Economy and Post-War Social Democracy', *English Historical Review*, 125/515 (2010), 912–13; Chris Rogers, 'Economic Policy and the Problem of Sterling under Harold Wilson and James Callaghan', *Contemporary British History*, 25/3 (2011), 339–63; Fred Hirsch, *The Pound Sterling: A Polemic* (London: Victor Gollancz, 1975); Michael Stewart, *The Jekyll and Hyde Years: Politics and Economic Policy in Britain since 1964* (London: J. M. Dent, 1977); Alec Cairncross and Barry Eichengreen, *Sterling in Decline: The Devaluations of 1931, 1949 and 196 7*(Oxford: Blackwell, 1983), 213–17.

system.[7] Kynaston describes in detail the fractious and frustrating nature of the attempt to prevent devaluation that derailed the modernization plan—noting in particular the conflict between the vocally deflationist preferences of the Earl of Cromer, as Governor of the Bank of England, and the desire of Wilson and the Cabinet to fulfil their electoral pledges.[8]

In the politics of post-war economic policymaking, the City's ability to derail the Labour government's 1960s economic strategy has been assessed at great length. Yet, in the tumultuous decade that followed, in which the macroeconomic norms of post-war Keynesianism gave way to a 'monetarist' macroeconomic policy, there has been little historical analysis of the role of the City. This chapter attempts to remedy this historiographical deficiency by demonstrating the complex and contingent ascent of 'monetarist' policies, which evolved as a product of the British state's interaction with the financial markets over the course of the 1970s.

FROM KEYNESIANISM TO MONETARISM

In his annual Budget statement to the House of Commons in March 1980, the Conservative Chancellor of the Exchequer, Sir Geoffrey Howe, revealed the government's plan to eradicate the high rate of inflation that had plagued the British economy since the mid-1970s. The Chancellor announced a series of four-yearly targets for the 'steadily declining growth of the money supply' and for a concurrent reduction in the state's budget deficit (see Table 5.1).[9] This Medium Term Financial Strategy (MTFS) was based on the central claim of 'monetarist' economic theory that inflation is caused by an excess supply of money; and a belief that a primary cause of this glut of money was government borrowing (known as the Public Sector Borrowing Requirement (PSBR)) (see Box 5.1).[10]

The MTFS was the apotheosis of the British monetarist experiment in macroeconomic policy, and it represented a radical break from the Keynesian norms of economic management that had prevailed since the Second World War. 'Price stability' superseded 'full employment' as the primary goal of

---

[7] Tomlinson, 'Labour Party and the City', 187; the Bretton Woods system is described later in this chapter.

[8] Kynaston, *The City of London*, iv. 298–362.

[9] Parliamentary Debates, Commons, vol. 981, col. 1443 (26 March 1980); David Smith, *The Rise and Fall of Monetarism: The Theory and Politics of an Economic Experiment* (Harmondsworth: Penguin, 1987), 93.

[10] For a brief summary of monetarism, see Philip Cagan, 'Monetarism', in Steven N. Durlauf and Lawrence E. Blume (eds), *The New Dictionary of Economics*, 2nd edn (Basingstoke: Palgrave Macmillan, 2008).

Table 5.1. Medium-term financial strategy targets, 1980

Year	Money supply (% increase)	PSBR (% of GDP)
1980/1	7–11	3.75
1981/2	6–10	3.00
1982/3	5–9	2.25
1983/4	4–8	1.5

Box 5.1. Money supply (£M3)

Money supply (£M3)	=	Public Sector Borrowing Requirement (PSBR)	+	Increase in domestic bank lending to private sector	+	Net external finance	−	Increase in bank's non-deposit liabilities

Note: There are many alternative measures of the 'money supply'. For a more detailed discussion of the various monetary aggregates, see Anthony Hotson, 'British Monetary Targets, 1976 to 1987: A View from the Fourth Floor of the Bank of England', LSE Financial Markets Group Paper, Special Paper 190 (April 2010), 30.

---

macroeconomic policy, and monetary policy became enshrined as the key control level of economic growth and stability.[11] The popular view of the monetarist experiment tends to stress its 'idealist' or 'ideological' nature. This perspective emphasizes the spread of Milton Friedman's monetarist theories (alongside other elements of 'New Right'/'neoliberal' thought) and their adoption by the right wing of the Conservative Party during the 1970s— influenced by journalists, think tanks, and a vocal minority of British economists.[12] The promoters of monetarist ideas are deemed to have been particularly effective, given the widespread hostility from most professional economists in Britain.[13] From an alternative materialist perspective, it has been argued that monetarist doctrine simply rationalized the long-standing Tory desire to overcome inflation; reduce public expenditure; and abandon

[11] This narrative has been challenged in Jim Tomlinson, 'Tale of a Death Exaggerated: How Keynesian Policies Survived the 1970s', *Contemporary British History*, 21/4 (2007), 429–48.
[12] Cockett, *Thinking the Unthinkable*, 148–58; Desai, 'Second-Hand Dealers in Ideas'; Brian Harrison, 'Mrs Thatcher and the Intellectuals', *Twentieth Century British History*, 5 (1994), 206–45; Middleton, 'Brittan on Britain'; D. W. Parsons, *The Power of the Financial Press: Journalism and Economic Opinion in Britain and America* (Aldershot: Edward Elgar, 1989).
[13] Mark Wickham-Jones, 'Monetarism and its Critics: The University Economists' Letter of Protest of 1981', *Political Quarterly*, 63/2 (1992), 171–85.

trade-union-negotiated incomes policies.[14] Alternatively, Tomlinson has argued that the Thatcher government's monetarist strategy was largely unplanned and incoherent.[15]

Although the MTFS was a definitive break with Keynesianism, we must recognize that this change was not simply the product of the first Thatcher Conservative government. In fact, the shift from nominal Keynesianism to monetarism had already begun to take place in the decade prior to Thatcher's election victory in 1979. This is most significantly asserted in the work of the political scientist Peter A. Hall, who has interpreted the ascent of monetarism as a 'paradigm shift' in economic policy norms during the 1970s. Hall argues that, as economic contradictions proliferated (notably the concurrent increase in inflation and unemployment), the established Keynesian paradigm was exposed to an accumulation of anomalies that challenged its basic assumptions. This failure of the post-war macroeconomic framework instigated a demand for a new economic model.[16] Jim Callaghan's speech to the 1976 Labour Party conference is often referred to as a critical moment in this evolution. His rejection of fiscal stimuli to overcome unemployment echoed the monetarist critique of full-employment goals.[17] Furthermore, in 1976 the Labour Chancellor, Denis Healey, began to announce yearly targets for the control of the money supply—four years before the famed MTFS. Why did a Labour government, which was committed to the economic strategy of post-war Keynesian social democracy, come to adopt monetary targets? What were the pressures and influences on economic policymaking during the 1970s that can account for the emergence of monetary targets?

During the 1970s and early 1980s it was commonplace for contemporaries to assert the key role of the City of London in developing, promoting, and ensuring the success of British monetarism.[18] In this context, 'the City' acts as a metonym for the markets in government

[14] Jim Bulpitt, 'The Discipline of the New Democracy: Mrs Thatcher's Domestic Statecraft', *Political Studies*, 34/1 (1986), 32; Jim Tomlinson, 'Thatcher, Monetarism, and the Politics of Inflation', in Ben Jackson and Robert Saunders (eds), *Making Thatcher's Britain* (Cambridge: Cambridge University Press, 2012), 62–77.

[15] Jim Tomlinson, 'Mrs Thatcher's Macroeconomic Adventurism, 1979–1981, and its Political Consequences', *British Politics*, 2 (2007), 3–19.

[16] Peter A. Hall, 'Policy Paradigms, Social Learning, and the State: The Case of Economic Policymaking in Britain', *Comparative Politics*, 25/3 (1993), 275–96; Michael J. Oliver and Hugh Pemberton, 'Learning and Change in 20th Century British Economic Policy', *Governance: An International Journal of Policy, Administration, and Institutions*, 17/3 (2004), 428–32.

[17] Kenneth O. Morgan, *Callaghan: A Life* (Oxford: Oxford University Press, 1997), 535.

[18] Jerry Coakley and Laurence Harris, *The City of Capital: London's Role as a Financial Centre* (Oxford: Blackwell, 1983), 190–214.

debt and international currencies, and those individuals and institutions (stockbrokers, pension funds, financial commentators, banks, and so on) that operated within them.[19] Writing in 1978 for the Centre for Policy Studies think tank, the journalist-turned-stockbroker Tim Congdon proclaimed that the City was 'the spiritual home of British monetarism'.[20] This was echoed in Nicholas Kaldor's scathing 1982 denunciation of 'a new epidemic of monetarism' promoted by financial journalists and stockbrokers.[21] Peter Hall's model of a paradigm shift itself relies on the importance of the 'marketplace for ideas' in providing policymakers with a new economic framework to replace the failed 'Keynesianism'. For Hall, writing in the early 1990s, the City was seen as vitally important in constructing and contributing to this marketplace. He claimed that the increased prevalence of monetarist ideas within the City coincided with institutional changes that ensured their ascendance. He asserts that, following the expansionary policies of the early 1970s, the government was increasingly exposed to the demands of its creditors. Simultaneously, the policy of Competition and Credit Control adopted in 1971, in which quantitative controls on bank lending were removed and credit was managed according to variations in the Bank of England lending rate, created a number of structural changes. First, it increased the behavioural cohesiveness of the gilt-edged market (the market in UK government bonds), with investors acting *en masse* to changes (predicted and actual) in interest rates. Secondly, it stressed to investors the vital need to anticipate interest rate changes—which encouraged financial institutions to employ economists to make predictions of future economic trends and policies. These economists became increasingly influenced by 'monetarist' thought and concerned with the behaviour of the money supply, and in turn shared their interpretations in client circulars.[22] His account of these changes led Hall to conclude that 'many of the ad hoc adjustments towards monetarism made by the 1974–79 Labour Government were forced on it by the behaviour of the financial markets, and the popularity of monetarist doctrine in these markets influenced both the Bank of

---

[19] See the Introduction for a more detailed discussion of changing definitions of 'the City'.

[20] Tim Congdon, *Monetarism: An Essay in Definition* (London: Centre for Policy Studies, 1978), 29.

[21] Nicholas Kaldor, *The Scourge of Monetarism* (Oxford: Oxford University Press, 1982), p. xi.

[22] Peter A. Hall, 'The Movement from Keynesianism to Monetarism: Institutional Analysis and British Economic Policy in the 1970s', in Sven Steinmo, Kathleen Thelen, and Frank Longstreth (eds), *Structuring Politics: Historical Institutionalism in Comparative Analysis* (Cambridge: Cambridge University Press, 1992), 100–3.

England and the Government'.[23] This chapter examines Hall's claim by analysing the relationship between the financial markets and policymaking authorities at the Treasury and Bank of England using previously unemployed archival documents. In doing so the chapter attempts to comprehend how and why Keynesian social democracy gave way to a specific form of British monetarism in the decade prior to the Medium Term Financial Strategy.

MONETARISM AND THE FINANCIAL MARKETS, 1968–1976

In March 1968 Milton Friedman gave his presidential address to the American Economic Association. His speech, on the role of monetary policy, received wide coverage in the British financial press.[24] Samuel Brittan, economics editor of the *Financial Times*, published an article in October entitled 'Money Supply: The Great Debate', which received a large response from the readership.[25] The debate continued in the letters pages of the paper until January 1969, with contributions that deliberated over the definition, size, and means of controlling the supply of money.[26] Meanwhile, the December 1968 issue of the *Banker* magazine dedicated a special issue to 'The Money Supply Debate', which included a contribution from Friedman himself.[27] To a degree this newfound interest was due to an intellectual curiosity, which demanded new ideas that might engage an informed readership. However, this intense focus had a greater imperative. The *Banker* noted that the concept of the money supply was becoming a topic of debate that was 'by no means academic'. 'Money' appeared to be taken seriously by many of the key economic bodies that influenced and directed British economic policy. The magazine cited a September meeting of the OECD that had been set up to discuss Britain's economic strategy following the 1967 devaluation of sterling; a meeting between the International Monetary Fund (IMF) and the 'UK monetary authorities' that had focused solely on the issue of monetary theory; and a recent speech by the Governor of the Bank of England in which he had

---

[23] Hall, 'Policy Paradigms, Social Learning and the State', 288.

[24] Milton Friedman, 'The Role of Monetary Policy', *American Economic Review*, 58/1 (1968), 1–17.

[25] Samuel Brittan, 'The Money Supply: The Great Debate', *Financial Times*, 25 October 1968.

[26] e.g. letter from E. B. Chalmers, 'Money Supply', *Financial Times*, 29 October 1968.

[27] 'The Money Supply Debate', *Banker*, 118/514 (1968), 1094–1116.

stressed the need for greater attention being paid to the money supply.[28] In addition, the US government and the IMF were seen to be increasingly dissatisfied with the 'rather old-fashioned' rejection of exogenous monetary theories embodied in the report of the 1959 Radcliffe Committee on the Working of the Monetary System.[29] This perceived influence of 'monetarist' theory emerged at a time, post-devaluation, in which the British economy was particularly susceptible to the institutional opinions of global economic bodies. Furthermore, the Bank of England took the challenge of evaluating the relevance of the new transatlantic theories seriously, establishing a Money Supply Group to work on the issue.[30]

The gilt-edged stockbrokers W. Greenwell & Co. sent a letter to their clients in October 1968 that asserted that it was vital to understand the money supply because 'the Basel bankers and the IMF attach[ed] considerable importance to the subject'.[31] This justified the firm's decision to undertake research into the influence of monetary aggregates on the gilt-edged market, and provoked the firm to send a detailed memorandum explaining how monetary aggregates were calculated. The belief that the authorities were concerned with the money supply was made concrete in May 1969, when the British government's Letter of Intent in exchange for IMF financial assistance promised to restrain Domestic Credit Expansion (DCE—a measure of the money supply adjusted for the balance of payments).[32] The formalization of DCE as a key component of the authorities' economic objectives, while in no way a firm assertion of the utmost centrality of money to the management of the economy (and certainly bearing no relation to the Friedmanite proposition of ensuring a fixed, stable growth of the money supply), served to valorize the monetary aggregate as a key component in the control of the British economy. Simultaneously, beginning in December 1968, the *Bank of England Quarterly Bulletin* had begun to publish data and accompanying comments on the money supply. Furthermore, the Bank

[28] 'The Supply of Money', *Banker*, 118/513 (1968), 971.
[29] Ibid.; N. H. Dimsdale, 'British Monetary Policy since 1945', in N. F. R. Crafts and Nicholas Woodward (eds), *The British Economy since 1945* (Oxford: Oxford University Press, 1991), 108.
[30] Needham, *UK Monetary Policy*, 24–9.
[31] Michael J. Oliver Personal Archive, Open University [Henceforward: MJO]: letter from W. Greenwell & Co., 'The Money Supply', 18 October 1968.
[32] Capie, *The Bank of England*, 396; Michael J. Oliver, 'Whatever Happened to Monetarism? A Review of British Exchange Rate Policy in the 1980s', *Twentieth Century British History*, 8/1 (1997), 52; 'Domestic Credit Expansion', *Bank of England Quarterly Bulletin*, 9/3 (1969), 363; for a discussion of the Labour government's negotiations with the IMF, see Schenk, *Decline of Sterling*, 185–204.

provided an accounting identity that could be used to calculate the money supply.[33]

What emerged after 1968 was a widely held view that international and domestic authorities were increasingly influenced by new theoretical ideas regarding the role of the money supply. It appeared to observers that these various authorities attached considerable importance to the money supply, and were thus liable to shape their policies in accordance with a strategy to control monetary growth. The academic development of Chicago mon-etarism created a new intellectual climate, which, while being conceptually stimulating for some, was more notable for its perceived influence on key international economic institutions and, by extension, Britain's macro-economic policymaking executive. This ensured that, for those involved in monitoring and assessing the activities of the government, such as the stockbrokers at Greenwell's, it was imperative that they were able to explain changes in the 'money supply' in order to provide high-quality investment advice to their clients. This resulted in the dislocation of the simplistic aggregate of monetary growth from the wider intellectual debates and disagreements in the academic community, ensuring that the importance of money relied not on a scientifically agreed certainty about the role of money, but simply on an increasingly shared belief among market participants that the money supply was important.

Though the government abandoned its commitment to controlling DCE in 1971, the intense focus on the money supply had forced the authorities at the Bank of England to take it seriously.[34] The extent to which the authorities were converted to 'monetarist' prescriptions during this period is debateable. Forrest Capie has argued that the Bank experi-enced no intellectual conversion, yet Duncan Needham has claimed that the authorities were engaged in an internal 'money supply experiment' after 1971, operating according to an unpublished 'monetary objective'.[35] Regardless of these competing accounts, what matters most is that to external observers in the financial markets the Bank and Treasury appeared committed to a practical and moderate goal of monitoring and controlling monetary growth. In October 1972 Gordon Pepper, the principal author of *Greenwell's Monetary Bulletin* and the most prominent City monetarist by the middle of the decade, noted that the Governor had

---

[33] 'Money Supply: April–September 1968', *Bank of England Quarterly Bulletin*, 8/4 (December 1968), 370.
[34] Charles Goodhart, 'The Importance of Money', *Bank of England Quarterly Bulletin*, 10/2 (1970), 159–98; Capie, *The Bank of England*, 452.
[35] Capie, *The Bank of England*, 460; Needham, *UK Monetary Policy*, 46–77; Duncan Needham, 'Britain's Money Supply Experiment, 1971–1973', *English Historical Review*, 130/542 (2015), 89–122.

stated: 'I accept, as most central bankers would, the control of the money supply is my principal, if not my most important, concern.'[36] This valorization had the effect of changing market behaviour. Financial markets began to shift their interpretative framework and align their investment expectations with changes in the monetary aggregates. In response to the official assertions of the importance of the money supply, investors altered their conception of the economy and thus changed the way in which they behaved as market participants. This was especially important in the market for government debt—a market in which 'practice and commercial greed meet theory and the academic'.[37] As described by Hall, it was realized in the wake of Competition and Credit Control that by monitoring the monetary aggregates it was possible to anticipate future changes in interest rates.[38] The authors of *Greenwell's Monetary Bulletin* identified that, if the authorities were 'operating a money supply policy' (that is, attempting to prevent excessive monetary growth) and the monetary aggregates were seen to increase beyond a desirable range, then it was the case that long-term interest rates would inevitably rise in the near future.[39] This dynamic enabled Greenwell's, drawing on the 'counterparts' accounting identity (see Box 5.1), to provide investment advice to their clients.[40] For example, in April 1973 the bulletin stated that 'the authorities will not be able to finance sufficiently the public sector borrowing requirement from the non-bank private sector and, therefore, the money supply will continue to grow excessively. Upwards pressure on interest rates will occur as the authorities battle unsuccessfully to control the money supply.'[41] Alongside this practical usage, monetarist interpretations began to proliferate more generally within the financial markets, providing clues to future economic growth and inflationary pressures likely to emerge. This was led by stockbroker circulars and bulletins such as those published by W. Greenwell & Co., Pember & Boyle

---

[36] MJO: Gordon Pepper (W. Greenwell & Co.), 'Investment Analysts Meeting. Gilt-Edged: The Future Outlook', 25 January 1973; Gordon Pepper, *Inside Thatcher's Monetarist Revolution* (Basingstoke: Macmillan; Institute of Economic Affairs, 1998), 6–19.

[37] Jeremy Wormell, *The Gilt-Edged Market* (London: Allen & Unwin, 1985), p. xiii.

[38] Hall, 'The Movement from Keynesianism to Monetarism', 101–2; David Gowland, *Controlling the Money Supply* (London: Croom Helm, 1982), 101.

[39] MJO: W. Greenwell & Co., 'Monetary Bulletins: An Explanation', October 1972.

[40] For an explanation of the counterparts approach to calculating the money supply, see Anthony Hotson, 'British Monetary Targets, 1976 to 1987: A View from the Fourth Floor of the Bank of England', LSE Financial Markets Group Paper, Special Paper 190 (April 2010), appendix 1.

[41] MJO: W. Greenwell & Co., 'The Financing of the Public Sector Borrowing Requirement in 1973/4', April 1973.

(written by Brian Griffiths), and Joseph Sebag & Co. (Alan Walters).[42] The writers of these circulars demonstrate the significant personal and conceptual overlap between academic-, City-, and political-monetarism. Brian Griffiths was a lecturer in Economics at the London School of Economics (LSE) (1968–76) and Professor of 'Banking and International Finance' at City University (1977–85). Alan Walters was a Professor of Economics at the LSE (1968–76). Both of them, alongside Gordon Pepper, were economic advisors to the Conservative Party in opposition and in government. These individuals were also linked to free market think tanks, such as the Institute of Economic Affairs and the Centre for Policy Studies.[43] *Greenwell's* was the most influential circular, as evidenced in a survey conducted among UK investment managers in 1975 by *Continental Illinois*, which ranked it as providing the best 'Fixed Interest Stock (Primarily gilt-edged market)' investment analysis, and the second-best analysis of 'General Economic Trends'.[44] Pepper explained to Greenwell's clients in October 1973 that the purpose of monitoring monetary aggregates was to 'detect accelerations and decelerations in the economy' and used the firm's bulletin as a means of explaining and predicting the course of monetary change during the post-DCE years.[45]

The strength of the monetarist interpretation of the economy gained a significant degree of validation with the onset of rapid inflationary growth after 1973. At the end of 1973 the Organization of Petroleum Exporting Countries (OPEC) progressively quadrupled the price of oil to almost \$12 a barrel, resulting in a global inflationary shock.[46] The primary method by which both Conservative and Labour governments in the 1970s sought to deal with the rapid increases in inflation was through negotiations over incomes with the trade-union movement. When the Conservative government rejected the National Union of Mineworkers' demand for increased wages in late-1973, the resultant industrial action led to energy shortages and an enforced three-day working week. The Prime Minister called an election in March 1974 in an effort to renew the government's mandate to resist wage

[42] Hall, 'The Movement from Keynesianism to Monetarism', 102; Smith, *The Rise and Fall of Monetarism*, 82.

[43] Brian Griffiths, *Monetarism and Morality: A Response to the Bishops* (London: Centre for Policy Studies, 1985); A. A. Walters, *Money in Boom and Slump: An Empirical Inquiry into British Experience since 1880* (London: Institute of Economic Affairs, 1970); Gordon Pepper, *Money, Credit and Inflation: An Historical Indictment of UK Monetary Policy and a Proposal for Change* (London: Institute of Economic Affairs, 1990).

[44] CPA: KJ 10/5, ' "Stockbrokers" Research: The Best of 1975', *Investors' Chronicle*, 24 October 1965, 6 November 1975.

[45] MJO: W. Greenwell & Co., 'Monetary Bulletin No. 17', October 1973.

[46] Jeffrey A. Frieden, *Global Capitalism: Its Fall and Rise in the Twentieth Century* (New York: W. W. Norton & Co., 2006), 364–6.

increases, but was unable to secure a majority in the face of a Labour Party that promised that it could bring the strike to an end through its closer relationship with the unions. The miners' strike was called off once a 35 per cent wage increase had been secured.[47] Wage increases of this scale—an attempt to accommodate the oil inflation—generated an inflationary spiral. When Labour re-entered government, the primary focus was on resisting this cycle by entering into a voluntary social contract with the unions and employers. As part of this effort, the government implemented statutory price controls to offset falling living standards. Meanwhile, despite the significant borrowing deficit bequeathed to them by their Conservative predecessors, the government made efforts to maintain economic growth, and avoid unemployment, through deficit-financed expenditure.[48]

In this context, financial commentators simplistically explained the rapid hike in the rate of inflation from a monetarist point of view, and popularized the interpretation through market circulars, in the press, and in direct communication with political parties. Gordon Pepper criticized the 'explosion in M3', which began at the end of 1971 and grew by 60 per cent in the next two years. According to Pepper, the origins of this rapid expansion could be primarily attributed to the Bank of England's failure to control bank lending, which was further exacerbated by the vastly expanding public-sector deficit. This interpretation placed the interventionist Heath government, under the Chancellorship of Anthony Barber, at the root of the rapid growth of the money supply.[49] In a speech dramatically entitled 'An Economic Threat to Democracy' (a theme recently considered by Peter Jay in *The Times*) given to the Conservative Bow Group in March 1974, Pepper chastised the Heath government for its 'growth at all costs' policy, informing the Conservative House of Commons Finance Committee later that year that 'the economic record of the last Conservative Government was almost unbelievably bad'.[50] As Needham demonstrates, the Heath government had in fact been operating according to a money supply target. Yet it is clear that Heath, in

---

[47] Kevin Hickson, *The IMF Crisis of 1976 and British Politics* (London: Tauris Academic, 2005), 53–4.

[48] Artis et al., 'Social Democracy in Hard Times', 40–4; Hickson, *The IMF Crisis*, 57.

[49] MJO: Gordon Pepper, 'Competition by Lack of Credit Control—a Paper given to the Money Study Group at a Monetary Policy Symposium held at the London School of Economics', 28 November 1973.

[50] MJO: Gordon Pepper, 'An Economic Threat to Democracy—Annual Conference of the Bow Group at Magdalen College, Oxford', 31 March 1974; Gordon Pepper, 'Address to the House of Commons Finance Committee of the Conservative Party', 25 November 1974; Peter Jay, 'How Inflation Threatens British Democracy with its Last Chance before Extinction', *The Times*, 1 July 1974.

accordance with the macroeconomic policy norms of the post-war social democratic settlement, was unwilling to commit the government to the deflationary policies necessary to adhere to the private target in 1973 and thus abandoned the nascent monetary experiment.[51]

As inflation soared throughout 1974 and 1975 (and PSBR growth continued apace), this broad monetarist interpretation of events was given a strong impetus. The modest cadre of British monetarist economists became particularly vocal, expressing their concerns in increasingly pessimistic terms. In an open letter to Harold Wilson in July 1974, Alan Walters and Harry Johnson urged the Prime Minister to take urgent action to ensure a gradual reduction in the rate of money supply growth with a return to a balanced budget. They warned:

> Every week you . . . postpone the necessary action the more difficult the task and the nearer we approach the abyss of hyperinflation . . . If you do not act speedily on the lines that we have urged, we are convinced that both inflation and unemployment will be massive, ugly, and cruel.[52]

These attacks popularized and politicized monetarism as it became increasingly favoured by many Conservative MPs. Yet it was the Labour Chancellor who did most to further the monetarist cause in British public discourse. The questions and proclamations of backbench Conservatives in the Commons regarding the state of the money supply handed Denis Healey a useful political stick with which to beat the opposition. Drawing on the monetarist critique of the Heath administration, Healey regularly responded to challenges in the Commons regarding the rate of monetary growth by comparing the Labour government's record with their predecessors. Healey told the House in March 1975: 'I think that there is now general agreement on both sides of the House that the major cause of the inflation now racking Britain is the excessive increase in the money supply which took place in the last year of the previous Conservative Government.'[53] In early 1976 he was quick to note that his record on controlling the money was 'four times superior' to that of the previous government, and that this was largely due to the Labour government's 'superior fiscal probity' (the Budget of April 1975 had cut public expenditure, and in July a system of 'cash limits' on spending had been introduced).[54] In continuing to stress success in preventing excessive monetary growth, and consistently wielding monetary growth under Heath as a

---

[51] Needham, *UK Monetary Policy*, 46–77.

[52] MJO: W. Greenwell & Co., 'Monetary Bulletin No. 26', July 1974.

[53] Parliamentary Debates, Commons, vol. 889, cols 667–73 (27 March 1975).

[54] Parliamentary Debates, Commons, vol. 904, cols 1396–8 (5 February 1976); Hickson, *The IMF Crisis*, 57–8.

political weapon to rile the opposition benches, Healey further legitimized the importance of the 'money supply' as a key economic indicator and gave the distinct impression that the government was making every effort to prevent its expansion. This was not a 'monetarist' approach to economic policy in any sense. Healey stressed: 'I think it is important to keep the matter under control and I have done so. However, I do not think that aspect is as important as many honourable Members believe.'[55] Yet it is clear that, by proclaiming successful control of the money supply as one of his government's achievements, the Chancellor served to cement a widespread belief within financial markets that the government did attach importance to the monetary aggregates and was operating a strict monetary policy. The result was to establish a situation in which the success or failure of the government's counter-inflationary policies could seemingly be measured according to the behaviour of the money supply.

THE EURODOLLAR MARKET AND COLLAPSE OF BRETTON WOODS

This domestic story of how the money supply became defined as an important economic indicator for the financial markets must also be placed in a global context. The role of the money supply as a key indicator of market confidence in the government was particularly influential as it had emerged within the vacuum left in the wake of the collapse of the Bretton Woods system of fixed exchange rates at the start of the decade.

The Bretton Woods system, which prevailed in the post-war decades, had not taken the form envisaged during its formation at the 1944 conference in New Hampshire. Instead of establishing a multilateral international monetary system with the IMF at its head, the system was based on the US dollar. Once the system had been formally established in 1958, the dollar was valued at one thirty-fifth of an ounce of gold, and currencies around the world were fixed to the dollar at a variety of exchange rates.[56] The purpose of the system was to ensure that the international monetary instability of the interwar period was not replicated, but also that exchange rates were flexible where necessary.[57] For the sake of the international order, changes to exchange rates were deemed acceptable only when alternative, domestic solutions had been exhausted. The system relied upon states controlling short-term movements of capital, so that flows of hot money did not undermine the exchange rates

---

[55] Parliamentary Debates, Commons, vol. 904, cols 1396–8 (5 February 1976).
[56] Frieden, *Global Capitalism*, 290.		[57] Ibid. 290.

determined and managed by governments pursuing domestic macroeconomic goals.[58] Where capital movements were restricted, international trade was encouraged as the means of producing stable, productive economic growth and prosperity. The Bretton Woods order was able to function effectively because international financial flows had been halted by the trauma of the 1930s and 1940s, and their reconstruction was hampered by controls on cross-border capital movements. This permitted governments the freedom and space to pursue domestic macroeconomic policies without the fear that capital movements might undermine them (for example, interest rate differentials between nations would not encourage equilibrating movements of capital that prevented their effectiveness).[59]

The Bretton Woods system collapsed in August 1971, when the Nixon administration decided to break with the fixed rate of exchange for gold and permitted the devaluation of the US dollar by 10 per cent. When the USA had previously experienced a payments deficit in 1959/60, the Federal Reserve had raised interest rates to defend the structure of the international order, thus pushing the domestic economy into recession. In the 1960s, the deficit spending engendered by the battle against Communism in south-east Asia, and the war on poverty at home, generated inflation. Foreigners began to lose trust in the US government's commitment to maintaining the value of the dollar and instead sought to hold inflation-proofed gold.[60] Rather than maintain its obligation as the hegemonic centre of the international monetary order, as the USA had done in 1959/60, the Nixon administration, fearful of the damaging effects on employment, output, and the nation's balance of payments, decided against the cuts to expenditure and increases in interest rates necessary to maintain the dollar–gold parity.[61] Following the breakdown of the post-war international monetary order, sterling was permitted to float in 1972.[62]

The breakdown of Bretton Woods generated the problem of how to monitor the performance of governments without a clear anchor; and how to ensure that responsible (non-inflationary) policies were undertaken.[63] The collapse of the international monetary system freed states from the

---

[58] Ibid. 290–2.
[59] Ibid. 343; John Gerard Ruggie, 'International Regimes, Transactions, and Change: Embedded Liberalism in the Postwar Economic Order', *International Organization*, 36/2 (1982), 379–415.
[60] Frieden, *Global Capitalism*, 344–5.   [61] Ibid. 339–42.
[62] Barry J. Eichengreen, *Globalizing Capital: A History of the International Monetary System*, 2nd edn (Princeton: Princeton University Press, 2008), 131.
[63] Oliver and Pemberton, 'Learning and Change in 20th Century British Economic Policy', 428.

constraints imposed by their obligation to maintain their fixed exchange rates, and as a result governments around the world used their new found freedom to stimulate economic growth.[64] As Pepper noted in 1971:

> the discipline of a fixed rate of exchange is one of the few factors which ensure that Governments react to excessive inflation. A Government may be reluctant to take unpopular measures to control excessive inflation. A deterioration in the balance of payments and foreign exchange pressures often force a Government to take early action. A movement towards either floating exchange rates or more flexible fixed exchange rates relaxes this most important discipline on Governments.[65]

In 1977, Paul Volcker (President of the Federal Reserve Bank of New York, and subsequent Chairman of the United States Federal Reserve) described this 'radical change in the game' and identified the value of monitoring the money supply for policymakers and investors in the new era of floating rates. He told the Toronto Bond Traders Association: 'the new focus on containing monetary growth can fill some of [the] void... It embodies an essential truth in a manner that can be clearly communicated. Performance can be readily monitored.'[66]

This structural change to the international monetary system coincided with the emergence of vast sums of 'highly mobile private money' in the form of institutional investment funds (pension, insurance, and trust funds) and the international Euromarkets (based in London) during the late 1960s and 1970s.[67] The size, speed, and concentration of this (in the words of Denis Healey) 'atomic cloud of footloose funds' overwhelmed the capacity for the government to intervene in the operation of the financial markets (primarily to influence exchange rates) and placed a greater onus on the state to meet the demands of its creditors.[68] The revival of international financial markets had eroded the institutional structure of the Bretton Woods system. The emergence of the Euromarkets outside the purview of capital controls caused increasing disruption to the monetary system, as speculative flows of hot money corroded its basic architecture. Increases in the regularity and intensity of exchange rate crises in the late 1960s were attributable to the capital market volatility

---

[64] Frieden, *Global Capitalism*, 364; Eichengreen, *Globalizing Capital*, 131; Schenk, *Decline of Sterling*, 317–56.

[65] MJO: Gordon Pepper, 'Is the Long Term Bear Market in Gilts Ending?', November 1971.

[66] MJO: W. Greenwell & Co., 'Mr Volcker's Speech to the Toronto Bond Traders' Association—22nd Feb. 1977—Monetary Bulletin No. 66', May 1977.

[67] Coakley and Harris, *City of Capital*, 206–8; Burn, 'The State, the City and the Euromarkets', 226–7.

[68] Denis Healey, *Time of my Life* (London: Michael Joseph, 1989), 412.

generated by the emergence of the Euromarkets. The unregulated pools of money that had accumulated outside the control of states responded to conventional market signals, and were thus oblivious to the domestic goals of governments facing speculative flows.[69] The Euromarkets offered a space in which investors and currency holders could switch quickly out of sterling and into dollars without restraint.[70] Newton has argued that, in the case of the 1967 sterling crisis, the speculation was not a response to poor trade performance, but was simply a crisis of confidence that created a 'negative feedback loop'.[71] This was an example of what the capital controls permitted by the Bretton Woods agreement were supposed to prevent—national economic policies being undermined by capital flows (irrational or otherwise). In the early 1970s West European nations attempted, unsuccessfully, to tighten their capital controls to support currency parities and retain control over domestic macroeconomic policies.[72]

THE STERLING CRISIS AND THE ADOPTION OF MONETARY TARGETS, 1976

Against the backdrop of vast inflationary pressures in 1975, it became increasingly evident within the Treasury and Bank of England that a greater degree of importance and value was being assigned, in both domestic and overseas financial markets, to the rate of monetary growth as a measure of inflation prospects. The formalized focus on monetary aggregates in the late 1960s, coupled with the popular critique of the deleterious effects of the expansionary Heath government, had ensured that investors and brokers in the gilt-edged and foreign exchange markets were heavily influenced by the behaviour of the money supply. Analysts in the financial markets had begun to employ the domestic money supply as a yardstick with which to measure confidence in the government's economic policies, and its credibility in being able to bring inflationary pressures under control.

In October 1975, a paper was presented to a subcommittee of the joint Treasury/Bank of England group undertaking a review of monetary policy. Produced by unnamed Bank officials, the brief stated that the Bank was becoming increasingly anxious about 'prospective monetary

---

[69] Harold James, *International Monetary Cooperation since Bretton Woods* (Oxford: Oxford University Press, 1996), 179.
[70] Newton, 'The Sterling Devaluation of 1967', 925–7.   [71] Ibid. 928–9.
[72] Helleiner, *States and the Reemergence of Global Finance*, 103.

developments'—namely, that an expanding PSBR was contributing to an upcoming rapid growth of the money supply. The paper stressed the importance of 'the climate of opinion, expectations and attitudes' and argued that there was a need to present a public display of commitment to controlling the monetary aggregates as a means of ensuring confidence within the financial markets. In attempting to achieve this, it was suggested that it might be useful to discuss establishing publicly announced monetary targets.[73] A responding note was prepared for discussion on the possible role that could be played in the adoption of the 'monetarist prescription' of setting a target for the growth of the money supply and holding to it 'irrespective of what was happening in the economy'.[74] The following week a brief was sent to Healey from the Bank that stressed the importance of demonstrating control of the money supply to the public in order to maintain the confidence of investors and to assert the government's anti-inflation credibility. The brief argued that sharp rises in the money stock would be interpreted simplistically by monetarist commentators as evidence that the government had 'given up the fight against inflation'—and so, to ensure that market confidence was retained, strong action on the monetary aggregates was required.[75]

This was a view supported in a draft of the Working Group's paper on 'The Review of Monetary Policy', which argued that it was not necessary to 'subscribe completely to monetarist arguments' to agree that monetary policy could produce inflationary pressure through the real economy and 'via its effect on confidence and expectations'. High money supply figures were clearly damaging to market confidence—made worse by financial commentators and much of the editorial comment in the press, which was 'overwhelmingly monetarist in a crude way'. In the light of this, the report stated that the Working Party had 'little doubt that a policy based on a declining monetary aggregates should be adopted and publicly stated' to demonstrate the government's commitment to reducing the money supply. However, the report expressed caution that strict monetary targets would undermine the authorities' discretion over interest rates. Furthermore, there was doubt that the authorities were sufficiently able actually to control the money supply.[76]

A submission on monetary policy formulated by Treasury officials J. M. Bridgeman and Kenneth Couzens argued that the 'monetarist

[73] TNA: T 364/274, 'Monetary Policy', October 1975.
[74] TNA: T 364/274, letter from Middleton to Bridgeman, 'Review of Monetary Policy', 31 October 1975.
[75] TNA: T 364/274, letter from Elstan to France, 'Monetary Implications of Fiscal Policy: A Holding Brief', 7 November 1975.
[76] TNA: T 386/122, 'Review of Monetary Policy', 17 December 1975.

approach' was 'neither proven empirically nor intellectually convincing'. However, the authors supported the development of an internal monetary target, which would be used as a yardstick with which to measure deviations in monetary growth that might signal a need for 'a reappraisal of macro-economic policy'. It was stressed that the target should not be fixed indefinitely but merely employed as a guideline, which would prove particularly useful to the Bank of England in providing a 'clearer frame of reference' in its market operations, and was certainly not designed for publication.[77] A published target was strongly resisted in a paper written a few days later by Treasury Under-Secretary Frank Cassell, which stated that, despite the ability of a published target to generate confidence in the markets (especially among the 'monetarists who have a significant influence on market attitudes'), an explicit public target would too rigidly commit the government to corrective actions. Furthermore, if it appeared that the targets were not likely to be met, market reactions would actually amplify the deviation from the target, as gilt-edged investors would force the authorities to borrow more from the banking sector—thus increasing the rate of monetary growth.[78] The authorities' perception of the markets was that they had become strongly influenced by monetarist ideas—or at the very least had begun to associate money supply figures with inflationary pressures. Civil servants and Bank officials consciously expressed the view that the influence of 'monetarist' ideas among investors was a significant limitation on the government's policies. In a note from the Downing Street Policy Unit in January 1976, the Prime Minister was informed that 'some people in the City...(whether correctly or incorrectly does not matter) believe that a rising money supply leads to inflation'.[79] Gordon Pepper in particular embodied what the authorities were 'up against from large sections of the City and external opinion'.[80] Yet there remained strong resistance to the constraints that would be imposed by a public monetary target.

Beginning in April 1975, the sterling exchange rate began to fall in response to inflationary pressures and a lack of international confidence in the Labour government's economic policies. In March 1976 the pound

[77] TNA: T 386/122, letter from Bridgeman to Wass, 'Draft Outline of Submission on Monetary Policy', 27 January 1976.
[78] TNA: T 386/122, letter from Cassell to Wass, 'Targets for Monetary Policy', 6 February 1976.
[79] TNA: T 386/115, letter from Wicks to Robson, 'Monetary Policy—a Note by the Policy Unit', 5 January 1976.
[80] TNA: T 386/115, letter from Posner to Wass, 'Mr Gordon Pepper', 22 April 1976; letter from Wass to Posner, 'Mr Gordon Pepper', 26 April 1976; letter from Middleton to Couzens, 7 May 1976.

went below the $2.00 mark, and, following Wilson's resignation from Downing Street, it eventually dropped to $1.70 by June.[81] The government was able to obtain a stand-by credit arrangement with the IMF, but confidence could not be restored until Healey demonstrated the government's serious commitment to bridging the payments gap, controlling inflation, and cutting government expenditure. After a few weeks of discussion within the Cabinet, in which Anthony Benn and Anthony Crosland both expressed distaste for deflationary measures, Healey announced a package of policies designed to revive confidence—a £1 billion cut to public expenditure, and a £1 billion increase in National Insurance contributions.[82]

It is widely noted in the extensive literature on this episode that the July package also included a commitment to adopt a publicly announced monetary target.[83] Yet this decision was not so straightforward. On 5 July a meeting of senior Treasury figures was held by Douglas Wass to discuss 'the desirability of setting targets for the monetary aggregates'. In the meeting, the Chief Economic Advisor to the Treasury, Sir Bryan Hopkin, explained how a published target could influence market behaviour in such a way as actually to fulfil the target, arguing that, if the government committed to a combined PSBR and monetary target, demand for gilt-edged stock would increase (thus reducing the amount that needed to be borrowed from the banking system). However, if it appeared that the monetary target was going to be surpassed and the markets expected the government to raise interest rates, then meeting the money supply target would be made more difficult. Kenneth Couzens also expressed concern that the adoption of a money supply target would cause political difficulties for the Chancellor, as the trade unions were likely to be suspicious of a policy 'propounded by the right wing of the Opposition'. It was agreed that there was a danger of setting a target that would be deemed too high, with J. M. Bridgeman stating that a target of greater than 10 per cent growth would be viewed as being too lenient. Treasury officials were broadly opposed to public targets, with Wass expressing hope that the contents of the existing plans for the 'July Package' would impress the markets sufficiently to encourage the sale of gilts.[84] Yet on

[81] Schenk, *Decline of Sterling*, 369–71; Kynaston, *The City of London*, iv. 529–31.

[82] Kathleen Burk and Alec Cairncross, *'Goodbye, Great Britain': The 1976 IMF Crisis* (New Haven: Yale University Press, 1992), 43–50; Hickson, *The IMF Crisis*, 96.

[83] Healey, *Time of my Life*, 432; Burk and Cairncross, *'Goodbye, Great Britain'*, 161; Mark D. Harmon, *The British Labour Government and the 1976 IMF Crisis* (Basingstoke: Macmillan, 1997), 155; Douglas Wass, *Decline to Fall: The Making of Macro-Economic Policy and the 1976 Crisis* (Oxford: Oxford University Press, 2008), 212–13.

[84] TNA: T 386/116, Wood, 'Note for the Record', 5 July 1976.

12 July Wass told the 'Second Secretaries Meeting' that the Chancellor wanted 'to incorporate a monetary target in his forthcoming statement'.[85] Treasury staff, alongside colleagues at the Bank of England, were charged with formulating this—with the Bank proposing a target range of 8–12 per cent for 1976/7.[86] Hopkin argued that a monetary target would 'add materially to the confidence-generating effect of the package'—despite acknowledging the future difficulties it might cause in constraining policy. However, Hopkin informed Wass that he was against the Bank's suggested target range, and preferred instead a single figure commitment of 'about 12%', which would decline to '"less" or "about 10%"'.[87]

A deep Treasury resistance to monetary targets remained in principle, which Wass has emphasized in his historical memoir of the crisis.[88] In a letter to the Chancellor's Parliamentary Private Secretary (PPS) on 16 July, the Permanent Secretary asserted his strong dissatisfaction with the idea of publishing a target. He felt that the government had 'come very close to overdoing the targetry business', and that there was a danger of producing an impossible target that lacked credibility. He also repeated the self-fulfilling nature of the monetary target, which, if appearing to be overshot, could generate an expansion in monetary aggregates as a result of reduced confidence in the gilt-edged market. Despite these objections Wass simply concluded that 'since we cannot afford failure we must have the target'.[89]

The absolute necessity of regaining the confidence of the financial markets made the adoption of a monetary target seemingly essential—regardless of the intellectual justifications or Treasury preferences. The Bank of England was generally more proactive in asserting a targets policy—aware that a public monetary restraint would place 'a tighter rope round the Chancellor's neck' to restrain public expenditure.[90] In a meeting held in the Chancellor's room at the Treasury on 20 July, the Governor of the Bank of England, Gordon Richardson, argued that adopting a target, alongside a firm commitment to a 'progressive reduction of inflation', would help confidence.[91] Reviewing the Chancellor's proposed statement the following day, Richardson stressed that the target

---

[85] Wass, *Decline to Fall*, 212.
[86] TNA: T 386/16, 'Speaking Note on Monetary Targets', 14 July 1976.
[87] TNA: T 386/116, letter from Hopkins to Wass, 'Monetary Targets', 15 July 1976.
[88] Wass, *Decline to Fall*.
[89] TNA: T 386/16, letter from Wass to PPS, 'Monetary Targets', 16 July 1976.
[90] BOE: EID 4/700, C. W. McMahon, 'Monetary Policy', 26 September 1975; quoted in Needham, 'Britain's Money Supply Experiment, 1971–1973', 25.
[91] BOE: EID 4/700, Monck, 'Note of a Meeting: A Monetary Target in the Package?', 20 July 1976.

must not exceed 12 per cent and that, 'consistent with your objective of lowering the rate of inflation', should be lower the following year.[92] On 22 July Healey made his statement to the House of Commons, stating simply:

> monetary growth *should* [emphasis added] amount to about 12 per cent. Such an outcome would be fully consistent with our objectives for reducing inflation. I repeat the assurances I have given that I do not intend to allow the growth of the money supply to fuel inflation either this year or next. If inflation and output move as now forecast I would expect the growth in money supply to be lower next year than this.[93]

The Chancellor justified his phraseology to Richardson by arguing that he felt he had gone 'a considerable way towards what [the Governor] wanted'. His reasoning for not going further was that he 'did not want to enter into commitments without being clear about the policy measures needed to meet them, and our ability to deliver them'. The use of the word 'should' was a deliberate attempt to provide manoeuvrability and to prevent being forced into automatic corrective action if aggregates appeared to be deviating from the target.[94] The vagueness of Healey's announcement, with its lack of rigid commitment, had a double effect. While serving further to valorize the money supply as something that the authorities were attempting to control, the statement did not convince investors that the commitment was serious. Writing in the *Phillips and Drew Market Review* for August, Chris Anthony described how the fiscal promises of the 'July Package' were met with 'scant enthusiasm in both the gilt-edged and foreign exchange markets'. The market had calculated that, with an estimated borrowing requirement of £9 billion, the money supply was certain to grow at a rate 'inconsistent with the Chancellor's aim of a sustained fall in the rate of inflation'. Confidence had not been restored by the package as a whole, with the money supply commitment providing little relief for the government.[95] Furthermore, the government's commitment to controlling the money supply was decidedly unconvincing in global markets. A letter sent from S. H. Broadbent at the 'United Kingdom Treasury and Supply Delegation' in Washington to Frank Cassell described the view:

[92] TNA: T 386/116, letter from Richardson to Healey, 21 July 1976.
[93] Parliamentary Debates, Commons, vol. 915, cols 2010–36 (22 July 1976), emphasis added.
[94] TNA: T 386/116, letter from Healey to Richardson, 22 July 1976.
[95] Chris Anthony, 'Spending Cuts and the Money Supply', *Phillips and Drew Market Review* (August 1976).

The Chancellor's public statements lay increasing emphasis on a 12% *target* [emphasis added], but amongst those who take an interest in these matters (i.e. the Wall Street Journal, a good deal of the foreign exchange market, and, to varying degrees a majority of the bank and business economists) our enthusiasm for targets is seen as lukewarm, our willingness to stick with them as slight, and the targets themselves as too high.

Broadbent stated that, regardless of the 'intellectual basis of monetarist arguments', 'the fact remains that there seems to be some yearning for a clear, and probably too low, set of monetary targets as an element of our policies—coupled, of course, with some evidence that we will actually follow them'.[96]

In the following months it was acknowledged within the Treasury that the hoped-for 12 per cent growth in money supply had actually 'assumed the properties of a target', and that market expectations were aligned to the notion that the government was attempting to achieve the 12 per cent rate or lower.[97] This was despite a deliberate effort on the part of the Chancellor not to commit to a rigid target. Failure to meet the 12 per cent figure would indicate to investors that the government was failing to get a grip of the situation, and thus the authorities were required to operate as if the figure described was actually a fixed target. Treasury officials realized that in the financial markets the behaviour of the monetary aggregates, in relation to the nominal target, had come to be formally regarded as 'an index of the "responsibility" of Government policy and hence ultimately of its credit-worthiness'.[98]

At the start of August 1976, in the midst of a hot summer drought, a balance of payments deficit of £524 million was revealed. This bad news was compounded in September when both British Leyland workers and the National Union of Seamen went on strike, and the Labour Party published its proposals for nationalizing the financial sector. This toxic combination triggered renewed pressure on the pound. A decision (without Cabinet approval) was taken to apply to the IMF for support at the end of the month.[99] The IMF originally recommended that the PSBR be

---

[96] TNA: T 386/116, letter from Broadbent to Cassell, 'Monetary Targets', 28 September 1976, emphasis added.

[97] HM Treasury Freedom of Information Disclosures <https://web.archive.org/web/20130123073026/http://hm-treasury.gov.uk/foi_sterling_imf_2006.htm> (accessed 20 December 2016) (HMT FOI), File 60, letter from Wiggins to Heigham, 'Briefing for Chancellor's Statement', 14 December 1976.

[98] TNA: T 386/117, letter from Britton to Hopkin, 'Objectives for the Money Supply', 17 November 1976; letter from Hopkin to Britton, 'Objectives for the Money Supply', 23 November 1976.

[99] Hickson, *The IMF Crisis*, 99–101.

cut by £6.5 billion–£7 billion (from a forecasted £11.2 billion), though Callaghan refused to go below a £9 billion PSBR, which had been agreed upon in July—a policy backed by the TUC and CBI in their support for the 'social contract'.[100] By late November the IMF proposed a £4.5 billion cut in the PSBR over two years. The Cabinet was divided. Anthony Crosland repeated the argument he had made in July that there was no need further to deflate the economy, because existing policies were working. Further cuts would increase unemployment, which in turn would counterproductively expand the PSBR through increased social security costs. If the IMF would not listen to sense, Crosland argued, the government should threaten to restrain imports and withdraw from military outposts in Germany and Cyprus. Crosland's Keynesian–Revisionist response to the crisis was supported by many of his Cabinet colleagues, including Harold Lever, Roy Hattersley, and Shirley Williams. A more radical solution was offered by Wedgwood Benn in pursuit of an 'Alternative Economic Strategy' of import quotas, exchange controls, expansion of state ownership, and greater freedoms for the TUC in forming national economic policy. Peter Shore, Crosland, and Hattersley all argued for a system of temporary import controls as a short-term solution to the balance of payments deficit, but did not support Benn's vision of using the crisis to implement his radical economic strategy. However, neither Benn, Shore, nor Crosland was able to garner Cabinet support in a meeting of the Cabinet on 1 December. When Crosland finally decided to support Callaghan and Healey in cutting public expend-iture in order to maintain the stability of the government, Healey was given the authority by Cabinet to negotiate with the IMF on the basis of £1.5 billion cuts in 1977/8. The eventual agreement with the Fund, made public in the Letter of Intent, was for expenditure cuts of £1 billion in 1977/8 and £1.5 billion in 1978/9, with £500 million to be generated by the sale of British Petroleum shares. In addition to this further round of spending cuts, the government committed itself to a DCE target to be achieved through a special deposits scheme to restrain bank lending.[101] It was asserted that the government's IMF Letter of Intent established a commitment to a target for domestic monetary growth (£M3), yet this was not the case.[102] Healey announced in the Commons that 'the growth of sterling M3 is likely to be between 9 per cent and 13 per cent. It is too early to give an estimate for 1977–78. But our target will now be in terms

---

[100] Ibid. 128–9.   [101] Ibid. 124–49.

[102] Bank of England Freedom of Information Disclosures <http://www.bankofengland. co.uk/publications/foi/disc060519.htm> (accessed 20 December 2016) (henceforward BOE FOI): document 4, Denis Healey, 'Letter of Intent', 15 December 1976.

of DCE, not M3.'[103] Indeed, a note prepared for Healey's attendance at Cabinet in advance of his Commons announcement described how the IMF team was persuaded that an M3 target was not needed in addition to DCE, on the basis that having to observe two targets would be problematic.[104] However, in announcing a 'likely outcome' for £M3, Healey essentially reaffirmed the monetary 'target' set in July (DCE was derived from £M3 anyway). The government had avoided committing itself to a formal monetary target with the IMF, but Healey gave legitimacy to what was interpreted and expected by the financial markets to be a treated as a formal target range. In March 1977 the Governor informed the Chancellor that, despite the latter's continued reluctance to announce any formal commitment to £M3 growth, the constraint was already in place, because the financial markets would react badly to growth above the 'likely' growth of 9–13 per cent—even if the formal DCE target was being fulfilled.[105] In his memoirs, Healey described the deliberate decision to publish monetary forecasts and describe them as targets in order to 'satisfy the markets'.[106] In reality, the emergence of targets was, as Bryan Hopkin has asserted, 'mostly luck'.[107]

With the established constraint of a fixed exchange regime no longer in place, financial markets looked to the money supply as a measure for indicating the anti-inflationary, 'sound' policies of the government. The sterling crisis of 1976 was a critical juncture in which the newly formed market metric for measuring confidence compelled the resistant Chancellor towards moderate concessions, which were translated into formal targets by a rational and inevitable market response.

THE OPERATION OF MONETARY
TARGETS, 1976–1979

The effect of having unwillingly established fixed monetary targets, which were given validity by the behaviour and expectations of the financial markets, was that the government was required to demonstrate publicly its long-term commitment to the targets. It became impossible for the

---

[103] Parliamentary Debates, Commons, vol. 922, col. 1534 (15 December 1976).

[104] HMT FOI: File 65, letter from Bridgeman to Isaac, 'Cabinet 14 December: Monetary Policy', 13 December 1976.

[105] TNA: T 386/118, 'Note of a Meeting Held in the Chancellor of the Exchequer's Room, Treasury Chambers', 16 March 1977.

[106] Healey, *Time of my life*, 434.

[107] Bryan Hopkin, 'Freedom and Necessity in Economic Policy: Britain 1970–1979', *Political Quarterly*, 70/3 (1999), 312.

authorities to cease operating according to targets, because any attempt to abandon them would be seen by the markets as failure to commit to the action markets believed was required to control inflation. The Governor informed Healey in October 1977 that 'any appearance of resiling' from holding to monetary targets would cause serious damage to confidence.[108] Wass also conceded that 'it was no longer practical politics to contemplate abandoning monetary targets'.[109] Targets were now 'locked in' and irreversible. Furthermore, in line with the Chancellor's promise to eradicate inflationary pressures, it was thought that the markets were expecting the government to set progressively lower yearly target ranges—regardless of other policy demands. The Governor was particularly keen, as in 1976, and attempted to persuade the Chancellor to commit to a percentage reduction on the previous 9–13 per cent target range for the financial year 1977/8.[110] Any attempt to *increase* the target range, regardless of any broader economic objectives, would send a damaging signal to the markets that the government did not have a convincing anti-inflationary strategy.[111]

Yet the obligation to continue announcing nominal targets was less onerous than the requirements of actually meeting them. By agreeing to adhere to the targets, the government accepted that action would be taken to ensure that they were not breached. From August until October 1977, the success of the government's attempts to maintain the stability of sterling by signalling a domestic monetary squeeze had the unintended outcome of generating significant foreign capital inflows. A high interest rate encouraged funds into Britain, which had the double effect of a significant appreciation of the exchange rate and an increase in the rate of monetary growth.[112] The effect of the increase in £M3 was to shake confidence in the gilt-edged market, as it seemed to signal that the authorities had been overwhelmed, giving the impression that the government lacked the ability and will to take the necessary steps to fulfil its promised anti-inflationary agenda. There was evident frustration within the Labour government, as the market was perceived to be over-reacting and misunderstanding the difference between domestic and 'inflow'

[108] TNA: T 386/120, 'Note of a Meeting Held at 11 Downing Street—"Money Supply, Exchange Rate Policies and Exchange Controls"', 11 October 1977.

[109] TNA: T 286/271, 'Note of a Meeting Held in Sir Douglas Wass' Room—Monetary Policy', 9 November 1977.

[110] TNA: T 386/118, 'Note of a Meeting Held in the Chancellor of the Exchequer's Room, Treasury Chambers', 16 March 1977.

[111] TNA: T 386/119, letter from Bridgeman to Isaac, 'Market Reaction to Package', 20 September 1977.

[112] Peter Riddell, 'Sterling Policy Threatening Monetary Target, Say Brokers', *Financial Times*, 28 October 1977; W. Greenwell & Co., 'Monetary Bulletin No. 69', August 1977.

generated monetary growth. Yet they were constrained by the targets. In a letter to the Chancellor, the Treasury Minster Denzil Davies expressed the view:

> we should do all we can do to keep M3 within the announced target during this financial year. It matters not, it seems to me, that the definition of M3 is arbitrary; that the commitment to the IMF is in terms of Domestic Credit Expansion (although everyone knows that DCE is irrelevant when a country is in a balance of payments surplus); and that an increase in the money supply caused by 'printing money' may be of a different nature to an increase caused by inflows. All this, no doubt, is good stuff for a seminar. Unfortunately, those people who have the power to move large sums of money across the international exchanges believe, on the whole, that 'money counts'. The fact that it may not count as much as they think it does, seems to me to be somewhat irrelevant.[113]

As described earlier, gilt-edged investors understood the practical use of monetary theory in an environment in which the authorities were seen to be acting to restrain monetary growth, by allowing investors to predict the future course of interest rates. Essentially, if monetary aggregates were seen to be increasing beyond the government's stated objectives, investors could be sure that interest rates were likely to rise. In the wake of the failure of Competition and Credit Control, the authorities had developed the Duke of York Strategy for selling government bonds, which acknowledged that the demand for gilts peaked when long-term interest rates were believed to be at their highest—meaning that the price of the stock was at its lowest and would increase as long-term interest rates were inevitably reduced over the medium term. If the authorities could engineer a situation of this kind, they would be able to ensure a successful sale of government debt.[114] The task of investors and their brokers was to predict when interest rates were at their peak in order to ensure the greatest capital return on their investment. The Duke of York Strategy gives the appearance that the authorities were able to establish a situation amenable to their funding programme, and thus investors were simply following the authorities' lead. Yet there was a fundamental communication problem in this strategy, which meant that the authorities were unable to announce freely when long-term interest rates were at their peak, because under a system of monetary targeting it remained up to gilt-edged brokers, looking after the interests of their clients, to decide when they had peaked.

---

[113] TNA: T 386/120, letter from Davies to Healey, 'Monetary Prospects', 27 October 1977.

[114] Hall, 'The Movement from Keynesianism to Monetarism', 101–2; TNA: T 386/406, 'Transcript from BBC2, *The Money Programme*', 28 February 1979.

As a result, the behaviour of gilt-edged investors could force interest rate changes on the government if they refused to purchase stock until they believed that rates were actually at their highest.[115] Hall has described this as holding the government 'to ransom'—though in reality they were simply assuming that the government would adhere to its targets.[116]

This process regularly took place under the post-1976 system of monetary targets. In late 1977, as £M3 grew beyond the intended 9–13 per cent annual rate, gilt-edged investors predicted that interest rates would have to increase to halt monetary expansion, and, given that an interest rate hike was inevitable, the rational investment decision was to hold off from buying gilt-edged securities until rates had peaked. The result was that market demand dried up completely, establishing a situation that forced the government to borrow directly from the banking system. In response, the government was forced to raise its Minimum Lending Rate (MLR) from 5 per cent to 7 per cent in order to meet expectations. This resulted in a large-scale selling operation.[117] Interest rate hikes resulted in the appreciation of the sterling, and forced the authorities to 'uncap' the exchange rate—that is, allow it to rise freely.[118] In other words, investors had collectively decided (not through a conspiracy, but in accordance with rational investor behaviour guided by the influential advice of a handful of brokers) not to purchase gilt-edged stock until rates had reached a certain level, thus forcing up interest rates, regardless of whether the government had really wanted this. Under the post-1976 system of monetary targeting, this process of pushing up interest rates to ensure that the PSBR could be funded became endemic.[119]

In July 1977 the Labour Minister Harold Lever had identified that gilt-edged strikes would become a protracted problem under monetary targets, and that interest rate volatility would wreak havoc on the real economy. In a note sent to Callaghan, Lever acknowledged:

> when we commit ourselves to fixed monetary targets, we commit ourselves to accepting the rates of interest determined by the market in absorbing the

---

[115] BOE: 3A927/7, letter from Fforde to Governors, 'Some Obiter Dicta, Old and New, on the Gilt-Edged Market', 13 June 1978.

[116] Hall, 'Policy Paradigms, Social Learning, and the State', 285; Hall, 'The Movement from Keynesianism to Monetarism', 102.

[117] 'The Monetary Targets', *Financial Times*, 23 December 1977; Chris Anthony, 'Gilt-Edged', *Phillips and Drew Market Review* (December 1977).

[118] TNA: T386/270, letter from King to Odling-Smee, 'Study of Macroeconomic Problems and Policies: Monetary Policy', 5 May 1978.

[119] Healey, *Time of my Life*, 397; Capie, *Bank of England*, 670; William Keegan and Rupert Pennant-Rea, *Who Runs the Economy?: Control and Influence in British Economic Policy* (London: Temple Smith, 1979), 133.

required amount of gilt-edged stock. These rates depend crucially on market expectations and the only control we have over them arises from any ability we have to affect these expectations. Without such ability we would be obliged to accept interest rates however high or unstable and whatever their consequences for exports, unemployment, finance for industry and housing costs.[120]

He argued that the solution was to establish a formal interest rate policy that would clearly and unequivocally inform the markets when interest rates were at their peak, handing the initiative back to the government. This would serve to align investor expectations with the government's aims, rather than allowing the gilt-edged market to determine rates.[121] This proposal fell on deaf ears, largely because it was incompatible with the logic of monetary targets in which commitment had to be backed by policies designed to meet them.

In early 1978 the process reignited as gilt-edged demand dried up once more. Callaghan confided in Wedgewood Benn, then Secretary of State for Energy, that there was 'a lot of funny business going on between the City of London and the Government over the gilt-edged market. The City are not buying gilts in an effort to force us to push up interest rates.'[122] The response of the Governor was to press for an increase in MLR up to 10 per cent, though Wass and Couzens at the Treasury were doubtful that such an increase would be sufficient.[123] By early June, as high money supply figures encouraged further growth of the money supply as a result of depressed demand for gilts, Richardson became equally pessimistic that monetary policy alone could revive confidence. Only monetary measures of 'exceptional severity' could be relied upon—a prospect that encouraged Healey to look into taxation measures and the reimposition of direct controls on bank lending ('the corset') as a means of bringing monetary growth under control.[124] Despite exhortations not to increase rates, nor to impose 'the corset', from Harold Lever—who instead favoured an attempt to communicate directly with investing institutions—it was emphasized by Gordon Richardson that there were 'greater risks to activity and employment if confidence was not restored'.[125] Once MLR had eventually been

[120] TNA: T 386/118, letter from Lever to Callaghan, 'Interest Rates and the Money Supply', 22 July 1977.
[121] Ibid.
[122] Tony Benn and Ruth WInstone, *Conflicts of Interest: Diaries 1977–1980* (London: Hutchinson, 1990), 305.
[123] TNA: T 386/270, 'Note of a Meeting Held at No. 11 Downing Street—Financial Markets', 17 May 1978.
[124] TNA: T 386/280, letter from Lever to Healey, 'The Meaning of 27 Per Cent Annualised Growth of £M3', 25 May 1978.
[125] TNA: T 286/270, 'Note of a Meeting Held at No. 11 Downing Street—Monetary Situation', 6 June 1978.

raised to 10 per cent, and the 'corset' on bank lending reintroduced, Rowe & Pitman chronicled an 'immediate euphoric response' in the City, which 'enabled the Government broker to enjoy a concentrated spell of substantial funding sales'.[126] The process occurred yet again in November 1979, when, under the new Conservative Chancellor Sir Geoffrey Howe, MLR was increased to 17 per cent in what Kit McMahon at the Bank of England described as going 'for overkill in interest rate terms' in order to sell gilt-edged stock.[127]

Writing in the *Phillips and Drew Market Review* in February 1979, the analyst Chris Anthony described the gilt-edged 'stop–go cycles' that had been taking place since 1976:

> In recent years it has become a feature of the UK financial system that market pressures have at times persuaded the authorities to introduce measures of either a fiscal or monetary nature, whether or not strict economic considerations initially dictated such moves. What might start out as a pessimistic view held by only a small minority on, for example, the outlook for the money supply may eventually develop into a majority opinion causing a 'funding deadlock' in the gilt-edged market. Consequently, a market faced with reasonably favourable medium-term prospects shifts rapidly into one locked in a self-perpetuating downward spiral where a decline in the level of official stock purchases by the non-bank private sector leads to a deterioration in the monetary background and heightens further the general degree of pessimism. As a result the authorities are forced to introduce measures, often containing a significant degree of 'overkill', to break the funding impasse.[128]

Throughout the remaining years of the Labour government, perennial attempts were made to try to extricate the government from the bind imposed on it by this process. In his February 1978 speech to the 'Johnian Society', Douglas Wass pleaded publicly with the financial markets, stressing that investors should not overemphasize the monetary targets—placing them instead within the context of the government's wider economic strategy.[129] Interestingly, Wass's speech was delivered less than a week after the Governor of the Bank of England's 'Mais Lecture', which had extolled the virtues of 'practical monetarism' in providing 'one element of stability in a turbulent world'.[130] Meanwhile, within the Downing Street

---

[126] Quoted in Kynaston, *The City of London*, iv. 555; Grant, *Business and Politics*, 78; Chris Anthony, 'Gilt Edged', *Phillips and Drew Market Review* (June 1978).

[127] Capie, *The Bank of England*, 701.

[128] Chris Anthony, 'Gilt-Edged Stop–Go Cycles', *Phillips and Drew Market Review* (February 1979).

[129] Peter Riddell, 'Treasury Head's Plea on Money Supply Targets', *Financial Times*, 15 February 1977.

[130] 'Governor's Philosophy', *Financial Times*, 10 February 1977, 16.

Policy Unit, Bernard Donoughue promoted new methods of gilt-edged market management that might produce 'a more even flow of gilt sales'— such as index-linked gilts and tender selling. These were rejected by the Bank on the basis that they could signal a lack of commitment on the part of the government to controlling inflation, and that the market might be disturbed by any changes to the current structure.[131] The failure to overcome the problem ensured that the Labour government was exposed to recurrent gilt-edged crises throughout its remaining period in office.

To understand why this situation evolved as it did it is necessary to refer to the conceptual framework of the macroeconomic 'trilemma' identified by Obstfeld and Taylor. This states that governments are able to pursue a maximum of two of the following policy goals at any given time:

1. full freedom of cross-border capital movements;

2. a fixed exchange rate; and

3. an independent monetary policy orientated toward domestic objectives.[132]

Under the post-war Bretton Woods system, governments around the world chose to fix their exchange rates and pursue independent monetary policies while controlling capital movements (conditions 2 and 3). Social democratic economic strategy for domestic development was insulated from the vicissitudes of hot money flows, so long as governments were committed to their exchange rate parities. This framework crumbled as a result of the unwillingness (or inability) of governments to deliver domestic policies that could uphold their exchange rates, but also because of the burgeoning of an uncontrolled international capital market, which made defending against speculation an extremely costly task (particularly for Britain).[133] The 1970s witnessed a transitional period of immense complexity and confusion in British macroeconomic policy. In 1976, despite the collapse of the international monetary system, the Labour government sought to manipulate the exchange rate, and pursue an independent monetary policy, on behalf of the domestic economy. By 1977, with the uncapping of the exchange rate, the government had ceded control of the former. Yet the government was unable to transition directly to a new equilibrium of floating exchange rates and independent monetary policy (conditions 1 and 3) because the latter remained hamstrung by the

---

[131] Kynaston, *The City of London*, iv. 555.
[132] Maurice Obstfeld and Alan M. Taylor, *Global Capital Markets: Integration, Crisis and Growth* (Cambridge: Cambridge University Press, 2004), 30.
[133] Ibid. 38–9, 157–60.

monetary targets that entirely dictated the willingness of the gilt-edged market to fund the government's large budget deficit.

CONCLUSION

The decade prior to the Conservative general election victory in 1979 saw significant adjustments towards a form of British monetarism embodied in the evolution of monetary targeting. This process of change was not the product of an intellectual conversion in government, nor was it a coherent package forced upon the Labour government by monetarist ideological fervour within financial markets. Instead, we see that after 1968 financial markets came to believe, understandably, that the government was operating a money supply policy, which ensured that investors started to align their investment decisions and expectations with the behaviour of the 'money supply'. Furthermore, set against the background of vast inflationary pressures and the collapse of the global fixed exchange rate regime after 1973, financial markets attached considerable value to the money supply by employing it as a yardstick with which to measure the government's commitment to countering inflation. This started a feedback loop in which the financial markets, by behaving as if the government was attempting to control the money supply, began to act on the assumption that the government would implement policies designed with that end in mind—which, in turn, placed pressure on the government to fulfil this expectation. When confidence in the Labour government waned in 1976, these expectations evolved into a demand for a public monetary target. Though the Chancellor sought to retain macroeconomic policy autonomy and resisted these formally announced targets, his announcement of an intended monetary outcome unintentionally provided figures that the markets adopted and interpreted as if they were targets. The result of this market formalization was to impose significant constraints on the government's economic policy, through fears of losing confidence in the foreign exchange markets; and by allowing purchasers of government debt to enforce the interest rate increases they deemed necessary for meeting those targets. By 1979 the government had ceded a large degree of its macroeconomic policy autonomy to the dominance of financial indicators centred on the monetary aggregates. In an attempt to retain favourable money supply figures, the government was left exposed to the short-term volatility of domestic and international investors. This resulted in the dismantling of the Keynesian policymaking apparatus, which had formed the basis of the social democratic macroeconomic consensus over the past three decades.

This account highlights the contingent and unintended nature of the macroeconomic policy changes that took place during the 1970s, which were the product of interests, ideas, and market expectations operating within the changing global and domestic structures that governed the relationship between the state and the financial markets. It poses a strong challenge to notions of intentionality in economic policymaking, and undermines the simplistic ideological accounts that have tended to dominate popular interpretations of the British monetarist moment. However, the fundamental dynamic that underpinned this process was the emergence and imposition of a new financial discipline on the state, which served to replace the collapsed strictures of the fixed exchange rate regime. This new framework was not designed as a coherent strategy for maintaining exchange rate stability and insulating national economies from uncontrolled international capital movements, but was imposed chaotically by the behaviour of increasingly globalized, liberalized, and highly capitalized financial markets seeking a new metric of government 'performance' and 'credibility'.

What can this account tell us about the 'Thatcherite monetarism' that was to follow? The influence of ideological monetarism on senior Conservative politicians (for example, Sir Keith Joseph) is certain. Furthermore, the convenient relationship between the PSBR and the money supply that justified radical curtailments to government expenditure (while also abandoning controls on bank lending) was undoubtedly influenced by a free-market intellectual tradition within the Tory Party. Yet, ultimately, the findings presented here support the notion that the monetarist experiment was an unplanned strategy.[134] One must be conscious that when the Conservatives entered government in 1979 they faced the intractable problem of managing a large budget deficit within volatile markets reacting to short-term economic data and short-term monetary targets. In this context, it is possible to interpret the 'Medium Term Financial Strategy' after 1980 as a strong signal designed to assure investors in the financial markets of the government's lasting commitment to constraining monetary growth, while also serving to restructure the time horizon of policy to force investors to assess successful monetary control in the long term rather than the short term. This suggests that the attempt to manage policy and inflationary expectations, which the monetarists in Thatcher's first government argued was the purpose of the

---

[134] Tomlinson, 'Mrs Thatcher's Macroeconomic Adventurism'.

strategy, was specifically directed at an audience in the financial markets, rather than to all economic agents.[135] The vast increase in the sterling exchange rate brought about by the Thatcher government's attempted monetary squeeze, and its devastating impact on industrial firms during the early 1980s, demonstrates the prioritization of managing financial indicators (upon which government credibility was defined) above indicators of the performance of the 'real' economy.[136] This seems to support the assertion made by Bryan Gould, John Mills, and Shaun Stewart in 1979 that 'monetarism means quite simply that the Government has chosen once again to put the City and its interests ahead of manufacturing industry'.[137] However, the argument outlined here suggests that it was not a simple choice, but the product of a chaotic transition in the macroeconomic policymaking environment over the previous decade, which corroded the space within which the state had been permitted to pursue a social democratic, industry-biased, macroeconomic strategy since the war.

[135] Ibid. 9–10.   [136] Oliver, 'Whatever Happened to Monetarism?', 58–60.
[137] Bryan Gould, John Mills, and Shaun Stewart, *The Politics of Monetarism*, Fabian Tract 462 (London: Fabian Society, May 1979), 3.

Conclusion

The aim of this book has been to evaluate the relationship between Britain's financial sector, based in the City of London, and the social democratic economic strategy of post-war Britain. The central argument presented in the book was that changes to the City during the 1960s and 1970s undermined a number of the key post-war social democratic techniques designed to sustain and develop a modern industrial economy. Financial institutionalization weakened the state's ability to influence investment, and the labour movement was unable successfully to integrate the institutionalized funds within a renewed social democratic economic agenda. The post-war settlement in banking came under strain in the 1960s as new banking and credit institutions developed that the state struggled to manage. This was exacerbated by the decision to introduce competition among the clearing banks in 1971, which further weakened the state's capacity to control the provision and allocation of credit to the real economy. The resurrection of an unregulated global capital market, centred on London, overwhelmed the capacity of the state to pursue domestic-focused macroeconomic policies—a problem worsened by the concurrent collapse of the Bretton Woods international monetary system. Against this background, the fundamental social democratic assumption that national prosperity could be achieved only through industry-led growth and modernization was undermined by an effective campaign to reconceptualize Britain as a fundamentally financial and commercial nation with the City of London at its heart.

FROM SOCIAL DEMOCRACY TO NEOLIBERALISM

The broader aim of undertaking this research has been to improve our understanding of the complex transition from social democracy to neoliberalism in Britain during the final third of the twentieth century. With regards to this much larger question, there are four key implications to be derived from the findings presented in this book.

i. The post-war social democratic settlement in Britain was contingent on a unique set of material conditions.

Chapters 1 and 2 both demonstrate that the fundamental framework of the social democratic settlement in managing credit and investment was built on a set of material conditions specific to the 1940s and 1950s. At that time, investment was predominantly undertaken within private firms using retained profits, and so was in large part divorced from the London capital market. Meanwhile, the banking system was dominated by a small number of uncompetitive clearing banks that were essentially willing to implement the government's monetary policy in exchange for stable profits and retained private ownership. Once these conditions began to erode, as they did in the 1960s and 1970s, the settlement in financial policy became less efficacious as it became increasingly divorced from the realities of the financial system. Chapter 5 also underlines the importance of international material conditions. Social democracy, in its attempt to expand and modernize the industrial economy, and to maintain full employment, could pursue the policies necessary to achieve these goals only because of a set of international rules and structures that insulated the domestic economy from the constraints that would have been imposed by free capital movements. The 'embedded liberalism' of the Bretton Woods system was designed for this purpose. When an international capital market outside the constraints of this settlement emerged in the 1960s, and with the collapse of the Bretton Woods system at the start of the 1970s, the space for social democracy on a national level was rapidly, and chaotically, eroded.

The fundamental shape of the social democratic project was formed in the 1940s, but the environment in which its practices were developed did not remain static. This statement is not only is true of the financial system, or of the economy as a whole, but can be applied equally to British society and culture in the same period. Such underlying shifts are not always appreciated in the histories of post-war Britain, which tend to emphasize party politics or the influence of ideas on policymaking. The material underpinnings of social democracy, and its subsequent neoliberal turn, should be central to our understanding of post-war Britain. However, that is not to say that historians should abandon politics and ideas in favour of a solely materialist conception of historical change. The focus on William Clarke and the Committee on Invisible Exports in Chapter 4 is an explicit challenge to the economistic analysis of the City's late-twentieth-century reinternationalization. Historians are fortunate in their capacity to engage in such a flexible approach to understanding political and economic change.

ii. Attempts were made to reconfigure social democratic economic strategy in response to material changes.

There is a popular tendency to view the 1970s in simplistic terms through the prism of the subsequent decade. It is particularly pervasive in contemporary political discourse to view the post-war social democratic project as moribund by the end of the 1970s, and to see the post-1979 Thatcherite project as an inevitable necessity. Such an understanding of the decade is, in large part, the product of the Thatcher government's ability to define and frame it in a way conducive to its own political agenda.[1] In this simplistic narrative the Labour Party's governing elite are seen to have been lacking in ideas, while the party's left-wing activists naively pursued a foolish strategy of electorally unpopular radicalism. In the more considered accounts of historians and political scientists this bipolarity is less pronounced, and there is less willingness to condemn the social democratic project as irrelevant. Yet the notion of a civil war in the party does continue to shape our understanding of the Labour movement in the 1970s. The findings presented in this book suggest that social democracy in the 1970s was more nuanced and varied than is often portrayed, and should be understood on its own terms within the context of the troubled decade. In particular, the findings suggest that:

1. The Labour left of the 1970s must be understood in its material context. Regardless of the political sensitivity of the left's policy proposals, its radical approach was rooted in an attempt to deal with the contemporary nature of the British economy. The demand for nationalization of the banking system is indicative of this, as the idea had been dormant since the 1940s, but was revived in response to the Heath government's deregulation of bank lending.

2. There were new and innovative ideas about how to respond to the crisis of the 1970s produced within the Labour movement that have not previously been recognized—notably the attempt to incorporate institutional investors within the left's economic strategy. Our understanding of the Alternative Economic Strategy, and the influence of Stuart Holland, is well established. However, the ideas of other figures, such as John Hughes, have not been studied in any depth. It is particularly interesting to see the trade-union movement's contribution to policy debates in this area. A valuable future

---

[1] See, e.g., Colin Hay, 'Chronicles of a Death Foretold: The Winter of Discontent and Construction of the Crisis of British Keynesianism', *Parliamentary Affairs*, 63/3 (2010), 446–70.

avenue of research would be to develop a more detailed understanding of social democratic economic strategy in the 1970s. The Labour Party archive, as well as various trade-union archives, offer an underutilized resource in this area.

3. The divisions in the Labour Party were not always clearly defined. Wilson's support for the trade-union proposals to reform the capital market put him on the side of radical change at the end of the decade. Hughes's resistance to wholesale nationalization did not make him a defender of the status quo. These grey areas between the party's left and right wings should be explored in further studies of Labour's economic policies in the 1970s.

iii. Interests mattered in the ascent of neoliberalism.

Historians attempting to understand the transition from social democracy to 'neoliberalism' in the 1970s and 1980s have tended to focus on the influence of neoliberal thinkers and their ideas. More recently, historians have focused on the way in which those ideas were transferred into political and public discourse, and subsequently into policymaking. This book has demonstrated that the material interests of economic actors and groups should not be forgotten in the transition. Historians should make every effort to avoid reductionism, but it is important not to lose sight of basic economic and political pressures that determined policymaking. Chapters 3 and 4 both suggest that the neoliberal agenda of reducing the role of the state in the economy, through reduced taxation and deregulation, was promoted by industrial and financial interests with little relation to the 'neoliberal thought collective'.[2] Chapter 3 reasserts the importance of the profitability crisis in the mid-1970s as the most significant factor underlying the formation of an anti-social democratic political coalition between industrial and financial interests. This is not to suggest that neoliberal thought had no influence, or was not important, but asserts that we should be careful not to view Thatcherism (as the British expression of neoliberalism) as an intellectual novelty based solely on ideas and principles, when in fact there were clear motivations rooted in material self-interest. It would be valuable to engage in further research into the relationship between business interests and neoliberal ideas in Britain, which would build on the work of Ben Jackson (on business funding of neoliberal think tanks) and Neil Rollings (on the influence of neoliberals

---

[2] Philip Mirowski and Dieter Plehwe (eds), *The Road from Mont Pelerin: The Making of the Neoliberal Thought Collective* (Cambridge, MA: Harvard University Press, 2009).

within the Federation of British Industry and the Confederation of British Industry).[3]

Chapter 5 demonstrated how interests and ideas interacted in financial markets to determine the shape of British macroeconomic policy in the second half of the 1970s. This challenges the notion that a key idea in the neoliberal revolution—monetarism—influenced policymaking because of its intellectual value, or even its usefulness to policymakers. However, it does not support a simplistic analysis of the power of financiers to impose their policy preferences on the government in a coherent and deliberate way. To improve our understanding of the transition to monetarism, it would be useful to broaden our analysis and to compare the British experience with other countries where monetary targets were simultaneously adopted, such as France, Germany, and the United States.

This thesis also touches on the underappreciated role of the Bank of England as a political actor in the post-war decades. The role of the Bank in placing pressure on Labour governments to reduce expenditure in order to satisfy the financial markets is well understood, and has been assessed by a number of historians (particularly regarding the Wilson governments in the 1960s). This view is given some support in Chapter 5. However, it is clear that the central bank operated in additional ways that have not been appreciated by historians. The Bank's political activism, in its detached management of the Committee on Invisible Exports, demonstrates its role as a supporter and promoter of the City of London's international role. The political activism of the Bank of England, as a representative of the interests of the City of London, is something that deserves greater attention from historians.

iv. The transition to neoliberalism was rooted in a cultural contest over the character and purpose of the British economy.

The social democratic project was rooted in an industrial society in which the production of primary and manufactured goods was central to the nation's economic activity. The purpose of social democracy was to secure employment, and improve the performance of the British economy as a whole, through industrial expansion and modernization. During the late-twentieth-century neoliberal age, the preoccupation with industry was significantly reduced in the discourse of British politics, particularly during the 'great moderation' of the 1990s and

---

[3] Jackson, 'The Think-Tank Archipelago'; Neil Rollings, 'Cracks in the Post-War Keynesian Settlement? The Role of Organised Business in the Rise of Neoliberalism before Margaret Thatcher', *Twentieth Century British History*, 24/4 (2013), 637–59.

early 2000s.[4] This has reflected a large reduction in industrial employment, and the rapid expansion of the financial services sector in London and the south-east. Chapter 5 suggests that, when we try to understand the transition from social democracy to neoliberalism in Britain, we must consider the way in which the national economy was conceptualized and defined in public and political discourse. The contest over what the British economy was, or was not, shaped the way in which economic policies were formed. The 'invisibles' campaign reformulated the 'gentlemanly capitalist' ideal of Britain's economic role in the world for the post-war age, and sought to undo the primacy afforded to industry in economic policy. The capacity to reconceptualize the British economy as an entrepôt island offering financial and commercial services to the rest of the world, in both a historic and a contemporary context, was a powerful rhetorical tool for pursuing policy goals amenable to the interests of the City of London. This offers a new perspective that has not been appreciated—that the liberal economic norms of Thatcherism were not simply the product of abstract ideas about the legitimate relationship between 'the market' and 'the state', but grew out of a long-standing tension between competing definitions of the British economy. For historians, this perspective allows us to gain a clearer understanding of why the global neoliberal turn has taken the specific form that is has done in Britain. The *idea* of the British economy during the post-war period, at both an elite and a popular level, is an area worthy of further investigation.

THATCHERISM, NEOLIBERALISM, AND THE CITY OF LONDON

This thesis has attempted to improve our understanding of the transition from social democracy to neoliberalism that took place in Britain during the final quarter of the twentieth century. It has done so by focusing on one of the chief beneficiaries of the regime change, the British financial sector, during the two decades prior to the election of Margaret Thatcher's first Conservative government in 1979. In confining itself to this time period, it has been concerned with trying to understand the multiple constraints imposed on post-war social democracy (as well as the attempts made by social democrats to overcome these) as a way of

---

[4] Ben S. Bernanke, 'The Great Moderation', at the meetings of the Eastern Economic Association, Washington DC (2004).

explaining the subsequent neoliberal turn. The Thatcher government was deliberately excluded from explicit analysis, in the hope that such an approach would give a clearer understanding of the context and environment in which it was elected at the end of the 1970s. This encourages us to avoid seeing Thatcherism as the sole product of the post-1975 Conservative Party, and to place it in a wider context of interests, institutions, and ideas that had evolved over the previous two decades. Future research into the enthusiastic application of neoliberal policies in the 1980s, and of the closely related financial sector deregulation and internationalization during the decade, could usefully draw on this pre-history of the financial aspect of British neoliberalism.

LABOUR AND THE CITY, *c.*1979–2008

This thesis highlighted the efforts made by many within the labour movement during the 1970s to reform the British financial system in order to advance the economic and political project of social democracy. Criticism of the City and its institutions was well established in the political economy of the Labour Party in the period. Yet by the 1990s we know that the party leadership (John Smith, Tony Blair, and Gordon Brown) became enthusiastic supporters of the City's role as an international financial centre. The famed 'prawn cocktail offensive', in which senior Labour figures sought to reconcile the party with the City and other business interests, exemplified this conversion.[5] How, and why, did this shift occur? Narratives of New Labour's 'modernization', or move to the 'centre ground' of politics, frame our contemporary understanding of the change, though such platitudes deserve far greater attention by historians. What was the Labour Party's relationship with the City in the 1980s? How did the left respond to the Thatcherite reforms to the City in the period? What impact did the party's internal fracturing have on its attitudes to the City? It is also particularly interesting to consider the influence on the New Labour project of Will Hutton's critique of the City in the mid-1990s.[6] How did Hutton's analysis, which we know had some influence on the early Blair leadership, interact with New Labour's attempted engagement with the financial sector?[7] These questions could

[5] Anatole Kaletsky, 'John Smith's Poisoned Prawns', *The Times*, 23 September 1991.
[6] Will Hutton, *The State We're In* (London: Jonathan Cape, 1995).
[7] Duncan Weldon, 'Beyond Living with Capitalism: The Labour Party, Macroeconomics, and Political Economy since 1994', *Renewal*, 21/2–3 (2013), 23.

form the basis of future research into the political economy of the Labour Party during the latter decades of the twentieth century.

The City of London is at the centre of contemporary political and economic debate in the wake of the 2007–8 financial crisis. These events, which have engendered public outrage over inappropriate or risky financial activities, bankers' pay and bonuses, and the transfer of private bank losses onto the public balance sheet, have posed a threat to the City, and to the neoliberal settlement in which it is embedded. This has taken the form of a notional political consensus on the apparent need to 'rebalance' the economy away from perceived over-reliance on the City and towards a revival of domestic industry and manufacturing—ideally outside the affluent south-east of England.[8] Critics have even begun to question whether the City's contribution to the nation is really so significant after all.[9] Raising taxes, and imposing new regulations on some financial sector activities, have become increasingly influential political proposals.[10] Concern with the capacity of the domestic banking system to provide quality services to personal and commercial clients has become a national scandal.[11] Meanwhile, the political movement of social democracy, in Britain and across Europe, is in the doldrums.[12] Although the Labour Party has been forced to reappraise the relationship it had with the City during the Blair and Brown years, it has failed to translate this into any political advantage.[13] By putting these contemporary concerns in a historical context, this book might read like a counsel of despair for social democrats seeking to reform the City of London. The findings presented suggest that

[8] e.g., 'George Osborne: UK must End its Reliance on the City', *Guardian*, 15 June 2013; 'We're too Dependent on London and the City is to Blame, warns Nick Clegg', *Independent*, 18 February 2013.

[9] Adair Turner, 'How to Tame Global Finance', *Prospect* (September 2009); Linda Prieg and Heather Stewart, 'Mythbusters: "The City is Vital to Britain"', *New Economic Foundation* (May 2013) <http://www.neweconomics.org/blog/entry/mythbusters-the-city-is-vital-to-britain> (accessed 18 March 2014).

[10] Independent Commission on Banking, *Final Report: Recommendations* (London: HM Treasury, 2011); Mikey Smith, 'Labour Plan Bankers' Bonus Tax to Fund 56,000 New Jobs for Young People', *Daily Mirror*, 9 February 2014; see also the campaign for an international financial transactions tax, aka 'The Robin Hood Tax' <www.robinhoodtax.org.uk> (accessed 18 April 2014).

[11] John Lanchester, 'Are We Having Fun Yet? On the Banks' Barely Believable Behaviour', *London Review of Books*, 35/13 (2013), 3–8.

[12] Piraeus Ludwigshafen and Valletta, 'Rose thou Art Sick: The Centre Left Is in Sharp Decline across Europe', *Economist*, 2 April 2016.

[13] 'Ed Balls "Deeply Sorry" over Banking Crisis', *BBC News*, 12 September 2011 <http://www.bbc.co.uk/news/uk-politics-14888933> (accessed 18 April 2014); Labour Party, 'Labour's Plan for Banking Reform', 13 February 2015 http://www.yourbritain.org.uk/uploads/editor/files/Banking_Reform.pdf (accessed 23 June 2016).

social democracy can operate only within a favourable material context that has long since vanished, and that attempts to undertake radical financial sector reform are doomed to fail in the face of a powerful and influential City. The task of achieving reform remains, undoubtedly, a difficult one. Yet social democrats should not be deterred. They should instead recognize that to achieve change it is essential to build a broad coalition of political support behind innovative, coherent, and credible proposals for financial sector reform. Moral outrage alone will not be enough.

Bibliography

I. MANUSCRIPT AND ARCHIVAL SOURCES

Bank of England Archive, Bank of England
Bank of England Freedom of Information Disclosures <http://www.bankofengland.
co.uk/publications/Pages/foi/disclosurelog.aspx> (accessed December 2016)
Bodleian Library, University of Oxford
    Conservative Party Archive
    Harold Wilson papers
British Library of Political and Economic Science, London School of Economics
    Committee to Review the Functioning of Financial Institutions papers
Labour Party Archive, People's History Museum, Manchester
London Metropolitan Archives
    British Bankers' Association papers
    National Association of Pension Funds papers
Margaret Thatcher Foundation Archive
Michael J. Oliver, Personal Archive, Open University
    W. Greenwell & Co. Monetary Bulletins
Modern Records Centre, University of Warwick
    Confederation of British Industry papers
    Trades Union Congress papers
The National Archives: Public Record Office
    Records of the Prime Minister's Office
    HM Treasury
HM Treasury Freedom of Information Disclosures <https://web.archive.org/web/
20130123073026/http://hm-treasury.gov.uk/foi_sterling_imf_2006.htm>
(accessed 20 December 2016)

II. PRINTED PRIMARY SOURCES

Newspapers and Periodicals
Bank of England Quarterly Bulletin
Banker
Bankers' Magazine
Daily Mirror
Daily Telegraph
The Economist
Evening Standard
Financial Guardian
Financial Times
Guardian
Investors Chronicle

Journal of the Institute of Bankers
London Review of Books
New Statesman
Phillips and Drew Market Review
Spectator
The Times
Socialist Commentary

OFFICIAL PAPERS

Central Office of Information, *British Banking and Other Financial Institutions* (1974).
Cmd 3282, *The Final Report of the Committee on Trade and Industry* (1929).
Cmd 3897, *The Report of the Committee on Finance and Industry* (1931).
Cmd 827, *Report: Committee on the Working of the Monetary System* (1959).
Cmd 2764, *The National Plan* (1965).
Cmd 3292, *National Board for Prices and Incomes. Report No. 34: Bank Charges* (1967).
Cmd 5391, *Company Law Reform* (1973).
Cmd 7937, *Report: Committee to Review the Functioning of Financial Institutions* (1980).
Committee to Review the Functioning of Financial Institutions: Evidence on the Financing of Industry and Trade, 8 vols (1977–8).
Committee to Review the Functioning of Financial Institutions: Second Stage Evidence, ii (London: HMSO, 1979).
Inter-Bank Research Organisation (Cabinet Office), *The Future of London as an International Financial Centre: A Report* (1973).
Parliamentary Debates (Hansard).

BOOKS AND ARTICLES

Alexander, Ken, and John Hughes, *A Socialist Wages Plan: The Politics of the Pay Packet* (London: Universities and Left Review/New Reasoner, 1959).
Benn, Tony, and Ruth Winstone, *Conflicts of Interest: Diaries 1977–1980* (London: Hutchinson, 1990).
Briston, Richard J., and Dobbins, Richard, The Growth and Impact of Institutional Investor: A Report to the Research Committee of the Institute of Chartered Accountants in England and Wales (London: Institute of Chartered Accountants, 1978).
Cairncross, Frances, and Hamish McRae, *The Second Great Crash: How the Oil Crisis could Destroy the World's Economy* (London: Methuen, 1975).
City Capital Markets Committee, *Evidence to the Wilson Committee* (London, 1977).
Clark, R. J., 'The Evolution of Monetary and Financial Institutions', in David R. Croome and Harry G. Johnson (eds), *Money in Britain: 1959–1969* (Oxford: Oxford University Press, 1970), 131–49.

Clarke, William M., *The City's Invisible Earnings: How London's Financial Skill Serves the World and Brings Profit to Britain* (London: Institute of Economic Affairs, 1958).

Clarke, William M., *The City and the World Economy* (Harmondsworth: Penguin, 1967; first published London: Institute of Affairs, 1965).

Clarke, William M., *Inside the City: A Guide to London as a Financial Centre* (London: George Allen & Unwin, 1979).

Clendenning, E. W., *The Eurodollar Market* (Oxford: Oxford University Press, 1970).

Committee of London Clearing Bankers, *The London Clearing Banks: Evidence by the Committee of London Clearing Bankers to the Committee to Review the Functioning of Financial Institutions, November 1977* (London: Longman, 1978).

Congdon, Tim, *Monetarism: An Essay in Definition* (London: Centre for Policy Studies, 1978).

Crosland, C. A. R., *The Future of Socialism* (Jonathan Cape: London, 1956).

Dobbins, R., B. Lowes, and C. L. Pass, 'Financial Institutions and the Ownership and Control of British Industry', *Managerial and Decision Economics*, 2/1 (1981), 16–24.

Drucker, Peter F., *The Unseen Revolution: How Pension Fund Socialism Came to America* (London: Heinemann, 1976).

Einzig, Paul, *The Euro-Dollar System* (London: Macmillan, 1964).

Financial Advisory Panel on Exports (British National Export Council), *Britain's Invisible Earnings: Report of the Committee on Invisible Exports* (London: 1967).

Friedman, Milton, 'The Role of Monetary Policy', *American Economic Review*, 58/1 (1968), 1–17.

Glyn, Andrew, 'Social Democracy and Full Employment', *New Left Review*, 211 (1995), 33–55.

Glyn, Andrew, and John Harrison, *The British Economic Disaster* (London: Pluto, 1980).

Glyn, Andrew, and Bob Sutcliffe, 'The Critical Condition of British Capital', *New Left Review*, 66 (1971), 3–33.

Glyn, Andrew, and Bob Sutcliffe, *British Workers and the Profit Squeeze* (Harmondsworth: Penguin, 1972).

Griffiths, Brian, *Competition in Banking* (London: Institute of Economic Affairs, 1970).

Griffiths, Brian, *Monetarism and Morality: A Response to the Bishops* (London: Centre for Policy Studies, 1985).

Hatfield, Michael, *The House the Left Built: Inside Labour Policy-Making, 1970–75* (London: Gollancz, 1978).

Healey, Denis, *Time of my Life* (London: Michael Joseph, 1989).

Hilferding, Rudolf, *Finance Capital: A Study of the Latest Phase of Capitalist Development*, ed. Tom Bottomore, trans. Morris Watnick and Sam Gordon (1910; London: Routledge, 2006).

Hirsch, Fred, *The Pound Sterling: A Polemic* (London: Victor Gollancz, 1975).

Hobson, J. A., *Imperialism: A Study* (London: John Atkins, 1902).

Holland, Stuart, *The Socialist Challenge* (London: Quartet Books, 1975).

Holmans, A. E., 'Invisible Earnings', in D. J. Robertson and L. C. Hunter (eds), *The British Balance of Payments* (Edinburgh: Oliver and Boyd, 1966), 42–64.

Hughes, John, 'Funds for Investment', *Fabian Research Series 325* (1976).

Independent Commission on Banking, *Final Report: Recommendations* (London: HM Treasury, 2011).

Kaldor, Nicholas, 'The Economics of the Selective Employment Tax', in *Reports on Taxation I: Papers Relating to the United Kingdom* (London: Duckworth, 1980), 200–29.

Kaldor, Nicholas, *The Scourge of Monetarism* (Oxford: Oxford University Press, 1982).

Keegan, William, and Rupert Pennant-Rea, *Who Runs the Economy?: Control and Influence in British Economic Policy* (London: Temple Smith, 1979).

Keynes, John Maynard, *The General Theory of Employment, Interest and Money* (London: Macmillan, 1936).

Let Us Face the Future: A Declaration of Labour Policy for the Consideration of the Nation (London, 1945).

Liberal Party, *Industrial Inquiry* (London, 1928).

Ludwigshafen, Piraeus, and Valletta, 'Rose thou Art Sick: The Centre Left Is in Sharp Decline across Europe', *The Economist*, 2 April 2016.

Macmillan, Harold, *The Middle Way* (1938; London: Pickering & Chatto, 1994).

Manser, W. A. P., *Britain in Balance* (Harmondsworth: Penguin, 1973).

Miller, Robert, and John B. Wood, *Exchange Control for Ever?*, IEA Research Monograph, 33 (London: IEA, 1979).

Minns, Richard, *Pension Funds and British Capitalism: The Ownership and Control of Shareholdings* (London: Heinemann, 1980).

Nevin, Edward T., and E. W. Davies, *The London Clearing Banks* (London: Elek Books, 1970).

Pass, C., 'The Industrial Reorganization Corporation—a Positive Approach to the Structure of Industry', *Long Range Planning*, 4/1 (1971), 63–70.

Pepper, Gordon, *Money, Credit and Inflation: An Historical Indictment of UK Monetary Policy and a Proposal for Change* (London: Institute of Economic Affairs, 1990).

Pimlott, Ben, *Labour and the Left in the 1930s* (Cambridge: Cambridge University Press, 1977).

Prais, S. J., *The Evolution of Giant Firms: A Study of the Growth of Concentration in Manufacturing Industry in Britain* (Cambridge: Cambridge University Press, 1976).

Raw, Charles, *Slater Walker: An Investigation of a Financial Phenomenon* (London: Deutsch, 1977).

Report of the Annual Conference of the Labour Party (London: Labour Party, 1972).

Roberts, Richard, 'What's in a Name? Merchants, Merchant Bankers, Accepting Houses, Issuing Houses, Industrial Bankers and Investment Bankers', *Business History*, 35/3 (1993), 22–38.

Shonfield, Andrew, *British Economic Policy since the War* (Harmondsworth: Penguin Books, 1958).

Stewart, Michael, *The Jekyll and Hyde Years: Politics and Economic Policy in Britain since 1964* (London: J. M. Dent, 1977).

Stock Exchange, *Evidence to the Committee to Review the Functioning of Financial Institutions: The Role and Functioning of the Stock Exchange* (London, 1977).

Stock Exchange, *The Stock Exchange Survey of Share Ownership: A Supplement to the Stock Exchange Fact Service* (London, 1983).

Su-Hu, Yao, *National Attitudes and the Financing of Industry* (London: Political and Economic Planning, 1975).

Titmuss, Richard, *The Irresponsible Society* (London: George Allen & Unwin, 1958).

Trades Union Congress, *The Role of Financial Institutions: TUC Evidence to the Committee to Review the Functioning of Financial Institutions* (London, 1979).

Walters, A. A., *Money in Boom and Slump: An Empirical Inquiry into British Experience since 1880* (London: Institute of Economic Affairs, 1970).

Wilson, Harold, *Final Term: The Labour Government, 1974–1976* (London: Weidenfeld & Nicolson, 1977).

Wormell, Jeremy, *The Gilt-Edged Market* (London: Allen & Unwin, 1985).

III. PRINTED SECONDARY WORKS.

Addison, Paul, *The Road to 1945: British Politics and the Second World War*, 2nd edn (London: Pimlico, 1994).

Anderson, Perry, 'Origins of the Present Crisis', *New Left Review*, 23 (1964), 26–53.

Anderson, Perry, 'Figures of Descent', *New Left Review*, 161 (1987), 20–77.

Artis, Michael, David Cobham, and Mark Wickham-Jones, 'Social Democracy in Hard Times: The Economic Record of the Labour Government 1974–1979', *Twentieth Century British History*, 3/1 (1992), 32–58.

Asteris, Michael, 'British Overseas Military Commitments 1945–47: Making Painful Choices', *Contemporary British History*, 27/3 (2013), 348–71.

Atkin, John, The Foreign Exchange Market: Development since 1900 (Routledge: Abingdon, 2005).

Augur, Philip, *The Death of Gentlemanly Capitalism* (London: Penguin, 2000).

Avrahampour, Yally, ' "Cult of Equity": Actuaries and the Transformation of Pension Fund Investing, 1948–1960', *Business History Review*, 89/2 (2015), 281–304.

Backhouse, Roger E., 'The Macroeconomics of Margaret Thatcher', *Journal of the History of Economic Thought*, 24/3 (2002), 313–34.

Backhouse, Roger E., The Rise of Free Market Economics: Economists and the Role of the State Since 1970', *History of Political Economy*, 37 (2005), 355–92.

Baker, Mae, and Michael Collins, 'English Commercial Banks and Business Client Distress, 1946–63', *European Review of Economic History*, 7 (2003), 365–88.

Baker, Mae, and Michael Collins, 'English Bank Business Loans, 1920–1968: Transaction Bank Characteristics and Small Firm Discrimination', *Financial History Review*, 12 (2005), 135–71.

Baker, Mae, and Michael Collins, 'London as an International Banking Centre, 1950–1980', in Youssef Cassis and Eric Bussière (eds), *London and Paris as International Financial Centres in the Twentieth Century* (Oxford: Oxford University Press, 2005), 247–64.

Baker, Mae, and Michael Collins, 'English Commercial Banks and Organization Inertia: The Financing of SMEs, 1944–1960', *Enterprise and Society*, 11/1 (2009), 65–97.

Bale, Tim, 'Dynamics of a Non-Decision: The "Failure" to Devalue the Pound, 1964–7', *Twentieth Century British History*, 10/2 (1999), 192–217.

Barnett, Corelli, *The Audit of War: The Illusion and Reality of Britain as a Great Nation* (Basingstoke: Macmillan, 1986).

Barnett, Corelli, *The Lost Victory: British Dreams, British Realities 1945–1950* (London: Pan Macmillan, 1996).

Bell, Geoffrey, *The Eurodollar Market and the International Financial System* (London: Macmillan, 1973).

Bellringer, Christopher, and Ranald Michie, 'Big Bang in the City of London: An Intentional Revolution or an Accident?', *Financial History Review*, 21/2 (2014), 111–37.

Best, M. H., and Jane Humphries, 'The City and Industrial Decline', in Bernard Elbaum and William Lazonick (eds), *The Decline of the British Economy* (Oxford: Clarendon Press, 1978), 223–39.

Billings, Mark, and Forrest Capie, 'Capital in British Banking, 1920–1970', *Business History*, 49/2 (2007), 139–62.

Blackburn, Robin, *Banking on Death: Or, Investing in Life: The History and Future of Pensions* (London: Verso, 2002).

Blackburn, Robin, *Age Shock: How Finance Is Failing us* (London: Verso, 2006).

Blyth, Mark, 'Moving the Political Middle: Redefining the Boundaries of State Action', *Political Quarterly*, 68/3 (1997), 231–40.

Booth, Alan, 'The "Keynesian Revolution" in Economic Policy-Making', *Economic History Review*, 36 (1983), 103–23.

Booth, Alan, 'Defining a "Keynesian Revolution"', *Economic History Review*, 37 (1984), 253–67.

Booth, Alan, 'The "Keynesian Revolution" and Economic Policy-Making: A Reply', *Economic History Review*, 38 (1985), 101–6.

Booth, Alan, 'Technical Change in Branch Banking at the Midland Bank, 1945–75', *Accounting, Business & Financial History*, 14/3 (2004), 277–300.

Bowden, Sue M., 'Ownership Responsibilities and Corporate Governance: The Crisis at Rolls Royce, 1968–71', *Business History*, 44/3 (2002), 31–62.

Bowden, Sue M., and Michael Collins, 'The Bank of England, Industrial Regeneration, and Hire Purchase between the Wars', *Economic History Review*, 44 (1991), 120–36.

Brooke, Stephen, 'Revisionists and Fundamentalists: The Labour Party and Economic Policy during the Second World War', *Historical Journal*, 32 (1989), 157–75.

Brooke, Stephen, 'Problems of "Socialist Planning": Evan Durbin and the Labour Government of 1945', *Historical Journal*, 34 (1991), 687–702.

Brooke, Stephen, *Labour's War: The Labour Party during the Second World War* (Oxford: Clarendon Press, 1992).

Brown, Joan C., and Stephen Small, *Occupational Benefits as Social Security* (London: Policy Studies Institute, 1985).

Buchanan, James M., 'Public Choice: The Origins and Development of a Research Program', Center for Study of Public Choice, George Mason University (Fairfax, VA: 2003).

Bulpitt, Jim, 'The Discipline of the New Democracy: Mrs Thatcher's Domestic Statecraft', *Political Studies*, 34/1 (1986), 19–39.

Burk, Kathleen (ed.), 'Witness Seminar on the Origins and Early Development of the Eurobond Market', *Contemporary European History*, 1/1 (1992), 65–87.

Burk, Kathleen, and Alec Cairncross, '*Goodbye, Great Britain': The 1976 IMF Crisis* (New Haven: Yale University Press, 1992).

Burn, Gary, 'The State, the City and the Euromarkets', *Review of International Political Economy*, 6/2 (1999), 225–61.

Burn, Gary, *The Re-Emergence of Global Finance* (Basingstoke: Palgrave Macmillan, 2006).

Burnham, Peter, 'The Politicisation of Monetary Policy in Postwar Britain', *British Politics*, 2 (2007), 395–419.

Burnham, Peter, 'Depoliticising Monetary Policy: The Minimum Lending Rate Experiment in Britain in the 1970s', *New Political Economy*, 16/4 (2011), 463–80.

Cagan, Philip, 'Monetarism', in Steven N. Durlauf and Lawrence E. Blume (eds), *The New Dictionary of Economics*, 2nd edn (Basingstoke: Palgrave Macmillan, 2008).

Cain, P. J., and A. G. Hopkins, 'Gentlemanly Capitalism and British Expansion Overseas II: New Imperialism, 1850–1945', *Economic History Review*, 40/1 (1987), 1–26.

Cain, P. J., and A. G. Hopkins, *British Imperialism, 1688–2000* (London: Longman, 2002).

Cairncross, Alec, *Years of Recovery: British Economic Policy, 1945–51* (London: Methuen, 1985).

Cairncross, Alec, 'The Heath Government and the British Economy', in Stuart Ball and Anthony Seldon (eds), *The Heath Government, 1970–1974: A Reappraisal* (London: Longman, 1996), 107–38.

Cairncross, Alec, and Barry Eichengreen, *Sterling in Decline: The Devaluations of 1931, 1949 and 1967* (Oxford: Blackwell, 1983).

Callaghan, John, *The Retreat of Social Democracy* (Manchester: Manchester University Press, 2000).

Callaghan, John, 'Rise and Fall of the Alternative Economic Strategy: From Internationalisation of Capital to "Globalisation"', *Contemporary British History*, 14/3 (2000), 104–30.

Capie, Forrest, *The Bank of England, 1950s to 1979* (Cambridge: Cambridge University Press, 2010).

Capie, Forrest, and Mark Billings, 'Profitability in English Banking in the Twentieth Century', *European Review of Economic History*, 5/3 (2001), 367–401.

Capie, Forrest, and Mark Billings, 'Evidence on Competition in English Commercial Banking, 1920–1970', *Financial History Review*, 11/1 (2004), 69–103.

Capie, Forrest, and Michael Collins, *Have the Banks Failed British Industry?: An Historical Survey of Bank/Industry Relations in Britain, 1870–1990* (London: Institute of Economic Affairs, 1992).

Carruthers, Bruce G., *City of Capital: Politics and Markets in the English Financial Revolution* (Princeton: Princeton University Press, 1996).

Cassis, Youssef, 'British Finance: Success and Controversy', in Jean Jacques van Helten and Youssef Cassis (eds), *Capitalism in a Mature Economy* (Aldershot: Edward Elgar, 1990), 1–22.

Cassis, Youssef, *City Bankers, 1890–1914* (Cambridge: Cambridge University Press, 1995).

Cassis, Youssef, *Capitals of Capital: The Rise and Fall of International Financial Centres, 1780–2009*, 2nd edn (Cambridge: Cambridge University Press, 2010).

Chambers, David, 'Gentlemanly Capitalism Revisited: A Case Study of the Underpricing of Initial Public Offerings on the London Stock Exchange, 1946–86', *Economic History Review*, 62/1 (2009), 31–56.

Chandler, Alfred D., Jr, *Scale and Scope: The Dynamics of Industrial Capitalism* (Cambridge, MA: Belknap Press, 1990).

Cheffins, Brian R., 'Mergers and the Evolution of Patterns of Corporate Ownership and Control: The British Experience', *Business History*, 46: 2 (2004), 256–84.

Cheffins, Brian R., *Corporate Ownership and Control: British Business Transformed* (Oxford: Oxford University Press, 2008).

Clark, Gordon, *Pension Fund Capitalism* (Oxford: Oxford University Press, 2000).

Coakley, Jerry, and Laurence Harris, *The City of Capital: London's Role as a Financial Centre* (Oxford: Blackwell, 1983).

Cockett, Richard, *Thinking the Unthinkable: Think-Tanks and the Economic Counter-Revolution, 1931–1983* (London: Harper Collins, 1994).

Coleman, D. C., 'Gentlemen and Players', *Economic History Review*, 26/1 (1973), 92–116.

Crafts, N. F. R., 'Forging Ahead and Falling Behind: The Rise and Relative Decline of the First Industrial Nation', *Journal of Economic Perspectives*, 12 (1998), 193–210.

Crafts, N. F. R., 'Long-Run Growth', in R. Floud and P. Johnson (eds), *The Cambridge Economic History of Modern Britain*, ii. *Economic Maturity, 1860–1939* (Cambridge: Cambridge University Press, 2003), 1–24.

Cunningham, Michael, '"From the Ground Up?": The Labour Governments and Economic Planning', in Jim Fryth (ed.), *Labour's High Noon: The Government and the Economy, 1945–51* (London: Lawrence & Wishhart, 1993), 3–19.

Daunton, Martin J., '"Gentlemanly Capitalism" and British Industry, 1820–1914', *Past and Present*, 122 (1989), 119–58.

Daunton, Martin J., *Just Taxes: The Politics of Taxation in Britain, 1914–1979* (Cambridge: Cambridge University Press, 2002).

Day, A. C. L., *The Future of Sterling* (Oxford: Clarendon Press, 1954).

Dell, Edmund, *A Strange and Eventful History: Democratic Socialism in Britain* (London: Harper Collins, 2000).

Desai, Radhika, 'Second-Hand Dealers in Ideas: Think-Tanks and Thatcherite Hegemony', *New Left Review*, 203 (1994), 27–64.

Dimsdale, N. H., 'British Monetary Policy since 1945', in N. F. R. Crafts and Nicholas Woodward (eds), *The British Economy since 1945* (Oxford: Oxford University Press, 1991), 89–140.

Dintenfass, Michael, *The Decline of Industrial Britain, 1870–1990* (London: Routledge, 1992).

Duménil, Gerard, and Dominique Lévy, 'Costs and Benefits of Neoliberalism. A Class Analysis', *Review of International Political Economy*, 8/4 (2001), 578–607.

Duménil, Gerard, and Dominique Lévy, *Capital Resurgent: Roots of the Neoliberal Revolution* (Cambridge, MA: Harvard University Press, 2004).

Durbin, Elizabeth, *New Jerusalems: The Labour Party and the Economics of Democratic Socialism* (London: Routledge and Kegan Paul, 1985).

Dutton, David, *British Politics since 1945: The Rise and Fall of Consensus* (Oxford: Basil Blackwell, 1991).

Edgerton, David, *Warfare State: Britain, 1920–1970* (Cambridge: Cambridge University Press, 2006).

Eichengreen, Barry J., *Globalizing Capital: A History of the International Monetary System*, 2nd edn (Princeton: Princeton University Press, 2008).

Elbaum, Bernard, and William Lazonick, 'The Decline of the British Economy: An Institutional Perspective', *Journal of Economic History*, 44/2 (1984), 567–83.

Eley, Geoff, *Forging Democracy: The History of the Left in Europe, 1850–2000* (Oxford: Oxford University Press, 2002).

Eley, Geoff, 'Corporatism and the Social Democratic Moment: The Post War Settlement, 1945–1973', in Dan Stone (ed.), *The Oxford Handbook of Postwar European History* (Oxford: Oxford University Press, 2012), 37–59.

Epstein, Gerald A. (ed.), *Financialization and the World Economy* (Cheltenham: Edward Elgar, 2005).

Evans, Eric J., *Thatcher and Thatcherism*, 3rd edn (London: Routledge, 2013).

Favretto, Ilaria, ' "Wilsonism" Reconsidered: Labour Party Revisionism 1952–64', *Contemporary British History*, 14/4 (2000), 54–80.

Ferguson, Niall, *High Financier: The Lives and Time and Siegmund Warburg* (London: Penguin, 2011).

Fielding, Steven, *The Labour Governments 1964–70*, i. *Labour and Cultural Change* (Manchester: Manchester University Press, 2003).

Foote, Geoffrey, *The Labour Party's Political Thought*, 2nd edn (London: Croom Helm, 1986).

Foxwell, Herbert S., 'The Financing of Industry and Trade', *Economic Journal*, 27/108 (1917), 502–22.

Fraser, Derek, *The Evolution of the British Welfare State: A History of Social Policy since the Industrial Revolution* (London: Macmillan, 1973).

Frieden, Jeffrey A., *Global Capitalism: Its Fall and Rise in the Twentieth Century* (New York: W. W. Norton & Co., 2006).

Gardner, Nick, *Decade of Discontent: The Changing British Economy since 1973* (Oxford: Basil Blackwell, 1987).

Garside, William, and Julian Greaves, 'The Bank of England and Industrial Intervention in Interwar Britain', *Financial History Review*, 3/1 (1996), 69–86.

Glennerster, Howard, 'Why was a Wealth Tax for the UK Abandoned? Lessons for the Policy Process and Tackling Wealth Inequality', *Journal of Social Policy*, 41/2 (2012), 233–49.

Glyn, Andrew, *Capitalism Unleashed: Finance, Globalization, and Welfare* (Oxford: Oxford University Press, 2006).

Godley, Wynne, and Ken Coutts, 'The British Economy under Mrs Thatcher', *Political Quarterly*, 60/2 (1989), 137–51.

Gould, Bryan, John Mills, and Shaun Stewart, *The Politics of Monetarism*, Fabian Tract 462 (London: Fabian Society, May 1979).

Gowland, David, *Controlling the Money Supply* (London: Croom Helm, 1982).

Grant, Matthew, 'Historians, the Penguin Specials and the "State of the Nation"' Literature', *Contemporary British History*, 17 (2003), 29–54.

Grant, Wyn, *The Political Economy of Industrial Policy* (London: Butterworth, 1982).

Grant, Wyn, *Business and Politics in Britain* (1st edn, London: Macmillan, 1987).

Green, E. H. H., 'Rentiers versus Producers? The Political Economy of the Bimetallic Controversy, c.1880–1898', *English Historical Review*, 103/408 (1988), 588–612.

Green, E. H. H., 'The Influence of the City over British Economic Policy, c.1880–1960', in Youssef Cassis (ed.), *Finance and Financiers in European History, 1880–1960* (Cambridge: Cambridge University Press, 1992), 193–218.

Green, E. H. H., 'Thatcherism: An Historical Perspective', *Transactions of the Royal Historical Society*, 6/9 (1999), 17–42.

Green, E. H. H., 'The Conservatives and the City', in Ranald Michie and Philip Williamson (eds), *The British Government and the City of London in the Twentieth Century* (Cambridge: Cambridge University Press, 2004), 156–66.

Green, E. H. H., *Thatcher* (London: Hodder Arnold, 2006).

Gregg, Pauline, *The Welfare State: An Economic and Social History of Great Britain from 1945 to the Present Day* (London: Harrap, 1967).

Hall, Peter A., 'The Movement from Keynesianism to Monetarism: Institutional Analysis and British Economic Policy in the 1970s', in Sven Steinmo, Kathleen Thelen, and Frank Longstreth (eds), *Structuring Politics: Historical Institutionalism in Comparative Analysis* (Cambridge: Cambridge University Press, 1992), 90–113.

Hall, Peter A., 'Policy Paradigms, Social Learning, and the State: The Case of Economic Policymaking in Britain', *Comparative Politics*, 25/3 (1993), 275–96.

Hannah, Leslie, 'A Failed Experiment: The State Ownership of Industry', in Roderick Floud and Paul Johnson (eds), *The Cambridge Economic History of Modern Britain*, iii. *Structural Change and Growth, 1939–2000* (Cambridge: Cambridge University Press, 2004), 84–111.

Harmon, Mark D., *The British Labour Government and the 1976 IMF Crisis* (Basingstoke: Macmillan, 1997).

Harris, Jose, 'Enterprise and Welfare States: A Comparative Perspective', *Transactions of the Royal Historical Society*, 40 (1990), 175–95.

Harrison, Brian, 'Mrs Thatcher and the Intellectuals', *Twentieth Century British History*, 5 (1994), 206–45.

Harrison, Brian, *Finding a Role? The United Kingdom, 1970–1990* (Oxford: Clarendon Press, 2010).

Harvey, David, *A Brief History of Neoliberalism* (Oxford: Oxford University Press, 2005).

Hay, Colin, 'Chronicles of a Death Foretold: The Winter of Discontent and Construction of the Crisis of British Keynesianism', *Parliamentary Affairs*, 63/3 (2010), 446–70.

Heim, Carol E., 'Limits to Intervention: The Bank of England and Industrial Diversification in the Depressed Areas', *Economic History Review*, 37/4 (1984), 533–50.

Helleiner, Eric, *States and the Reemergence of Global Finance: From Bretton Woods to the 1990s* (Ithaca, NY: Cornell University Press, 1994).

Helleiner, Eric, 'Explaining the Globalization of Financial Markets: Bringing States back in', *Review of International Political Economy*, 2/2 (1995), 315–41.

Hickson, Kevin, *The IMF Crisis of 1976 and British Politics* (London: Tauris Academic, 2005).

Holmes, Martin, *The Labour Government, 1974–79: Political Aims and Economic Reality* (Basingstoke: Macmillan, 1985).

Hopkin, Bryan, 'Freedom and Necessity in Economic Policy: Britain 1970–1979', *Political Quarterly*, 70/3 (1999), 305–18.

Howell, David, *British Social Democracy: A Study in Development and Decay* (London: Croom Helm, 1976).

Hughes, John, 'New Left Economic Policy', in Oxford University Socialist Discussion Group (ed.), *Out of Apathy: Voices of the New Left Thirty Years on* (London: Verso, 1989).

Hutton, Will, *The State We're In* (London: Jonathan Cape, 1995).

Ingham, Geoffrey, *Capitalism Divided? The City and Industry in British Social Development* (Basingstoke: Palgrave Macmillan, 1984).

International Labour Organization, *World of Work Report 2009: The Global Jobs Crisis and Beyond* (Geneva, 2009).

Jackson, Ben, 'Revisionism Reconsidered: "Property-Owning Democracy" and Egalitarian Strategy in Post-War Britain', *Twentieth Century British History*, 16/4 (2005), 416–40.

Jackson, Ben, *Equality and the British Left: A Study in Progressive Political Thought, 1900–64* (Manchester: Manchester University Press, 2011).

Jackson, Ben, 'Property-Owning Democracy: A Short History', in Martin O'Neill and Thad Williamson (eds), *Property-Owning Democracy: Rawls and Beyond* (Oxford: Wiley-Blackwell, 2012), 33–52.

Jackson, Ben, 'The Think-Tank Archipelago: Thatcherism and Neo-Liberalism', in Ben Jackson and Robert Saunders (eds), *Making Thatcher's Britain* (Cambridge: Cambridge University Press, 2012), 43–61.

Jackson, Ben, 'Social Democracy', in Michael Freeden, Marc Stears, and Lyman Tower Sargeant (eds), *The Oxford Handbook of Political Ideologies* (Oxford: Oxford University Press, 2013), 348–63.

James, Harold, *International Monetary Cooperation since Bretton Woods* (Oxford: Oxford University Press, 1996).

Jefferys, Kevin, *The Churchill Coalition and Wartime Politics, 1940–1945* (Manchester: Manchester University Press, 1991).

Jones, Harriet, and Michael Kandiah, *The Myth of Consensus: New Views on British History, 1945–64* (Basingstoke: Macmillan, 1996).

Jones, Tudor, 'Labour Revisionism and Public Ownership, 1951–63', *Contemporary Record*, 5/3 (1991), 432–48.

Judt, Tony, *Post-War: A History of Europe since 1945* (London: Vintage, 2010).

Kalecki, Michał, 'Political Aspects of Full Employment', *Political Quarterly*, 14/4 (1943), 322–30.

Kavanagh, Dennis, *Thatcherism and British Politics: The End of Consensus?* (Oxford: Oxford University Press, 1987).

Kavanagh, Dennis, 'The Post-War Consensus', *Twentieth Century British History*, 3 (1992), 175–90.

Kavanagh, Dennis, and Peter Morris, *Consensus Politics from Attlee to Thatcher* (Oxford: Blackwell, 1989).

Kennedy, William P., *Industrial Structure, Capital Markets, and the Origins of British Economic Decline* (Cambridge: Cambridge University Press, 1987).

Kenny, Michael, *The First New Left: British Intellectuals after Stalin* (London: Lawrence & Wishart, 1995).

Krippner, Greta R., 'The Financialization of the American Economy', *Socio-Economic Review*, 3 (2005), 173–208.

Kynaston, David, *The City of London*, i. *A World of its Own 1815–1890* (London: Chatto & Windus, 1994).

Kynaston, David, *The City of London*, ii. *Golden Years 1890–1914* (London: Chatto & Windus, 1995).

Kynaston, David, *The City of London*, iii. *Illusions of Gold, 1914–1945* (London: Chatto & Windus, 2000).

Kynaston, David, 'The Long Life and Slow Death of Exchange Controls', *Journal of International Financial Markets*, 2/2 (2000), 37–42.

Kynaston, David, *The City of London*, iv. *A Club No More 1945–2000* (London: Chatto & Windus, 2002).

Landes, David S., *The Unbound Prometheus* (Cambridge: Cambridge University Press, 1969).

Lapavitsas, Costas, *Profiting without Producing: How Finance Exploits Us All* (London: Verso, 2013).

Lisle-Williams, Michael, 'The State, Finance and Industry in Britain', in Andrew W. Cox (ed.), *State, Finance and Industry: A Comparative Analysis of Post-War Trends in Six Advanced Industrial Economies* (Brighton: Wheatsheaf, 1986), 231–73.

Longstreth, Frank, 'The City, Industry and the State', in Colin Crouch (ed.), *State and Economy in Contemporary Capitalism* (London: Croom Helm, 1979), 157–90.

Lowe, Rodney, 'The Second World War, Consensus, and the Foundations of the Welfare State', *Twentieth Century British History*, 1 (1990), 152–82.

McBriar, A. M., *Fabian Socialism and English Politics, 1884–1918* (Cambridge: Cambridge University Press, 1962).

McCloskey, Donald, 'Did Victorian Britain Fail?', *Economic History Review*, 23/3 (1971), 446–59.

MacDougall, Donald, *Don and Mandarin: Memoirs of an Economist* (London: John Murray, 1987).

McKibbin, Ross, 'Why was there no Marxism in Britain?', *English Historical Review*, 99 (1984), 297–331.

Michie, Ranald, *The City of London: Continuity and Change, 1850–1990* (Basingstoke: Macmillan, 1992).

Michie, Ranald, *The London Stock Exchange: A History* (Oxford: Oxford University Press, 1999).

Middlemas, Keith, *Power, Competition, and the State*, i. *Britain in Search of a Balance, 1940–61* (Basingstoke: Macmillan, 1986).

Middlemas, Keith, *Power, Competition, and the State*, ii. *Threats to the Post-War Settlement: Britain, 1961–74* (Basingstoke: Macmillan, 1990).

Middlemas, Keith, *Power, Competition, and the State*, iii. *The End of the Postwar Era: Britain since 1974* (Basingstoke: Macmillan, 1991).

Middleton, Roger, 'Brittan on Britain: "The Economic Contradictions of Democracy" Redux', *Historical Journal*, 54/4 (2011), 1141–68.

Mikardo, Ian, *Back Bencher* (London: Weidenfeld & Nicolson, 1988).

Milner, Henry, *Sweden: Social Democracy in Practice* (Oxford: Oxford University Press, 1989).

Mirowski, Philip, and Dieter Plehwe (eds), *The Road from Mont Pelerin: The Making of the Neoliberal Thought Collective* (Cambridge, MA: Harvard University Press, 2009).

Moran, Michael, *The Politics of Banking: The Strange Case of Competition and Credit Control* (London: Macmillan, 1984).

Morgan, Kenneth O., *Callaghan: A Life* (Oxford: Oxford University Press, 1997).

Moschonas, Gerassismos, *In the Name of Social Democracy: The Great Transformation: 1945 to the Present* (London: Verso, 2002).

Needham, Duncan, 'Britain's Money Supply Experiment, 1971–1973', *English Historical Review*, 130/542 (2015), 89–122.

Needham, Duncan, *UK Monetary Policy from Devaluation to Thatcher, 1967–82* (Basingstoke: Palgrave Macmillan, 2014).

Nesbitt, Steven, *British Pensions Policy Making in the 1980s: The Rise and Fall of a Policy Community* (Aldershot: Avebury, 1995).

Newton, Scott, 'The Two Sterling Crises of 1964 and the Decision not to Devalue', *Economic History Review*, 62/1 (2009), 73–98.

Newton, Scott, 'The Sterling Devaluation of 1967, the International Economy and Post-War Social Democracy', *English Historical Review*, 125/515 (2010), 912–45.

Newton, Scott, and Dilwyn Porter, *Modernization Frustrated: The Politics of Industrial Decline since 1900* (London: Unwin Hyman, 1988).

Nickell, Stephen, and Richard Layard, 'The Thatcher Miracle?', *American Economic Review*, 79/2 (1989), 215–19.

Nicholls, David, 'Fractions of Capital: The Aristocracy, the City and Industry in the Development of Modern British Capitalism', *Social History*, 13/1 (1988), 71–83.

Noon, Ron, 'Goodbye, Mr Cube', *History Today*, 51/10 (2001), 40–1.

Notermans, Ton, *Money, Markets, and the State: Social Democratic Economic Policies since 1918* (Cambridge: Cambridge University Press, 2000).

O'Hara, Glen, ' "Dynamic, Exciting, Thrilling Change": The Wilson Government's Economic Policies, 1964–70', *Contemporary British History*, 20/3 (2006), 383–402.

O'Hara, Glen, *From Dreams to Disillusionment: Economic and Social Planning in 1960s Britain* (Basingstoke: Palgrave Macmillan, 2007).

Obstfeld, Maurice, and Alan M. Taylor, *Global Capital Markets: Integration, Crisis and Growth* (Cambridge: Cambridge University Press, 2004).

Offer, Avner, 'Empire and Social Reform: British Overseas Investment and Domestic Politics, 1908–1914', *Historical Journal*, 26/1 (1983), 119–38.

Offer, Avner, 'Narrow Banking, Real Estate, and Financial Stability in the UK, c.1870–2010', *University of Oxford Economic and Social History Working Papers*, 116 (2013), 1–29.

Oliver, Michael J., 'Whatever Happened to Monetarism? A Review of British Exchange Rate Policy in the 1980s', *Twentieth Century British History*, 8/1 (1997), 49–73.

Oliver, Michael J., 'From Anodyne Keynesianism to Delphic Monetarism: Economic Policy-Making in Britain, 1960–79', *Twentieth Century British History*, 9 (1998), 139–50.

Oliver, Michael J., and Hugh Pemberton, 'Learning and Change in 20th Century British Economic Policy', *Governance: An International Journal of Policy, Administration, and Institutions*, 17/3 (2004), 415–41.

Padgett, Stephen, and William E. Paterson, *A History of Social Democracy in Post-War Europe* (London: Longman, 1991).

Parsons, D. W., *The Power of the Financial Press: Journalism and Economic Opinion in Britain and America* (Aldershot: Edward Elgar, 1989).

Pelling, Henry, *A Short History of the Labour Party* (Basingstoke: Macmillan, 1991).

Pemberton, Hugh, 'Politics and Pensions in Post-War Britain', in Hugh Pemberton, Pat Thane, and Noel Whiteside (eds), *Britain's Pensions Crisis: History and Policy* (Oxford: Oxford University Press, 2006), 39–63.

Pemberton, Hugh, '"What Matters is what Works": Labour's Journey from "Superannuation" to "Personal Accounts"', *British Politics*, 5/1 (2010), 41–64.

Pemberton, Hugh, 'The Failure of "Nationalization by Attraction": Britain's Cross-Class Alliance against Earnings Related Pensions in the 1950s', *Economic History Review*, 65/4 (2012), 1428–49.

Pepper, Gordon, *Inside Thatcher's Monetarist Revolution* (Basingstoke: Macmillan; Institute of Economic Affairs, 1998).

Plender, John, *That's the Way the Money Goes: Financial Institutions and your Savings* (London: André Deutsch, 1982).

Plender, John, and Paul Wallace, *The Square Mile: A Guide to the New City of London* (London: Century Publishing, 1985).

Pollard, Sidney (ed.), *The Gold Standard and Employment Policies between the Wars* (London: Methuen, 1970).

Pollard, Sidney, 'The Nationalisation of the Banks: The Chequered History of a Socialist Proposal', in David E. Martin and Martin Rubenstein (eds), *Ideology and the Labour Movement: Essays Presented to John Saville* (London: Croom Helm, 1979), 167–90.

Pollard, Sidney, 'Capital Exports, 1870–1914: Harmful or Beneficial?', *Economic History Review*, 38/4 (1985), 489–514.

Porter, Dilwyn, 'Government and the Economy', in Richard Coopey and N. Woodward (eds), *Britain in the 1970s: The Troubled Economy* (London: University College London Press, 1996), 34–54.

Przeworski, Adam, *Capitalism and Social Democracy* (Cambridge: Cambridge University Press, 1985).

Reid, Margaret, *The Secondary Banking Crisis, 1973–75* (London: Macmillan, 1982).

Ritschel, Daniel, *The Politics of Planning: The Debate on Economic Planning in Britain in the 1930s* (Oxford: Clarendon Press, 1997).

Roberts, Richard, and David Kynaston, *City State: How the Markets Came to Rule our World* (London: Profile Books, 2001).

Rogers, Chris, 'Economic Policy and the Problem of Sterling under Harold Wilson and James Callaghan', *Contemporary British History*, 25/3 (2011), 339–63.

Rollings, Neil, 'The "Keynesian Revolution" and Economic Policy-Making: A Comment', *Economic History Review*, 38 (1985), 95–100.

Rollings, Neil, 'British Budgetary Policy, 1945–1954: A "Keynesian Revolution"?', *Economic History Review*, 41 (1988), 283–98.

Rollings, Neil, '"The Reichstag Method of Governing"?: The Attlee Governments and Permanent Economic Controls', in H. Mercer, Neil Rollings, and Jim Tomlinson (eds), *Labour Governments and Private Industry: The Experience of 1945–51* (Edinburgh: Edinburgh University Press, 1992), 15–36.

Rollings, Neil, 'Poor Mr Butskell: A Short Life, Wrecked by Schizophrenia?', *Twentieth Century British History*, 5 (1994), 183–205.

Rollings, Neil, 'Multinational Enterprise and Government Controls on Outward Foreign Direct Investment in the United States and the United Kingdom in the 1960s', *Enterprise and Society*, 12/2 (2011), 398–434.

Rollings, Neil, 'Cracks in the Post-War Keynesian Settlement? The Role of Organised Business in the Rise of Neoliberalism before Margaret Thatcher', *Twentieth Century British History*, 24/4 (2013), 637–59.

Ross, Duncan M., 'Domestic Monetary Policy and the Banking System in Britain 1945–1971', in Ranald Michie and Philip Williamson (eds), *The British Government and the City of London in the Twentieth Century* (Cambridge: Cambridge University Press, 2004), 298–321.

Rubinstein, W. D., *Men of Property: The Very Wealthy in Britain since the Industrial Revolution* (London: Croom Helm, 1981).

Ruggie, John Gerard, 'International Regimes, Transactions, and Change: Embedded Liberalism in the Postwar Economic Order', *International Organization*, 36/2 (1982), 379–415.

Sassoon, Donald, *One Hundred Years of Socialism: The West European Left in the Twentieth Century* (London: I. B. Tauris, 2010).

Schenk, Catherine, *Britain and the Sterling Area: From Devaluation to Convertibility in the 1950s* (London: Routledge, 1994).

Schenk, Catherine, 'The Origins of the Eurodollar Market in London, 1955–63', *Explorations in Economic History*, 2 (1996), 1–19.

Schenk, Catherine, *The Decline of Sterling: Managing the Retreat of an International Currency, 1945–1992* (Cambridge: Cambridge University Press, 2010).

Seldon, Anthony, 'Conservative Century', in Anthony Seldon and Stuart Ball (eds), *Conservative Century: The Conservative Party since 1900* (Oxford: Oxford University Press, 1994), 17–68.

Smith, David, *The Rise and Fall of Monetarism: The Theory and Politics of an Economic Experiment* (Harmondsworth: Penguin, 1987).

Stedman Jones, Daniel, *Masters of the Universe: Hayek, Friedman, and the Birth of Neoliberal Politics* (Princeton: Princeton University Press, 2012).

Stopford, John M., 'The Origins of British-Based Multinational Manufacturing Enterprises', *Business History Review*, 48: 3 (1974), 303–35.

Supple, Barry, 'Official Economic Inquiry and Britain's Industrial Decline: The First Fifty Years', in M. Furner and B. Supple (eds), *The State and Economic Knowledge: The American and British Experiences* (Cambridge: Cambridge University Press, 1990), 325–53.

Supple, Barry, 'Fear of Failing: Economic History and the Decline of Britain', *Economic History Review*, 47 (1994), 441–58.

Sutcliffe-Braithwaite, Florence, 'Neo-Liberalism and Morality in the Making of Thatcherite Social Policy', *Historical Journal*, 55/2 (2012), 497–520.

Talani, Leila Simona, *Globalization, Hegemony and the Future of the City of London* (London: Palgrave Macmillan, 2012).

Tanner, Duncan, 'Ideological Debate in Edwardian labour Politics: Radicalism, Revisionism and Socialism', in Eugenio F. Biagini and Alastair J. Reid (eds), *Currents of Radicalism: Popular Radicalism, Organised Labour and Party Politics in Britain, 1850–1914* (Cambridge: Cambridge University Press, 1991), 271–93.

Thompson, E. P., *The Making of the English Working Class* (New York: Random House, 1964).

Thompson, E. P., 'The Peculiarities of the English', *Socialist Register*, 2 (1965), 311–62.

Thompson, Noel, *Political Economy and the Labour Party: The Economics of Democratic Socialism, 1884–1995* (London: University College London, 1996).

Thorpe, Andrew, *A History of the British Labour Party* (Basingstoke: Macmillan, 1997).

Tolliday, Steven, *Business, Banking, and Politics: The Case of British Steel, 1918–1939* (Cambridge, MA: Harvard University Press, 1987).

Tomlinson, Jim, 'Why was there Never a Keynesian Revolution in Economic Policy?', *Economy and Society*, 10 (1981), 72–87.

Tomlinson, Jim, 'A "Keynesian Revolution" in Economic Policy-Making', *Economic History Review*, 37 (1984), 258–62.

Tomlinson, Jim, 'The Attlee Government and the Balance of Payments, 1945–1951', *Twentieth Century British History*, 2 (1991), 47–66.

Tomlinson, Jim, 'Mr Attlee's Supply-Side Socialism', *Economic History Review*, 46/1 (1993), 1–22.

Tomlinson, Jim, 'Attlee's Inheritance and the Financial System: Whatever Happened to the National Investment Board?', *Financial History Review*, 1/2 (1994), 139–55.

Tomlinson, Jim, *Government and the Enterprise since 1900: The Changing Problem of Efficiency* (Oxford: Clarendon Press, 1994).

Tomlinson, Jim, 'Inventing "Decline": The Falling behind of the British Economy in the Post-War Years', *Economic History Review*, 49/4 (1996), 731–57.

Tomlinson, Jim, 'Conservative Modernisation, 1960–64: Too Little, Too Late?', *Contemporary British History*, 11/3 (1997), 18–38.

Tomlinson, Jim, *Democratic Socialism and Economic Policy: The Attlee Years, 1945–1951* (Cambridge: Cambridge University Press, 1997).

Tomlinson, Jim, *The Politics of Decline: Understanding Postwar Britain* (Harlow: Longman, 2000).

Tomlinson, Jim, 'The British "Productivity Problem" in the 1960s', *Past and Present*, 175 (2002), 188–210.

Tomlinson, Jim, 'Economic Policy', in Anthony Seldon and Kevin Hickson (eds), *New Labour, Old Labour: The Wilson and Callaghan Governments, 1974–79* (London: Routledge, 2004), 55–69.

Tomlinson, Jim, *The Labour Governments 1964–70*, iii. *Economic Policy* (Manchester: Manchester University Press, 2004).

Tomlinson, Jim, 'The Labour Party and the Capitalist Firm, c.1950–1970', *Historical Journal*, 47/3 (2004), 685–708.

Tomlinson, Jim, 'The Labour Party and the City, 1945–1970', in Ranald Michie and Philip Williamson (eds), *The British Government and the City of London in the Twentieth Century* (Cambridge: Cambridge University Press, 2004), 174–92.

Tomlinson, Jim, 'Mrs Thatcher's Macroeconomic Adventurism, 1979–1981, and its Political Consequences', *British Politics*, 2 (2007), 3–19.

Tomlinson, Jim, 'Tale of a Death Exaggerated: How Keynesian Policies Survived the 1970s', *Contemporary British History*, 21/4 (2007), 429–48.

Tomlinson, Jim, '"A Failed Experiment"? Public Ownership and the Narratives of Post-War Britain', *Labour History Review*, 73/2 (2008), 228–43.

Tomlinson, Jim, 'Balanced Accounts? Constructing the Balance of Payments Problem in Post-War Britain', *English Historical Review*, 124/509 (2009), 863–84.

Tomlinson, Jim, 'Thrice Denied: "Declinism" as a Recurrent Theme in British History in the Long Twentieth Century', *Twentieth Century British History*, 20/2 (2009), 227–51.

Tomlinson, Jim, 'Thatcher, Monetarism, and the Politics of Inflation', in Ben Jackson and Robert Saunders (eds), *Making Thatcher's Britain* (Cambridge: Cambridge University Press, 2012), 62–77.

Tomlinson, Jim, and Nick Tiratsoo, *Industrial Efficiency and State Intervention: Labour, 1939–1951* (London: Routledge, 1993).

Tooze, Adam, 'Imagining National Economies: National and International Economic Statistics, 1900–1950', in Geoffrey Cubitt (ed.), *Imagining Nations* (Manchester: Manchester University Press, 1998), 212–28.

Toye, Richard, 'Gosplanners versus Thermostatters: Whitehall Planning Debates and their Political Consequences, 1945–49', *Contemporary British History*, 14/4 (2000), 81–106.

Toye, Richard, *The Labour Party and the Planned Economy, 1931–1951* (Woodbridge: Boydell Press, 2003).

Tribe, Keith, 'Liberalism and Neoliberalism in Britain', in Philip Mirowski and Dieter Plehwe (eds), *The Road from Mont Pelerin: The Making of the Neoliberal Thought Collective* (Cambridge, MA: Harvard University Press, 2009), 68–97.

Turner, Adair, 'How to Tame Global Finance', *Prospect*, 27 September 2009.

Tweedale, G., 'Industry and Deindustrialization in the 1970s', in Richard Coopey and N. W. C. Woodward (eds), *Britain in the 1970s: The Troubled Decade* (London: UCL Press, 1996), 251–72.

Vernon, James, 'The Local, the Imperial and the Global: Repositioning Twentieth-Century Britain and the Brief Life of its Social Democracy', *Twentieth Century British History*, 21/3 (2010), 404–18.

Wass, Douglas, *Decline to Fall: The Making of Macro-Economic Policy and the 1976 Crisis* (Oxford: Oxford University Press, 2008).

Weldon, Duncan, 'Beyond Living with Capitalism: The Labour Party, Macroeconomics, and Political Economy since 1994', *Renewal*, 21/2–3 (2013), 23.

White, Stuart, 'The Economics of Andrew Glyn', *Renewal*, 6/3–4 (2008), 134–8.

Whiting, Richard, 'Ideology and Reform in Labour's Tax Strategy, 1964–1970', *Historical Journal*, 41/4 (1998), 1121–40.

Wickham-Jones, Mark, 'Monetarism and its Critics: The University Economists' Letter of Protest of 1981', *Political Quarterly*, 63/2 (1992), 171–85.

Wickham-Jones, Mark, *Economic Strategy and the Labour Party: Politics and Policy-Making, 1970–83* (Basingstoke: Macmillan, 1996).

Wickham-Jones, Mark, 'The Debate about Wages: The New Left, the Labour Party and Incomes Policy', *Journal of Political Ideologies*, 18/1 (2013), 83–105.

Wickham-Jones, Mark, 'The New Left's Economic Model: The Challenge to Labour Party Orthodoxy', *Renewal*, 21/1 (2013), 24–31.

Wiener, Martin J., *English Culture and the Decline of the Industrial Spirit, 1850–1980* (Cambridge: Cambridge University Press, 1981).

Williamson, Adrian, *Conservative Economic Policymaking and the Birth of Thatcherism, 1964–1979* (London: Palgrave Macmillan, 2015).

Williamson, Philip, 'A "Bankers' Ramp"? Financiers and the British Political Crisis of August 1931', *English Historical Review*, 99/393 (1984), 770–806.

Williamson, Philip, 'The City of London and Government in Modern Britain: Debates and Politics', in Ranald Michie and Philip Williamson (eds), *The British Government and the City of London in the Twentieth Century in the Twentieth Century* (Cambridge: Cambridge University Press, 2004).

Wilson, John F., *British Business History, 1720–1994* (Manchester: Manchester University Press, 1995).

Zweiniger-Bargielowska, Ina, 'Rationing, Austerity and the Conservative Party Recovery after 1945', *Historical Journal*, 37 (1994), 173–97.

IV. REFERENCE WORKS

Oxford Dictionary of National Biography (60 vols; Oxford: Oxford University Press, 2004).

Who's Who and *Who Was Who*; online edn (Oxford: Oxford University Press, 2012).

V. UNPUBLISHED PAPERS

'30 Years of the LOTIS Committee', *TheCityUK.com* <http://www.thecityuk.com/media/latest-news-from-thecityuk/30-years-of-the-lotis-committee/> (accessed 16 April 2014)].

Bernanke, Ben S., 'The Great Moderation', at the meetings of the Eastern Economic Association, Washington DC (2004).

Hotson, Anthony, 'British Monetary Targets, 1976 to 1987: A View from the Fourth Floor of the Bank of England', LSE Financial Markets Group Paper, Special Paper 190 (April 2010).

Kotz, David M., 'Neoliberalism and Financialization', paper given to the Political Economy Research Institute, University of Massachusetts (2008) <http://people.umass.edu/dmkotz/Neolib_and_Fin_08_03.pdf> (accessed 18 April 2014).

Labour Party, 'Labour's Plan for Banking Reform', 13 February 2015 <http://www.yourbritain.org.uk/uploads/editor/files/Banking_Reform.pdf> (accessed 23 June 2016).

Peacock, Alan, 'A Career as an Economic Advisor' (10 May 2011) <http://www.iea.org.uk/blog/a-career-as-an-economic-adviser> (accessed 22 March 2012).

Prieg, Linda, and Heather Stewart, 'Mythbusters: "The City is Vital to Britain"', *New Economic Foundation* (2013) <http://www.neweconomics.org/blog/entry/mythbusters-the-city-is-vital-to-britain> (accessed 18 March 2014).

Index